SINGER IN THE SHADOWS

SINGER IN THE SHADOWS

The Strange Story of Patience Worth

BY

Irving Litvag

AN AUTHORS GUILD BACKINPRINT.COM EDITION

Singer in the Shadows:
The Strange Story of Patience Worth
All Rights Reserved © 1972, 2001 by Irving Litvag

No part of this book may be reproduced or transmitted in any form or by any means, graphic, electronic, or mechanical, including photocopying, recording, taping, or by any information storage or retrieval system, without the permission in writing from the publisher.

AN AUTHORS GUILD BACKINPRINT.COM EDITION

Published by iUniverse.com, Inc.

For information address:
iUniverse.com, Inc.
5220 S 16th, Ste. 200
Lincoln, NE 68512
www.iuniverse.com

Originally published by Macmillan

ISBN: 0-595-19805-8

Printed in the United States of America

Sincere appreciation is expressed to the following for permission to quote from copyrighted materials:

Quotations from the book *Beyond The Reach of Sense* by Rosalind Heywood. Copyright © 1959 by Rosalind Heywood. Published by E. P. Dutton & Co., Inc. and reprinted with their permission. Quotation from *Time* magazine reprinted by permission from TIME, The Weekly Newsmagazine; Copyright Time Inc. 1970. Quotations from *The Man in The Mirror: William Marion Reedy and His Magazine* by Max Putzel used by permission of the publisher, Harvard University Press. Quotations from *Harper's Magazine* used by permission of Harper & Row, Publishers, Incorporated. Quotation from *Anatomy of Me* by Fannie Hurst, Copyright © 1958 by Fannie Hurst, used by permission of the publisher, Doubleday & Company, Inc. Quotations from *The Saturday Evening Post* reprinted by permission of THE SATURDAY EVENING POST © 1919, The Curtis Publishing Co. Quotation from *ESP: A Scientific Evaluation* by C.E.M. Hansel used by permission of the publisher, Charles Scribner's Sons. Quotations from article by Dr. Louisa E. Rhine in the FRNM *Bulletin* used by permission of the author. Quotations from *The Extra-Sensory Mind* by Kenneth Walker used by permission of the publisher, Emerson Books, Inc. Quotations from book review in the *Proceedings* of The Society for Psychical Research used by permission of the S.P.R. Quotations from *The Personality of Man* by G.N.M. Tyrrell, Copyright © G.N.M. Tyrrell, 1947, used by permission of the publisher, Penguin Books Ltd. Quotations from *The Unpartizan Review*, issues of March-April, 1920, and October-December, 1920. Copyright 1920, 1948 by Holt, Rinehart and Winston, Inc. Reprinted by permission of Holt, Rinehart and Winston, Inc.

*To my wife Ilene and to our
children, Julie and Joe, this book
is dedicated with love*

*And, gratefully, to Patience . . .
whoever and wherever she may be*

CONTENTS

	PREFACE	ix
1.	"Many moons ago..."	1
2.	The Devout Publicist	33
3.	Enter "Fatawide"	40
4.	Patience vs. the Scientific Man	65
5.	The Verdict of the Critics	86
6.	Patience's Blessed Event	115
7.	The Top of the Hill	148
8.	"A Nut for Psychologists"	186
9.	"Patience has shown me the end of the road..."	213
10.	The Analysts	245
11.	Who Was Patience Worth?	265
	NOTES	277
	INDEX	287

PREFACE

I DISCOVERED PATIENCE WORTH (or, as true believers in the occult would say, she discovered me) by the flimsiest of coincidences.

My training and proclivities have been journalistic; my career in recent years has been educational public relations.

If I have had any interest in the supernatural or the occult, in that half-lit world of so-called psychic phenomena, it has been the kind of tangential, curious interest possessed by most people. I have read an occasional book or article on the subject and, probably like yourself, have wondered, Could there possibly be anything to all this?

I have been openminded, in a disinterested sort of way, willing to be convinced—but leaning rather markedly to the skeptical side.

I am obsessed by books. A bookstore to me is like the candy store to a plumpish matron or the neighborhood bar to the alcoholic. The clerks hate me. I rarely buy, but I cannot keep my hands off the volumes. You can have the runs at Snowmass and the breakers at Makaha; just give me two weeks in a bookstore and I would be content.

During one lunch hour, wandering among the treasure-packed shelves of a local emporium, I came across a book with the simple yet eye-stopping title *Communicating with the Dead*.

If somebody has been doing that, I figured, it might be a good idea to find out about it. You never know when a talent like that might come in handy. So I picked up the book and, with the dexterity of a veteran bookstore browser, gave the contents a fast skim.

The book, I quickly found, was not what I had thought it might be—a startling revelation about contacting those who have gone before us. Rather, it was a collection—compiled and edited by Martin Ebon, a veteran writer on psychic subjects—of reported instances of spirit communication. Some of the individual reports went back many years. No headline-making new breakthroughs. Disappointed, I was about to put the book back on the shelf when my eye was caught by a familiar name: Casper S. Yost. I looked at the book with renewed interest. Was that St. Louis's Casper S. Yost? There is an old friend of my wife's parents named Mrs. Casper S. Yost. Could it be that her late husband had been involved somehow in efforts to talk to the dead? I was tantalized by the thought that someone I knew might be connected with the arcane world of spiritualism.

I browsed a bit further in the book and found that Casper S. Yost (it developed that he was the father-in-law of the Mrs. Yost we know) had written something many years ago about someone named Patience Worth. The piece in this book was excerpted from a book by Yost about Patience Worth.

I began reading the excerpt and thereby discovered Patience for myself.

I have lived in St. Louis for all my more than forty years and have taken a somewhat greater than average interest in my city and its history. Yet I had never heard of Patience and her mysterious appearance in St. Louis. Propelled initially by my curiosity over the appearance of a familiar name in this collection of occult writings, I read on about Patience and found myself growing more and more intrigued.

An avocation of mine has been free-lance writing, mainly magazine articles and feature stories for a St. Louis newspaper. Obviously here was a provocative subject for a newspaper feature. The headline quickly popped into my mind: "The Great St. Louis Ghost Story."

I found Mr. Yost's original book in the library of Washington University, where I am on the staff, and read it. No doubt about it—a prime subject for a reminiscing sort of feature article. I did more research, began digging into old magazines, began uncovering more and more evidence of the national, even international, interest aroused by the Patience Worth case. I searched St. Louis for additional source materials.

The realization came gradually that there was far more here than just a newspaper article.

I had stumbled onto one of the most bizarre mysteries of this century—a riddle with startling supernatural implications according to some, an unparalleled literary puzzle, a psychological whodunit that has completely befuddled experts.

It has never been satisfactorily explained, never has really been described in its full dimension. Now it has been virtually forgotten, except for those relatively few people who are acquainted with the history of psychic phenomena in this century.

Two books previously have been written about Patience Worth. The seminal book by Yost was published in 1916, just three years after the beginnings of the case. It incorporated only the first phase of the mystery.

In 1927 came Walter Franklin Prince's *The Case of Patience Worth*. Published originally by the Boston Society for Psychical Research, the book was actually an exhaustive report of Prince's careful investigation of the case. (It was reissued in 1964 by University Books.) While this book is extremely valuable to any study of the case and is highly recommended to anyone desiring to go into the case in great depth, it had two major deficiencies as I saw it. It was essentially a compilation of Prince's research findings and analyses, not a descriptive history of the case; and, secondly, it was written some twelve years before the death of the prime figure in the case and therefore covered actually only the first half of this strange phenomenon, which lasted for almost a quarter of a century.

In short, no complete account of the entire Patience Worth case had been written. What follows herewith is my effort to remedy this omission.

A few words are necessary concerning the personification of Patience Worth in this book. Very early in the game I had to decide how to refer to Patience. The cards in the library card catalogues invariably describe her as an "imputed author."

Persistent use of the terms *allegedly*, *purportedly*, or *supposedly* would be clumsy and tiresome. Yet to speak of Patience as a *her*, as a person, would seem to imply that I fully accept her as a separate and distinct being, presumably the discarnate spirit that spiritualists insist she was.

At the risk of being misunderstood, I chose the latter course. No matter what her real origin, Patience had many of the attributes of a vivid, unforgettable, distinct personality. For this, and for the sake of simplicity, I shall refer to her as "Patience" and shall write "she said" and "she answered" and "she snapped" and will hope that no value judgments are assumed by the reader, for none is intended.

Another brief word of explanation is necessary. This book is intended for that vast army of my brothers and sisters—the general readers. It is not written for scholars or philologists, although hopefully a stray savant or two might happen across it.

Even though it is aimed at a general, non-scholarly audience, however, I was determined that the book would be the product of careful, thorough research and that it would be based, insofar as possible, on documented fact rather than hearsay, supposition, or legend. This determination led me to spend more than nine months researching the Patience Worth case before writing one word of the book. Additional months of research followed, concurrent with the writing.

The sources of the book's rather extensive documentation, which would be useful to anyone desiring to pursue the case further, are given in the chapter notes. The notes are indicated throughout the text, but are relegated to the back of the book, where they will be less obtrusive.

A few brief acknowledgments: Writing this book was possible for me only because I live in St. Louis, where Patience first appeared and where most of the source material is located. My initial groundwork research was done at Washington University's magnificent John M. Olin Library, and I am grateful for my opportunity to utilize that fine source. I thank the library staff for its unfailing courtesy and help. The official Patience Worth Record (the complete compilation of her writings save for several full-length books published separately) is in the archives of the Missouri Historical Society, along with other valuable Patience Worth materials, and I express my sincere gratitude to the Society for being permitted to delve deeply into these all-important sources.

I have spent many months going carefully through the twenty-nine bound volumes of Patience Worth writings, totaling 4,375 single-spaced pages of materials. I am deeply grateful to the staff members of the Society, especially those in the archives and library, for making me feel at home and for so graciously meeting my needs. Special and heartfelt thanks to Mrs. Ernst A. Stadler, archivist of the Society, for her help and encouragement.

The other major source of research materials and microfilms was the St. Louis Public Library, and my warm appreciation is expressed to Miss Elizabeth Tindall of the library's Reference Department for her interest and valuable assistance.

A special word of thanks, too, to Mrs. Casper S. Yost, Jr., whose enthusiasm for my idea was important in encouraging me to go ahead with such an ambitious project.

Writing a book, particularly one requiring copious research, while working full time at regular employment is a killing task, and I would warn anyone against it who asked me, but no one ever has. Only a fool would try it. It surely cannot be done, if one has a family, without a massive amount of forbearance on the part of the family. To my wife, Ilene, and our children, Julie and Joe, I express my profound gratitude for their willingness to surrender hundreds of hours that properly belonged to them so that this book might be written.

IRVING LITVAG
St. Louis, Missouri

Oh, I hae come, such a wee finch, wi' a great Singin'; a Singin' which wert nay mine but tuned o' Him. And out the Great Silence I came forth, callin' not thee and thee and thee, but singin', singin' love.

And thy hearts leapt, and thou didst harken, and behold! the cloth hath sprung out thy faith. Verily a cloth made o' thy love; a thing which may be laid before men to look 'pon and to shew the magic of love. . . .

Look, the magic is *Thine*. There be nay word which thy handmaid hath brought which she hath not sung as a love song o' Him. And thou hast become the vessels unto which she pours the singin', thereby—think ye 'pon it—we together have added unto the store of love for Him!

PATIENCE WORTH

July 19, 1919

1

"Many moons ago..."

IT WAS A TYPICALLY torrid, airless summer night in St. Louis. Tuesday. July 8, 1913.

The temperature had climbed to ninety degrees that afternoon. Now, well past the dinner hour, with the sun gone, the heat was still within a degree or two of the day's high mark. It was humid as well, and shirts and blouses plastered themselves damply to the skin.

In the parlor of a comfortable, upper-middle-class flat in the 6000 block of Kingsbury Avenue in the city's West End, three women fanned themselves and gave their attention to a ouija board that rested between them. In the dining room nearby sat the husbands of two of the women. They smoked cigars and played pinochle.

Mrs. John H. Curran was tired and hot—and quite bored. Across the table from her sat her guest and close friend, Mrs. C. Edwin Hutchings. It was Emily Grant Hutchings who had persisted in this ouija-board business. Pearl Curran didn't believe in it and was tired of it. The third woman was Mrs. Curran's mother, Mrs. Mary Pollard, who sat alongside with paper and pencil ready, in case the board produced anything interesting and worth jotting down.

Mrs. Curran and Mrs. Hutchings lightly rested their fingertips on the movable part of the ouija board. Mrs. Curran exhaled a soft sigh. There were so many things she would rather be doing than playing around with this spiritualist nonsense. But Emily was very insistent about it. And Emily was a dear friend.

Under their fingertips the pointer suddenly began to move. It moved briskly, strongly, with certainty. It moved to a letter, then to another. Mrs. Hutchings began calling the letters out as the pointer moved to each.

"M-a-n-y—Many!"

Mrs. Pollard wrote down the word. The pointer continued its quick passage from one letter to the next. Mrs. Hutchings called out individual letters, then complete words, becoming more excited as she went on.

"Many moons ago I lived. Again I come—Patience Worth my name."

All three of the women expressed wonder at the statement, but quickly the pointer began again its movements across the face of the ouija board, and Mrs. Pollard wrote down this passage: "Wait, I would speak with thee. If thou shalt live, then so shall I. I make my bread by thy hearth. Good friends, let us be merrie. The time for work is past. Let the tabby drowse and blink her wisdom to the fire log."[1]

Three women idly passing a lazy summer evening with an ancient occult toy. So began one of the most puzzling literary and psychic episodes on record, a phenomenon that was to continue for almost a quarter of a century. It was destined to attract worldwide notice. It would bring forth plaudits from some of the most discerning men of the time. It would be condemned as a hoax by others. It would inspire a cult of utterly devoted admirers; it would amuse or anger or, at the least, tantalize millions of other persons.

For July 8, 1913, marked the first full-scale "appearance" of Patience Worth.

In a literary "career" of nearly twenty-five years she would produce the astounding total of almost four million words, seven full-length books, thousands of poems ranging from a few lines in length to hundreds, uncounted numbers of epigrams and aphorisms, short stories, a few plays, and thousands of pages of witty, trenchant conversation with the hundreds of guests who came to call on her.

Of one of her books a distinguished historian would later say: "Unquestionably this is the greatest story of the life and times of Christ penned since the Gospels were finished."

A noted professor at Oxford would call her "a philological marvel."

"She has produced," a book reviewer for one of the nation's biggest newspapers would write, "literature of extraordinary beauty and significance."

The New York Times would attest to her "flashes of genius."

A Canadian literary scholar would applaud another of her books as "one of the most powerful character novels I have ever read."

A professor of English literature would proclaim that her poetry achieved heights never attained by Shakespeare, Chaucer, or Spenser.

And one of the most famous of psychic investigators would blast the whole case as a "fool adventure" and charge that "notoriety and making a fortune . . . were the primary influences acting on the parties concerned."

The story of Patience Worth generally disappeared from public and popular view many years ago. However, it continues in the present day to rate major attention from researchers and writers in the field of psychic phenomena.

A British writer, Arthur Osborn, in his book *The Meaning of Personal Existence*, published in 1966, states: "There are literally hundreds of cases of mediumistic communications available for study in the proceedings and journals of the English and American Societies for Psychical Research. But of course it is not only in these journals that accounts of mediumistic phenomena may be found. . . . Sometimes a case is so remarkable that it becomes a classic in the records. Such a one is that of 'Patience Worth.'"

Osborn goes on to say: ". . . in cases such as these we are faced with a profound psychic riddle. The clue to its solution will only be found in a deeper understanding of human personality."[2]

Another British writer, Rosalind Heywood, in her excellent summary of psychic research over the past ninety years, *Beyond the Reach of Sense*, published in 1961, devotes an entire chapter to Patience Worth.[3]

Still another major figure in psychic research in Britain, G. N. M. Tyrrell, devoted eight full pages to his consideration of Patience Worth, whom he called "an outstanding product of automatic writing" in his book *The Personality of Man, New Facts and Their Significance*, published in 1948.[4]

Kenneth Walker, in his *The Extra-Sensory Mind*, published in 1961, also discusses the case in detail, taking most of his information from Tyrrell's account.

Charles Luntz, a long-time official of the Theosophical Society in St. Louis, has lectured on the topic "Patience Worth: Greatest E.S.P. of the Century."

Yet, despite the attention given to her case by all manner of writers on psychic phenomena, the general public in the 1970s is largely unacquainted with the strangest author of this century and perhaps of all time.

From the inception of the Patience Worth case, the life of its main participant would be radically altered. She would be an object of curiosity and speculation until her death. She would shape a mystery that today—almost sixty years after it began—remains unsolved and baffling.

The women who sat at the ouija board that hot July night in 1913 were the quintessence of upper-middle-class respectability. Pearl Lenore Curran, thirty years old, a tall, handsome woman, was born on April 15, 1883, in Mound City, Illinois, a small town near the extreme southern tip of the state. She was the only child of George and Mary Pollard.[5] Her father had tried art without great success, worked for a while in Texas for railroads and newspapers, and eventually became an official of a lead company in the "lead belt" of south-central Missouri, where Pearl spent her mid-teen years.

Her mother, described as "nervous, keen, ambitious," was a singer and passed on her love of music to her daughter, who also was an accomplished singer and pianist and later taught piano. The mother, Mrs. Pollard, remembered once having some ambitions to write, but forgot them after her marriage at eighteen.

Pearl admitted to being a mediocre student throughout her school years. She suffered what apparently was a nervous collapse at the age of thirteen and did not return to school after that. Living with her parents in several small Missouri towns and for a while with relatives in Chicago, she taught piano and voice and continued her own musical studies. At the age of twenty-four, in 1907, she was married to John H. Curran.

"I had made no effort to write," Mrs. Curran later told an interviewer, "never thought of it."[6]

Her good friend had thought of writing, however, and had done fairly well at it. Emily Grant Hutchings, born at Hannibal in the heart of Missouri's Mark Twain country, was the daughter of a railroad official, an ex-Methodist minister forced by ill health to give up the pulpit. Her mother was one of the early women physicians in the Mississippi Valley. After studying for a year in Germany, Emily had attended the University of Missouri, taught Latin, Greek, and German for two years, then came to St. Louis and got a job as feature writer for the *St. Louis Republic*. In 1897 she married C. Edwin Hutchings, a former newspaperman who was secretary of the Board of Commissioners of Tower Grove Park, a major unit in the St. Louis city park system.

Although she gave up her newspaper job when she married, Emily Grant Hutchings had lost none of her zest for writing and was an energetic and prolific free-lance writer. She regularly contributed feature articles to the Sunday magazine of the *St. Louis Globe-Democrat*. For four years she also had been the anonymous writer of newspaper articles signed by the "mysterious woman about town." She had contributed poetry and fiction to *Cosmopolitan*, *The Atlantic Monthly*, and other magazines, had written on art and home decoration for a monthly magazine published in St. Louis, and had served on the editorial staffs of several other magazines.

She had written a novel called *Chriskios—Divine Healer*, which had been published in the *Sunday Associated Magazine* of Chicago.[7]

John H. Curran, who played cards in the next room with C. Edwin Hutchings while their wives and his mother-in-law amused themselves with the ouija board, was associated with a land-development company in St. Louis. He was a well-known, highly respected businessman. An Iowan by birth, he grew up in Kansas and had been a cowboy, timber inspector, and a creamery superintendent before going into land development and investment. He had unsuccessfully run for Kansas Secretary of State in 1904.

From 1909 to 1911 he had served by appointment of Governor Hadley of Missouri as the state's Immigration Commissioner, helping to promote the influx of new residents to the state. He had been president of the National Land Exposition Company, secretary of the National Farm Homes Association, president of the Arcadia Country Club, a member of the Knights of Pythias, Elks, and other civic, fraternal, and athletic organizations. He apparently had some writing ability, for a biography credits him with having written (presumably articles) "The Business Man Back to Land" in 1910 and "The People and the Railroads" in 1911. Almost twelve years older than his wife, he had been married previously and was the father of a daughter by that marriage.[8]

In keeping with their station in life, the Currans lived in a quiet, comfortable residential area. A few blocks to the south was Forest Park, the huge city park that had housed the fabulous Louisiana Purchase Exposition—the unforgettable St. Louis World's Fair of 1904. An equally short distance to the west and south was the new campus of Washington University, a school already making a national reputation for itself.

Their home was in a red brick, two-family structure typical of the well-to-do neighborhood. A wide porch ran across the front of the building, and white columns bordered the doors at either end of the porch. Above the small front yard towered a second-floor dormer window rising to a circular peaked roof.

St. Louis had settled down from the exhilaration and enchantment of the World's Fair into the torpor of pre-World War I America. The local newspapers on that day in July reflected the attitudes of their readers: a vague, slowly increasing concern over the intensifying war in Europe, but a concern that was unfocused and weak. The people were parochial, much more interested in the concrete, the close-at-hand, than in some strange fighting in the Balkans.

So although the *St. Louis Globe-Democrat* on that July day carried the headline SERVIAN LINE OF RETREAT MENACED; SOFIA CONFIRMS MOVEMENT OF LARGE BULGARIAN FORCE, a more prominent display was given, with front-page pictures, to the problems of a young couple, aged nineteen and seventeen, fighting to marry despite the objections of his older brother-guardian.

Waiters at hotel cafés and restaurants were on strike, and, in Atlantic City, a woman accused by twenty of her neighbors of being a common scold and dubbed the "woman with the serpent tongue" was ordered to jail and threatened with banishment from the city. On the other coast, author Jack London had entered a hospital in preparation for an appendectomy.

Readers of the sports page on that day got scant consolation from the fact that the St. Louis Browns had won the final game of their series with Detroit—both the Browns and Cardinals were mired in sixth place in their respective leagues.

It was an easygoing time, an interlude between wars, a period of relative economic stability. Americans looked for fun, for gimmicks to pass the time away. And one of these was the ouija board.

Actually the ouija board was just one manifestation of an interest in spiritualism and the occult that had been intensifying since the formation, about thirty years earlier, of the Society for Psychical Research in England. Spiritualism, like the stock market, goes through repeated up-and-down cycles of popularity. It had burst into a flourishing period in the United States in the late 1840s with the appearance of the Fox sisters and their claims of "spirit rappings." After some years of notoriety, the sisters finally admitted that the mysterious rapping sounds (indicating yes or no answers to questions) actually came not from the realm of the spirits, as claimed, but from their own ankle and toe bones, which they had learned to manipulate so as to produce the requisite popping sounds on cue. Thus disillusioned, the public at large lost some of its enthusiasm for the ghostly communicators, although spiritualist cults survived and multiplied.

Another up-cycle began during the last twenty years of the nineteenth century, mainly because of the interest aroused by the painstaking research undertaken by a number of prominent Britons, including leading scientists and scholars, who had banded together as the Society for Psychical Research. Although the British investigators were generally cautious in making dramatic claims concerning their findings and were not loathe to call a hoax by its proper name, public interest in spiritualism and the possible survival of the human personality after death was renewed. The fact that respectable, even famous, men were taking part in these investigations seemed to lend an over-all credibility to the whole business.

With claims periodically being made, by careful investigators such as those in the S.P.R. as well as by some others far less qualified, that communication with the dead seemed possible, the cyclical pattern began a new upswing and the occult again became a fad.

One type of psychic activity, known as "automatic writing," began to attract attention through the activities of a group of mediums, mostly English, in the late nineteenth and early twentieth centuries. Automatic writing involves the reception and transcription of various types of communications in written form. The medium claims to have no control over the writing that is produced. Spiritualists insist that the material comes from spirits of the dead. Others, including many persons who affirm the reality of psychic phenomena of various kinds, are just as insistent that the writings originate in the subconscious or subliminal mind of the medium.

Rosalind Heywood, an active member of the S.P.R. in recent years, wrote in 1961:

> They [people using automatic writing] did get apparent messages from some source which was not that of their conscious minds. And they had little conception of the subconscious, of its love of drama, or of its power of storing up memories of observations which the surface mind had never consciously made or had forgotten. Neither did they know that a number of normal persons, by means of techniques varying from the inducement of slight dissociation to deep trance, can cause statements to emerge from beneath the threshold of consciousness which are quite unexpected by their surface selves. And since it is beneath that threshold that E.S.P. appears to function, it is not surprising that at times they achieved items of information which to them genuinely appeared to come from "the beyond." They were thus encouraged to accept as coming from an exterior source much else which probably originated in their own subconscious as a result of wishful thinking or frustration.[9]

Such an explanation of automatic writing is still very much in dispute among psychic researchers, however, and in the early years of this century most of them tended to view such activity as more likely to reflect communication with the dead.

An American medium, Mrs. Leonora Piper, spent some time in

England, was carefully investigated by the S.P.R. during this period, and became quite famous.

Around 1901 Mrs. A. W. Verrall, wife of a British classical scholar, began to receive automatic scripts, mostly in Latin and Greek and presumably coming from Frederic Myers, a deceased classicist and poet and an early leader in psychical research in England. Other mediums, among them Mrs. Verrall's daughter, also began receiving communications that purported to come from Myers.

A system known as "cross correspondences" became of major interest to psychic researchers as various mediums received messages that seemed to make sense when properly fitted together.

"A number of automatists were engaged in the cross correspondences," Rosalind Heywood has written, "and their reactions and methods of producing scripts were varied. Mrs. Wilson 'saw' pictures and then described them. Others spoke of their interior impressions; others would both speak and write; others again, Mrs. Verrall for instance, would only write. . . . Mrs. Holland said that she was always conscious when writing but that the pencil moved too quickly for her to grasp any meaning. . . . Her scripts, she said, had always come at a great speed; she once wrote fourteen poems in an hour."[10]

During the same period that Patience Worth made her first appearance in St. Louis through a form of automatic writing, much publicity was given to the work of another British medium, Mrs. Willett (pseudonym for a Mrs. Coombe-Tennant). Starting about 1910 Mrs. Willett received a series of communications purportedly from Professor Verrall and a friend, Professor Henry Butcher. The communications continued for about five years. Among those who made a careful study of Mrs. Willett's writing was Gerald, Earl of Balfour, who reported that, in his view, she ". . . showed a power of thought on difficult and abstruse subjects which he would not have expected from her normal self."[11]

We do not know whether the people gathered in that St. Louis parlor were aware of Mrs. Willett's activities or of the other writings by various mediums that supposedly emanated from the spirit world. But there are certain clear similarities between some of the English cases that had been widely reported in the press and magazines and the Patience Worth case. Yet, as we shall see, there also were great differences—especially in terms of the quality of the materials produced.

In addition to automatic writing directly with pen or typewriter, another method of establishing written communication (with the spirit world or subconscious, or what have you) uses that strange old device called the ouija board. Many people through the centuries, despite skepticism and sneers, have retained a dogged faith that the wooden board has some magical ability to bring forth the otherwise unheard voices of those who have died and yet still live. The ouija board is an ancient device, "made in various shapes and designs, some of them used in the sixth century before Christ."[12] Its odd name is simply a composite of the French and German words for "yes."

Casper S. Yost, a major figure in the Patience Worth case, described the board this way:

> The ouija board is a rectangular piece of wood about 16 inches wide by 24 inches in length and half an inch thick. Upon it the letters of the alphabet are arranged in two concentric arcs, with the ten numerals below, and the words "Yes" and "No" at the upper corners. The planchette, or pointer, is a thin heart-shaped piece of wood provided with three legs, upon which it moves about upon the board, its point indicating the letters of the words it is spelling. Two persons are necessary for its operation. They place the tips of their fingers lightly upon the pointer and wait. Perhaps it moves; perhaps it does not. Sometimes it moves aimlessly about the board, spelling nothing; sometimes it spells words, but is unable to form a sentence; but often it responds readily enough to the impulses which control it, and even answers questions intelligibly, occasionally in a way that excites the wonder and even the awe of those about it. Its powers have been attributed by some to supernatural influence, by others to subconsciousness, but science has looked upon it with disdain. . . .[13]

The devices of modern technology are born and die, and new ones come along to take their place. But the ouija board lives on and apparently it thrives. As recently as 1969, according to the *Wall Street Journal*, ouija boards were selling at the rate of two million a year.[14]

So it was in an atmosphere of rising worldwide interest in reputed spiritualist phenomena, with cases of supposed communication with the dead frequently reported in the popular magazines and press, and with the ouija board sweeping the country as a faddish plaything which some claimed to have real occult importance, that three semi-bored housewives sat in a humid St. Louis parlor and sought to commune with the beyond.

The communication on July 8, in which the name Patience Worth was mentioned for the first time, was by no means the first intelligible language that had been received by Mrs. Curran and Mrs. Hutchings via the ouija board. They had begun their rather idle experimentation about a year earlier, mainly in order to occupy their time while their husbands enjoyed games of pinochle. The impetus in securing the board and persisting in its use came from Mrs. Hutchings, who insisted that deep, dark, and quite marvelous things had resulted from such boards.

Mrs. Curran had firmly protested her disbelief in such things. A distasteful experience as a youngster in her uncle's spiritualist church in Chicago, she said, had turned her emphatically against such beliefs. She wanted nothing to do with it. But Mrs. Hutchings was insistent and begged her friend to humor her. Anyway, she would argue, what else did they have to do? So, during August 1912, they began placing their fingers on a ouija-board pointer and waiting to hear from someone.

An occasional intelligible word was spelled out by the pointer, but what came through was mostly gibberish—unrelated letters that spelled nothing understandable. Once in a great while several words came through—a phrase, a sentence. Each time Mrs. Hutchings became very excited, insisting that they were in the process of contacting the spirit world, that they were on the verge of a truly miraculous confrontation. Mrs. Curran remained skeptical. She wished she could persuade Emily to put aside the toy and find a new interest.

In the early summer of 1913, however, the situation began to change. Intelligible phrases and sentences began to come more often, understandable ideas were received. But there was still no indication from where the words came or who was sending them.

On June 22, 1913, the board spewed out a long series of disconnected letters and phrases, then a few fragmentary sentences. The pointer began a series of aimless rotary movements, then began to spell out, over and over again, the letters P-A-T . . . P-A-T . . . P-A-T. Then it began to move again and these lines came:

> Oh, why let sorrow steel thy heart?
> Thy bosom is but its foster-mother,
> The world its cradle and the loving home its grave.[15]

The participants were surprised at the intelligence of the utterance and also impressed and somewhat shaken by its poetic style and graceful expression. At that point, after hasty consultation with the husbands who had been excitedly summoned from their card game, it was decided to keep a written record of any further statements issuing from the ouija board. In order not to disturb the arrangement that had produced the "sorrow steel thy heart" passage, all agreed that Mrs. Curran and Mrs. Hutchings should continue to operate the board, while Mrs. Pollard would again sit alongside and take notes.

Before continuing with a description of the session, it is necessary here to explain some possible discrepancies with regard to the first few months of the Patience Worth literature. The procedure followed during that period involved notes being taken by Mrs. Pollard, who then turned the notes over to Mrs. Hutchings. She took them home, typed them up, and punctuated them, since the letters produced by the ouija board were turned out in serial fashion, unpunctuated and unparagraphed. This procedure was understood by all concerned. Apparently, however, Mrs. Hutchings was doing more than just typing and punctuating.

In January 1915 John Curran took over the responsibility of maintaining a complete record of the sittings. At that time he prefaced the compilation of the Patience Worth literature with this statement:

> Mrs. Hutchings or someone else have always been at the board with Mrs. Curran, Mrs. Pollard transcribing the words as they come from the board. Mrs. Hutchings would then take them home and rewrite and punctuate the matter. Also she would make interpolations of her own in the record and, we found since, she would add to and take from and change ad libitum. She kept one copy of the record and gave us the carbon copy. In making up this preliminary record it is well to state that these interpolations have been eliminated entirely as has everything else that in our

judgment has not come from Patience Worth, in the effort to make this entirely a record of the words of Patience Worth. We have no desire to hear from any other and none other has come to us as far as we know.[16]

In addition to its implications of a split between the two women who together had given birth to Patience Worth, the statement was frank enough to admit that there was some doubt as to the authenticity of the records until the time that Curran himself took responsibility for them. However, it appears that an honest effort was made to expunge any language deemed un-Worthy and to label as "doubtful" any words of questionable origin. In a few of the passages that follow, such a label will be used as it appears in the Patience Worth Record.

After those first three rather lyrical lines were given by the ouija board on June 22, the women—having settled on the need to record the language—turned their attention back to the board. Again the pointer began to move rapidly, spelling out one word after another. Individual statements, some aphoristic in nature, began to come forth:

> Rest, weary heart. Let only sunshine light the shrine within. A single ray shall filter through and warm thy frozen soul.
>
> A leaf falls and nestles close to the earth, but oh, the message she once sent to Spring! So 'tis with thee. Then nestle close on thy last day, but leave a message, like the leaf, to come again in Spring.
>
> Touch, taste and smell are homely facts, but thy heart-beats are a record for Him. [doubtful]
>
> Your deeds are nothing. Often the heart prompts what the circumstances will not permit. [doubtful][17]

Interspersed with these short statements, poetic in style, were a few other phrases which made little sense and seemed in no way related to the sentences given above. A few times one of the women tried to ask a question of the ouija board, but there was no response. Finally it was decided to set the board aside for a few days and then try again. Mrs. Hutchings was convinced by this time that a miracle was taking place. Mrs. Curran remained skeptical but confessed to some bewilderment over what had happened. The phrases meant nothing to her; she could detect little meaning in them. Inarguably some understandable sentences had actually been produced by this strange little wooden device—and she had no ready explanation for it. She felt a sinking feeling in her stomach. Somehow she wished the whole thing could just be stopped, right here and now. She wasn't at all certain she wanted to go on with this, yet, she had to admit, it was beginning to fascinate her. Who possibly could be speaking to them through a ouija board? Well, she thought, next time probably we'll get more gibberish and perhaps I can persuade Emily to drop the whole thing.

Next time was July 2, again at the Curran residence. Mrs. Curran and Mrs. Hutchings took their seats at the board and again placed their fingertips lightly on the pointer. Mrs. Pollard poised her pencil over her paper. Without hesitation the pointer began moving to one letter after another, and Mrs. Hutchings briskly called them out. The following messages were received:

> Dust rests beneath, and webs lie caught among the briars. A single jewel gleams as a mirrored vision of rising Venus in a mountain lake.
>
> One hovers near, whose flower-like face and sorrow-laden eyes reflect on the golden cup. One tear falls, and from the spot the tendrils of a tiny vine springs forth.
>
> A tiny form appears, as delicate as the tracery on a leaf of Fall, and fades as the rainbow, hidden from the sun.
>
> As windblown clouds appear, a face as twisted as an oaken limb, leers like a drunken seaman and laughs at storm.
>
> A bluet springs from 'neath the moss, and the eyes of her who trod thereon are bluer far. A lazy zephyr fans the curls she wears.
>
> Around come trooping myriad forms, and plucking all the flowers, cast wide upon the lake their wanton plunder, and lo, a wreath appears.[18]

Although impressed by the poetic feeling of the phrases and their lyric quality, the women could detect no theme or meaning. They again asked the board to be more enlightening. Here, for the first time, the record indicates that a response was made to questions—that some type of communication was being established.

The responses themselves, however, are labeled "doubtful" and seem to reflect Mrs. Hutchings' own inclinations toward spiritualism:

> All those who so lately graced your board are here, and as the moon looks down, think ye of them and their abode as a spirit lake, a spirit song, a spirit friend, and close communion held 'twixt thee and them. 'Tis but a journey, dost not see? [doubtful]

At this point the record notes: "We asked again for a clearer meaning." The board responded: " 'Tis all so clear behind the veil. A glimpse of life with us, and portraits, should convince." Someone asked who was sending these messages. The board said: "Should one so near be confined to a name? The sun shines alike on the briar and the rose. Do they make question of a name?"

The women excitedly speculated over the possible identity of their unseen correspondent. They agonized over those letters P-A-T, P-A-T that had come through several times at the first sitting.

Mr. Curran, vastly amused by the whole situation, solemnly insisted that P-A-T undoubtedly referred to a friend of his named Pat McQuillan, who recently had died and was trying to get in touch with him.[19] The women gobbled with excitement for a few moments until they realized he was kidding. Ordering him back to his card game, they resumed their analysis, over and over again, of the mysterious words they had produced, trying to determine their deepest meaning, trying to pierce the cloudiness of their origin.

On July 8, by now trembling with expectation when they sat at the board, the women again waited further word. And this time their shadowy friend proclaimed her name: "Many moons ago I lived. Again I come—Patience Worth my name."

Patience Worth. The three women looked at one another and shrugged their shoulders in puzzlement. It was a name unknown to any of them. They agreed that they liked the sound of it. It had dignity—a kind of Puritan honesty. And, of course, now they were convinced that the P-A-T they had been receiving was an effort to spell out the name Patience.

Here is the verbatim record of the remainder of that July 8 session. Here, and from here on in this account, the words produced by the ouija board will be attributed to Patience Worth.

PATIENCE: Wait, I would speak with thee. If thou shalt live, then so shall I. I make my bread by thy hearth. Good friends, let us be merrie. The time for work is past. Let the tabby drowse and blink her wisdom to the fire log.
MRS. CURRAN: How queer that sounds!
PATIENCE: Good Mother Wisdom is too harsh for thee, and thou shouldst love her only as a foster mother.
[This was one of the earliest samples of Patience's sarcasm. One of the refreshing things about this character is her astringent, sometimes caustic wit. There is nothing goody-goody about her, and she often displays a tongue like a stinging whip.]
MRS. POLLARD: Patience Worth must surely be the party who is delivering these messages. It sounds like a Quaker name. Let's ask her when she lived.
PATIENCE: (The board hesitates, swings to and fro, seems uncertain. Finally, numbers are indicated): 1-6-4-9 . . . 9-4 . . .
MRS. HUTCHINGS: Patience, where was your home?
PATIENCE: Across the sea.
MRS. HUTCHINGS: In what city or country?
PATIENCE: About me you would know much. Yesterday is dead. Let thy mind rest as to the past.
MRS. POLLARD (jokingly): She doesn't want us to inquire into her past. Perhaps it wasn't creditable.
PATIENCE: Wilt thou but stay thy tung! On rock-ribbed walls beat wisdom's waves. Why speak for me? My tung was loosed when thine was yet to be.
MRS. POLLARD: I suppose she was a regular type, rather hard and severe in her ideas and speech.
PATIENCE: This overwise, good-wife knows much that thrashing would improve. Am I then so hard?
[The sitters laughed and asked Patience if she had singled out Mrs. Pollard for this rebuke.]
PATIENCE: A secret held too close may inflame quite as sorely as one talked over-much.
[This, notes the record, was interpreted as a general rebuke, and Mrs. Curran laughed her appreciation, evidently annoying the unseen partner.]
PATIENCE: Wilt thou, of too much speech pray silence the witch? Much clatter from a goose. An owl is silent and credited with much wisdom. A wise hen betrays not its nest with a loud cackle.
[The record notes: The continued rebukes caused the sitters to believe she wished consideration, and in respect they asked if she would kindly continue.]

PATIENCE: If the storm passes. Thanks, good souls. Could I but hold your ear for the lesson I would teach! A striving for truth will not avail thee. Watch and listen. We are ever near. Thy paltry prayers are but a comforter to heal the wounds of thine own conscience. Mistake not their true worth, but live, and work and work and work. This alone can earn thee rest. [doubtful][20]

Before going further it seems necessary at this point to discuss the general style of the Patience Worth utterances and to offer some suggestions for reading them.

The first reaction by most modern readers to the language of Patience Worth probably will be one of irritation, frustration, and impatience. It was my reaction. The language, obviously, is archaic. It apparently is a type of Old English—that is, English as spoken in Great Britain several hundred years ago. Pinning it down any more definitely than that becomes a problem. Those who later became involved in the case—the loyal supporters of Patience and her critics—argued bitterly over the exact origin of her language, and some of those arguments will be discussed later in this book. There was general agreement, however, that her statements did not represent the language of a particular time and place in English history but rather were a weird composite of languages spoken in many times and places. Whatever its philological properties, the language was difficult for readers in 1913, as it is for those in the 1970s.

Strangely, as the years passed and Patience continued to speak, her language tended to become less archaic and easier to grasp at first reading. Patience was asked about this and gave what seem to be logical reasons for the transition. This will be discussed later. In any case, I would strongly suggest that you do not give up on it too quickly. Do not cop out by just skimming over those verbal stumbling blocks in an effort to pass on to something meatier. For in time, if you persevere, you will perceive a pattern, a consistency of rhythm and phrasing; you will understand at a glance the meanings of unusual words which at first only puzzled and irritated you.

Gradually, after some effort, you will find rewards. The meaning of the words will be more readily apparent, and—with the major difficulties of understanding having been overcome—the language will begin to have its effect on you. You will come upon passages of haunting beauty and a pristine kind of expression that at times is awesome.

The purpose of this book is to describe the Patience Worth case, not to compile her writings. Yet, obviously, it is necessary to quote extensively from those writings, if the full flavor of the entire mystery is to be made explicit. So, in the pages to come, you'll be reading much of the language of Patience Worth. If you meet Patience with patience (and that will be the last of that ploy) I think you'll be rewarded.

It might simplify things a bit if I mention here a few of Patience's favorite phrases and expressions and attempt to interpret them for you. The word "put" is often used. It is used as a verb, with "to put" meaning "to write," and as a noun—the product of that writing being referred to by Patience as her "put."

One of my favorite Patience Worth remarks, for its sheer incomprehensibility, is this: "Nay, 'tis not the put o' me, the word hereon. 'Tis the put o' me at see o' her. I put athin the see o' her, aye and 'tis the see o' ye that be afulled o' the put o' me, and yet a put thou knowest not." One observer noted, "It is no easy task to untangle that putting of puts, but, briefly, it seems to mean that Patience does not put her words on the board direct, with the hands of Mrs. Curran, but transmits her words through the mind or inner vision of Mrs. Curran, and yet it is the word of Patience and not of Mrs. Curran that is recorded."[21]

She refers to her writings often as the "bread o' me" and her readers or hearers as those who "eat o' my loaf." Obviously she favors contractions, and "o'" is used for "of," "athin" for "within," "e'en" for "even." "Thee"s and "thy"s are hurled about with great abandon, along with such archaisms as "canst" and "dost" and "pleg" for "plague." Some critics later challenged some of the "thee"s and "thy"s as being grammatically incorrect.

Whenever Patience was challenged about her choice of words, her reply was a blunt "I be dame," meaning I am a woman and therefore not subject to the usual rules of grammar or logic.

Later on, when Patience began creating some longer works such as short stories and novels, she tended to refer to such works as her "weaving," while her poems and aphorisms and epigrams constituted her "sweets," almost as if they represented a sort of pleasant refreshment coming between the real substance of her production.

Her favorite image for herself was that of a singer, and her poems were her songs.

Rural references abound, with innumerable mentions of flowers, trees, insects, farm and wild animals and the homely chores of farm life. Someone's home often is called his "hut."

Her speech is punctuated by exclamations, presumably Old English in origin, that haven't been heard since Dame May Whitty left the movies. You'll come across a periodic " 'Lor!" or "Alawk!" or even an occasional "Gad-zooks!"

It is the language of another world, very possibly a world that never actually existed. Yet it *is* a language; it has meaning and sense and beauty. It is not randomly thrown together. There is design and form and intelligence. I hope you will take the time and effort to find it. It is a struggle—but worth it.

After the productive session of July 8 the three women agreed that something definitely most unusual was happening, something possibly of historical significance. Even Mrs. Curran by now had abandoned her skepticism and was eager to hear more from the being calling herself Patience Worth and to question her about her origin and present whereabouts. They had no hesitation in agreeing to continue to meet regularly and to keep careful records of everything that transpired.

On July 13 they sat again. And again Patience Worth joined them. She gave them a series of epigrams:

> Professing piety can heal too foul a conscience as surely as a sunny summer saves the wheat when rain is shy.
>
> Shadows to the weary are cooling balm; but as youth basks in the sun, so at twilight comes shade and rest.
>
> Cradle thy heart in love, cloak thy deeds in pity, strengthen thy soul with long draughts of wisdom, culled from the vine of truthful knowledge, and go forth, a warrior indeed.
>
> Put faith in meager efforts, and I promise ye much.[22]

The women held several more sessions during the days that followed, and Patience continued her regular appearances, producing a series of random poems. Although there had been a vaguely religious and devout cast to many of the utterances, there had been no specific religious content, no direct linkage with Christianity, until July 31, when Patience asked, "Dost crave to touch the wounded side or kiss the quivering flesh from whence those precious drops were wrung, to prove the love song sung in Galilee?"

Gradually, as the sessions continued and the written record began to lengthen, recurrent themes and ideas became distinguishable. There apparently was a Patience Worth philosophy, and she was in the process of delivering it, in bits and pieces.

One of her most common themes over the years concerned her reverence and deep love for children contrasted with man's tendency to intellectualize and verbalize, which she despised. On August 8, she said this:

"Wouldst thou inquire into the universal truth, and make a culture of the tissue of thy long diseased pouch of knowledge? Oh, rest from the heated sands of the desert of thine own make, and study thou the smile of an infant's lips in sleep, where hallowed angels whisper the world lore thou wouldst choose to believe that thou hast taught, and clasp one tiny hand. The whole secret is sealed in one rosy palm, and the answer lies within each dimple kissed by thee. Dost need to cry for proof, O, thou of word-ridden creed?"[23]

The three women no longer felt any shyness about asking questions of Patience, and they sought persistently to obtain more information about her personal history. But she was always evasive and vague. On August 25, for example:

MRS. HUTCHINGS: What do you mean?
PATIENCE: Mean-ness is not o' my making.
MRS. HUTCHINGS: Patience, won't you please put this into more modern English?
PATIENCE: Oh, worry, worry, canst thou understand the purring of the cat?
MRS. HUTCHINGS: I truly did not mean to offend.
PATIENCE: I oft have seen the tung split for less.
[The women again pressed Patience for the dates when she had lived.]
PATIENCE (confusedly): 1 . . . 4 . . . 6. [pause] 1-6-4 . . . 9. Thou art over-wise. Then use of thy store.[24]

So far there had been no indication that any one of the three women was the specific target for Patience or, to put it better, was the particular conduit for her words. The messages had been addressed to no one in particular. Then, on September 11, some two months after Patience had first identified herself, the three women expressed irritation over the apparent reluctance of the board to deliver any messages and asked it to hurry up.

> PATIENCE: Beat the hound and lose the hare.
> MRS. POLLARD: That seems to be a rebuke. I wonder if she is particularly fond of Pearl and if that is her reason for coming always to her.
> PATIENCE: To brew a potion, needs must have a pot.

This homely reference, unflattering as it must have been to Mrs. Curran, was the first indication that she was somehow connected to these mystifying communications in a way that the other two women were not.

In that same September 11 session Mrs. Pollard again became the victim of Patience's rapier tongue:

> MRS. CURRAN: She seems to have very little use for us. I wonder what she thinks of the women of this day.
> PATIENCE: A good wife keepeth the floor well sanded and rushes in plenty to burn. The pewter should reflect the fire's bright glow.... Clip the wings of a goose. 'Twill teach thee clever tricks and brush the dust of long standing away.
> MRS. POLLARD: I wish we could get something besides sarcasm. I wish—
> PATIENCE: From constant wishing, the moon may tip for thee!
> MRS. POLLARD: I don't wish for anything, but I do want a lot of things.
> PATIENCE: The swine cry, "Want, want, want."
> MRS. POLLARD: I yield to Patience. She's cleverer than all three of us.
> PATIENCE: Some folk, like the bell without a clapper, go clanging on in good faith believing the good folks can hear.
> MRS. POLLARD: I hardly think I needed that scolding.
> PATIENCE: Nor does the smock need the wimple.
> MRS. HUTCHINGS: Just what do you think of Mrs. Pollard?
> PATIENCE: The men should stock her!
> MRS. POLLARD: She should not select me for her sarcasm. It's you two who interrupt and laugh at her. It's that that makes her angry.

MRS. HUTCHINGS: Do you mean that Mrs. Pollard should be put in the stocks?
PATIENCE: Aye, and leave a place for two!
MRS. POLLARD: I knew she didn't mean all that solely for me. I wish, though, that she would give us something nice.
PATIENCE: Mayhap thou wouldst have a pumpkin tart!
MRS. POLLARD: If she cannot forego sarcasm, then I wish she would stop all together.
PATIENCE: Then beat the hound.
MRS. CURRAN: We ought to be satisfied with what is given us.
MRS. POLLARD: Well, I don't feel as though I am to blame. I have been trying all evening to encourage you to be nice to her so that she would give us a nice message.
PATIENCE: Gad-zooks, hear her!
[A bit later in the session Patience suddenly exclaimed, "Dost know what war is? Hell."]
MRS. CURRAN: That is the first thing she has ever said that was out of keeping with her time. That expression originated during our own Civil War.
PATIENCE: Does thou flatter thyself that today's thoughts and deeds were born today, by such a fledgling as thou?

Mrs. Hutchings again asked Patience her age, but in the evasive way she responded to almost every question about her own history, Patience replied, " 'Tis odd, I forget it."[25]

Another session on September 19 brought more verbal missiles for poor old Mrs. Pollard:

MRS. POLLARD: Her tongue is sharp. I should like to have her show us her amiable side.
PATIENCE: A lollypop is but a breeder of pain.
[Obviously misinterpreting, Mrs. Pollard thought the comment a reflection on her appetite.]
PATIENCE: An old goose gobbles the grain like a gosling.
MRS. POLLARD: I can't say that that is an improvement over the last! The idea of her calling me an old goose!
PATIENCE: Youth taketh a homestead at early and late life.
MRS. POLLARD: Whew! She is rather hard on me, but I am getting used to it. . . . I'll take all the bitter doses you give me, Patience, if you will reward me afterward with something that I may love.
PATIENCE: Love hath shining eyes. Dost flatter thyself to be his chosen?

MRS. CURRAN: I believe I should prefer to have her call me an old goose!
MRS. POLLARD: I don't believe that she really means to be uncomplimentary.
PATIENCE: A timber, falling, to thee would be a splinter.[26]

For about three months after Patience's first manifestation in early July, the three women communed with the ouija board at least one evening a week, sometimes twice. By this time their husbands had begun to show somewhat more interest in the proceedings, although they still were reluctant to admit that anything really out of the ordinary was under way.

Mrs. Hutchings, an eager free-lance writer, had been quick to realize the possibilities of the situation in terms of its readership value. She was already making plans to write a book about the strange visitor to the Curran home and had broached the subject to Mrs. Curran and Mrs. Pollard, who thought it was an exciting idea.

During late September, after much discussion as to whether the whole affair should remain a closely guarded secret for the time being, Mrs. Curran and Mrs. Hutchings decided to invite others to attend the sittings in order to determine how the ouija board would respond to the new presences and in order to determine the reaction of outsiders. A few friends of the Currans and Hutchingses were discreetly invited to visit the Curran home and observe.

The following month, also more or less in the nature of an experiment, it was decided to take the ouija board to the homes of other people in order to see if the communications could still be obtained in different surroundings.

On October 17, the record discloses, the board was brought to the home of friends, Mr. and Mrs. Fred Arnold. Mr. Arnold was skeptical and kept demanding that Patience reveal secrets of the other world.

PATIENCE: Thou wouldst untie the knot tied by the Master Hand.
MR. ARNOLD: If she has been in the spiritual world all these years, she ought to be able to explain some of those secrets.
PATIENCE: Believe me, good souls, life is there as here.

This was a characteristic expression of Patience's. "There" means on earth, in the everyday lives of the people she is addressing. "Here" refers to wherever she is.

Mr. Arnold, apparently losing some of his skepticism, then asked to be allowed to join Mrs. Curran at the board.

PATIENCE: Wash thy hands. Wash thy hands! . . . Pleg the stupid! The stock for him![27]

As the winter wore on, more friends came into the Curran house to observe the strange goings-on there. The activities of the women and their ouija board became the topic of lively conversation among many of their friends. There was some speculation about the mental health of the ladies, but a single visit to the varnished board and its loquacious voice was usually enough to quell such muttering and to widen eyes and pale faces.

A session with the board on December 20 produced mostly trivial conversation about Christmas plans and presents. But there was one unusual twist:

MRS. HUTCHINGS: What has Mrs. Curran for me for Christmas?
PATIENCE: Fifteen pieces and one cracked.

The record states that the set of kitchen jars that Mrs. Curran had ordered for her friend was delivered the following day. As Patience had predicted, the vinegar jar was broken. Mrs. Curran obviously knew what she had ordered, but she had no way of knowing until the following day that one of the jars was cracked.

Although clairvoyance or precognition were never a major factor in the Patience Worth case (Patience persistently refused to answer questions about the future), there were a few claims that she had made predictions that proved to be startlingly true. This was one of the first of such claims.

After the comment about the cracked jar, Mrs. Hutchings asked, "Do you know what I have for her?"

Patience answered, "Table store, cross-stitched. Nay, then, stitched across."

This also was correct. Mrs. Hutchings had purchased a gift of table linen for her friend. Again this was something that Mrs. Curran—if Patience was a reflection of her subconscious—would have no way of knowing.

Finally, the record says, Mrs. Pollard requested, "Give me an inscription for my gift to Mrs. Curran."

Patience responded, "A burning desire never to be snuffed; a waxing faith, ever to burn."

Mrs. Pollard's gift to her daughter, unknown to Mrs. Curran at the time, was a Bayberry candle and shade and stick.[28]

It was now 1914. The sittings went on, one and two evenings a week. Patience never failed to make an appearance—a verbal one—and continued to dictate poems and epigrams and to engage in conversation with her partners and with anyone else who visited the sessions.

On February 15 the unseen visitor dictated the following poem, which was to become one of the better known compositions in the collection. The title, as in all other cases, was supplied by those who wrote down the words:

THE FAREWELL SONG

Heed I the sighting of my soul
For truth? Am I a mighty tempest,
Breaking all barriers and laying low the forest,
Distrust, where lingers mine undoing?
Or but the night breeze gently blowing
And only piling leaves as mine own barrier?

Ah, for my last rest and farewell song
To this, my stalk. Let me rest upon twigs
Of mine own breaking, lulled by the soughing
Of the echo of my last tempest.
Wrap me then, in sweet herbs
Of deeds well done, that, like
The rose of seasons gone, breathes back
A scent and smile of yesteryear.
Pillow not my head upon my good intent,
For rest would surely flee.
A stone would better be.

Ah, Peaceful Vale, wherein my soul
May be my soul and call not
As the night-bird his mate, who but re-echoes
His song. Nay, as cold stars warm
The heavens to light, so must coldly culled
Truth warm my soul, and I
Shall show myself, myself, not a fanged

Or painted thing, not yet the gently smiling
Oily thing I would crave the world to believe.

Strike ye the sword or dip ye
In an inken well, smear ye a gaudy color
Or daub ye the clay? Aye, beat
Upon thy bosom then and cry,
'Tis mine, this world-love and vainglory!
Ah, master-hand, who guided thee?
Stay! Dost know that through the ages,
Yea, through the very ages, one grain
Of Hero-dust, blown from afar,
Hath lodged and moveth thee?

Wait, wreathe thyself and wait.
The green shall deepen to an ashen brown,
And crumble then and fall into thy
Sightless eyes, while the mouldering flesh
Droppeth away. Wait, and catch thy dust.
Mayhap thou canst build it back!
Ah, World! Ah, Folly, thou art king of her!
She will not, but is like unto the monk
Who prays within his cell, unheedful
Of the timid sunbeams who would light
The page his wisdom so befogs.[29]

This message, some of it vague and elliptical, some of it fairly pulsing with strength and directness, is typical of the writings of Patience Worth. It is unrhymed, but in its lyricism and imagery it is incontestably poetry. Whether or not it was poetry of rare quality was to be the subject of prolonged controversy during the years ahead.

After the shock of Patience's first appearances faded, the recipients of the gleanings from the ouija board did not seem overawed by what was happening. They were quite willing to challenge Patience, to criticize her, even to argue with her. For instance this exchange on February 28:

PATIENCE: Weep thou a rosary of tears. Count thou the beads with smiles whose warmth shall vanish the string e'en in thine own hand.
MRS. CURRAN: The thought is both trite and old.
PATIENCE: So then, the rose may fear to bloom lest the ghosts of

sisters prove their right to foremost in the garden! . . . Ye expect a fox's brush upon an ass' tail.
MRS. CURRAN: I still maintain that the "rosary of tears" is not original.
PATIENCE: All your cunning hath gone for naught. A prayer was ne'er known to curd the milk.
MRS. HUTCHINGS: I don't believe Patience said that about the rosary. She was not a Catholic.
PATIENCE: To catch a flea needs be a dog?
MRS. POLLARD: She meant the very first part of her lecture for me, I feel sure. I haven't been in any too pleasant a frame of mind today and I believe she knows it. She evidently thinks me a bad egg.
PATIENCE: Should I blow an egg 'twould still remain puffed.
MRS. POLLARD: Her wits are always at their best when she is giving me a drubbing.
PATIENCE: Prod ye the donkey's rump thou art sure of a kick.[30]

By now the writings had been coming from the ouija board for eight months. During all this time Mrs. Curran and Mrs. Hutchings had operated at the board together. Except for a hint here and there, it had not been made really clear whether the presence of both was necessary for the communications or whether one or the other was the principal receiver.

About this time apparently some friction began to develop between the two women. Possibly it was an ego situation—a question of who was more important to the project. Perhaps the entity calling itself Patience Worth had become so real to both of them by now that they were beginning to compete for her favor.

The cooling of the friendship was shown in John Curran's introductory note to the complete Patience Worth Record when he wrote (as of January 5, 1915): "At first, Mrs. Curran believed in the idea conveyed by Mrs. Hutchings that it was absolutely necessary for Mrs. Hutchings to be at the board with Mrs. Curran in order that anything might come. At this date this has been entirely disproven and the following people have already sat with us, there being no difference in the character or quality of the result no matter who sat."[31]

He went on to list a dozen other people who had sat at the board, in addition to the Currans and Mrs. Pollard, and in the absence of Mrs. Hutchings.

The first attempt to contact Patience without Mrs. Hutchings was made on March 1, 1914. Mrs. Curran was joined at the ouija board by her husband. It is easy to imagine their nervousness as they wondered whether the poetic stranger would visit them again. Would she fail to appear without Emily's commanding presence? Would she possibly be so angered by their disloyalty to their friend that she would never return?

With the fingers of the husband and wife on the pointer, it began to move and they called out the letters to Mrs. Pollard. A new poem was dictated, beginning: "When I would sing, thou hast struck me dumb! When I would make a glorious noise, my lute respondeth not. O, e'en the songbird thou hast favored more."[32]

It was the same style, the same quality as before. Patience Worth had returned to them. Now they knew that Mrs. Hutchings had been only an incidental bystander in this whole unreal charade. She was not really needed.

The following day Mr. and Mrs. Curran held another session without Mrs. Hutchings. The board was slow to speak, and Mrs. Curran said with some impatience, "I wish we could get something from Patience Worth!" Patience replied, "Wait. A goodly lesson is Patience and Worth a wait," thus demonstrating that even wraiths of a ouija board are not immune to strained humor better left unsaid.

Another persistent tendency of Patience was her waspish downgrading of Mrs. Curran. Patience seemed determined to keep Mrs. Curran from getting a swelled head over the proceedings and periodically deflated her, albeit with an underlying sense of tenderness, as if a favorite niece was being chastised. She usually referred to Mrs. Curran as the "follied 'un." At the session on March 15 Mrs. Curran said, "I confess I don't understand it at all. It worries me." Patience replied, "My kerchief-holder would hold thy faith. Ah, weary, weary me from trudging and tracking o'er the long road to thy heart. Wilt thou not let me rest a while therein?"

The record notes here that Mrs. Curran expressed some resentment at the evident questioning of her faith and remarked that some credit was due her for having been the means of producing the writing.

Patience responded, "So doth the piggie who scratcheth upon

an oak deem his fleas the falling acorns' cause. The soap kettle needeth not a shape. I cut my soap to fancy."[33]

The sittings continued throughout the spring and summer. Mrs. Hutchings attended most of the sessions, but it was now quite clear to the Currans, and presumably to Mrs. Hutchings as well, that her involvement was only incidental. Patience Worth would come to Pearl Curran whether or not Mrs. Hutchings was present; the reverse was not true.

Visitors frequently participated in the sessions, sometimes just sitting to the side as awe-struck witnesses, sometimes actually joining Mrs. Curran at the ouija board. The output of the sessions continued to be a mélange—poems of varying lengths on diverse subjects, epigrams, aphorisms, and conversation with those manning the board. Patience often would dictate poems requested for specific guests. Occasionally, the record claims, a poem would be written on a specific subject and—a moment later—a thunderstruck guest would insist that she had silently petitioned Patience for a poem on that very theme.

At the sitting on August 28, 1914, Patience produced a short poem that became her most famous single utterance. It was given the title "Patient God."

> *Ah, God, I have drunk unto the dregs,*
> *And flung the cup at Thee!*
> *The dust of crumbled righteousness*
> *Hath dried and soaked unto itself*
> *E'en the drop I spilled to Bacchus,*
> *Whilst Thou, all-patient,*
> *Sendest purple vintage for a later harvest.*[34]

Some partisans of Patience Worth, with credentials as fanciers of fine language, regarded this poem as one of the most powerful ever written in English and cited the first two lines especially as stunning in their effect.

By October the Curran family had moved to a new house on Union Boulevard in the same West End area of St. Louis. More visitors were coming to their home for the sessions, now regularized on a twice-weekly basis. The guests were all friends, or persons brought by friends with the Currans' permission. The news was beginning to spread around the community about the unusual activities, although the transmission was strictly word-of-mouth. Just how Mrs. Curran regarded Patience Worth at this time, whether as an emissary from the spirit world, or a living being communicating with her somehow by telepathy, or even as a figment of her own personality, is difficult to ascertain from the documents. What is clear is that Mrs. Curran reacted to Patience as if to a totally separate being. As she manipulated the ouija board, Mrs. Curran could be moved to anger or laughter or even to tears by the words that came to her.

On October 18 Patience gave this poignant message:

"Ah, wake me not, if 'mong the leaves where shadows lurk, I fancy conjured faces of my loved, long lost; And if the clouds to me are sorrow's shroud; and if I trick my sorrow then to hide beneath a smile, or build of wasted words a key to wisdom's door—wouldst thou deny me?

"Ah, let me dream! The day may bring fresh sorrows but the Night will bring new dreams."[35]

The sadness of the poem caused Mrs. Curran to break down and cry. The pointer immediately began to move again, and Patience changed the mood with a teasing little poem called "The Weeper," which brought a smile back to Mrs. Curran.

The date of November 26, 1914, is one of some significance in the Patience Worth chronicle. Until that date Patience had dictated only short pieces of great diversity. On this particular day, however, came the first longer work—the forerunner of the full-length literary creations that were to create a whole new dimension in the case and bring worldwide notice.

In two sessions of two hours each on November 26, Patience dictated "The Fool and the Lady," a sort of medieval Pagliacci. A fool, hunchbacked and ugly, vainly loves the Lady Lisa. His only companion is his monkey, Beppo. To make it possible for the lady's beloved knight to win her in a tournament, he charges into the fray and gives up his own life.

The opening of the work is worth quoting because it is a good example of the descriptive power and skill frequently demonstrated in the play, using language that is clear and simple:

And there it lay asleep!
A mantle, gray as monk's cloth, its covering. Dim glowing tapers

shine like glowflies down the narrow, winding streets. The sounds of early morning creep through the thickened veil of heavy mist like echoes of the day afore.

The wind is toying with the threading smoke, and still it clingeth to the chimney pot.

There stands, beyond the darkest shadow, the Inn of Falcon Feather, her sides becracked with sounding of the laughter of the kind and gentle-folk who barter song and story for the price of ale. Her windows sleep like heavy-lidded eyes and her breath doth rock with wine, late drunk by a merry party there.

The dialogue went like this:

FOOL: Hear, Beppo, how she prates! Would I were a posey wreath and Beppo here a fashioner of song. We then would lend us to thy hand to offer as a token. But thou dost know a fool and ape art ever but a fool and ape. I'm off to chase thy truant laugh. Who cometh there? The dust doth rise like a storm cloud along the road ahead and 'tis shot with glinting! Ah, I see the mantling flush of morning put to shame by the flushing of thy cheek! See, he doth ride with helmet ope; its golden bars do clatter at the jolt and—but stop Beppo, she heareth not. We, poor beggars, thee and me—an ape with a tail and a fool with a heart.

The play, with the fool lying mortally injured, ends this way:

FOOL: Aday my lady fair! And has thee lost the silver of thy laugh and bid me fetch it thee? The world doth hold but fools and lovers, folly sick.
LISA: His eye grows misty. Fool, I know thee as a knave and love thee as a man.
FOOL: 'Tis but a patch, Beppo, a patch and tassel from a lance—but we did ride, eh? Laugh, Beppo, and prove thou art the fool's! I laugh anew, lest my friends should know me not. Beppo, I dream of new roads but thou art there! And I do faint, but she—did kiss my hand —aday—L-a-d-y.[36]

Whatever you may think of this as drama or as poetry—and admittedly it is hardly suited to the tastes of today's Broadway theatergoer—it must be conceded that there is power here and deep feeling and a gift for language. And it came from whom—a conventional, unliterary, presumably untalented St. Louis housewife?

Mrs. Curran's stepdaughter some years later made this comment to an interviewer: "I know nothing in Mrs. Curran's surroundings to give her the knowledge in the Patience Worth writings. There was no opportunity during my acquaintance with her to converse with scholars or overhear their talk. Before Patience Worth, housework mostly occupied Mrs. Curran's time in the forenoon; in the afternoon she might take a nap, do some fancy work, and perhaps make calls; in the evening she would sing to entertain the family or, very often, the whole family went to a picture show. She read little and almost never aloud."[37]

Could it be this woman, whose reading had been confined almost entirely to women's magazines and romantic novels, who now was producing poetic medieval dramas?

Was it this woman, who insisted that her childhood pleasure reading had been limited to stories like *Black Beauty* and books by Louisa May Alcott and who swore that she had never read a book of history or a complete Bible chapter, who was able to paint a verbal scene like this?

> Thick stands the hill in garb o' fir, and winterstripped the branching shrub. Cold gray the sky, and glistened o'er with star dust, pulsing tremorously.
>
> Snow, the Lady of the Winter Knight, hath danced her weary and fallen to her rest. She lieth stretched in purity and dimpled neath the trees.
>
> A trackless waste doth lie from hill to valley neath, and winter's knight doth sing a wooing lay unto his love.

On October 16, 1914, the record had indicated a first visit to Patience Worth by a prominent St. Louisan named Casper S. Yost. He was puzzled and fascinated by what he saw and was a frequent visitor thereafter.

Yost was one of two men who were responsible for dramatically transforming the case of Patience Worth from a neighborhood curiosity—a source of idle speculation and some amusement—into a captivating enigma for people throughout the world.

For the past eighteen months Patience had been a kind of offbeat parlor game. Now she was about to become a celebrity.

2

The Devout Publicist

CASPER SALATHIEL YOST was a newspaperman, but he was hardly an eager young newshawk, out to make a name and looking for an oddity on which to capitalize. Quite the opposite.

When he first encountered Patience Worth, Yost had been on the staff of the *St. Louis Globe-Democrat* for twenty-five years and had risen to the post of Sunday Editor. The son of a minister, born in southwest Missouri, he had learned to set type for a small-town paper at the age of eight, standing on a bench to reach the type cases.

In 1915, shortly after he became involved in the Patience Worth case, he was elevated to editor of his paper's editorial page, a position he held until his death in 1941. A deeply religious man, his editorials on Christmas, Easter, and Thanksgiving annually attracted wide notice.

He wrote six books, received honorary degrees from four colleges (he had never attended college), and in 1936 was given the national award for scholarship in journalism by Sigma Delta Chi, the national journalism society. He founded the prestigious American Society of Newspaper Editors and was its president from 1922–26.[1]

33

It is necessary to cite these seemingly incidental biographical facts to make clear that Casper Yost was a distinguished, universally respected journalist, nationally known and admired. Yet his interest in Patience Worth was to bring him, from some quarters at least, ridicule and imputations of dishonesty for the purpose of personal gain.

When Casper Yost died in 1941 at the age of seventy-seven, his newspaper, which he had served almost fifty-two years, said of him: "To those who worked with him, he was not merely a gentleman. He was in the authentic and original sense of that word a gentle man. Slight, modest, soft-spoken, courteous . . . he thought and weighed and wrote. Beneath the scholar was the thinker, beneath the thinker, the poet, and beneath the poet a deeply religious spirit. . . ."[2] An editorial the same day described him as "an omnivorous reader . . . and a student of the classics."[3] He was one of thirty-three noted Missourians for whom a Liberty Ship was named in World War II.[4]

More to the point, he was a man of unimpeachable honesty and integrity. He was the old-fashioned man of virtue, the sort of old newspaperman who sat at a roll-top desk and wrote everything in longhand. He was the kind of man of whom a fellow St. Louisan would say at a memorial service: "If ever, in our day, there lived and labored among us a man of fearless intellectual honesty, it was Casper Yost."[5]

And he was the man who came to believe passionately in the reality of Patience Worth and who first gave her words to the world.

Just how Casper Yost originally became interested in the Patience Worth case is uncertain. The record mentions that he attended one of the ouija-board sessions on October 16, 1914. He and his wife were frequent visitors at the Curran home thereafter. There is some indication that Yost had known Mrs. Curran for some time. A long-time friend of Mr. and Mrs. Yost told me that Mrs. Curran had lived with the Yosts for a time before her marriage. This could not be otherwise documented. He may have learned of Patience Worth directly from the Currans; he may have been told about the ouija-board writings by Mrs. Hutchings, a frequent contributor to the Sunday newspaper edited by Yost. It is interesting, though, that Yost didn't pay a call on Patience until some fifteen months after her first appearance. Whether the delay was due to an innate skepticism on his part, a reluctance to get involved in something that sounded so questionable, or whether he simply hadn't heard what was going on until October 1914 we don't know. But he finally did come and quickly was convinced that something truly remarkable was happening. This trained, seasoned newspaperman, wise in the ways of fraud and deception, soon became a devoted admirer of Patience Worth. The feeling was mutual. Patience soon began referring to him as "Brother" and made it clear to all that he held a special place in her affections.

During his repeated visits Yost took careful notes of the proceedings. Occasionally he would join Mrs. Curran at the board and sometimes would ask questions of their unseen visitor. His efforts to dig into Patience's personal history met with little more success than anyone else's. Yost spent additional hours poring over the records of the sessions dating back to the summer of 1913. A self-made scholar, with more than a passing acquaintance with poetry, he carefully analyzed the works that had been laboriously given by the ouija board, seeking out their derivation, checking for any clues that would indicate their source. He began also to look for common themes, to sort out and tie together any strands of ideas that would point to a coherent philosophy in the writings. Soon certain fundamental perspectives became apparent. There was, he decided, something that could be reasonably described as a Patience Worth Philosophy.

As the weeks went on Yost discussed with Mr. and Mrs. Curran their feelings about arranging a wider dissemination of the writings of Patience Worth. This, in turn, would obviously mean the revelation of the entire affair, of the identity of the Currans and the highly unusual, to say the least, manner in which the writings had been produced. He warned them that it would not necessarily be pleasant. There would be notoriety. They would be laughed at by some and probably ridiculed. They would be accused of running some sort of elaborate con game. Yes, they were eager to tell the world of Patience Worth and bring her writings to as wide an audience as possible. But were they willing to pay the price?

On Tuesday, February 2, 1915, a large display ad appeared in the *Globe-Democrat*. It was headed: THE MYSTERY OF "PA-TIENCE WORTH." The ad read: "Next Sunday, the *Globe-Democrat* will begin publication of a series of articles on what is perhaps the most marvelous psychical phenomenon the world has ever known. An 'intelligence' which claims to be the spirit of a woman who lived over two hundred years ago is composing, here in St. Louis, poems and story-plays whose beauty amaze all who read them. Nothing like them has ever been published and no matter what one may think of the claim of supernatural origin, one must be profoundly impressed by the intellect which produces them. Do not fail to get next Sunday's *Globe-Democrat!*"

The same ad was run in all editions for the rest of the week. The promotional campaign, considering the superlatives of the ad copy and the frequent repetition of the ad, presumably provided a large audience for the long-awaited public announcement of the "marvelous psychical phenomenon."

On the following Sunday, February 7, in the Sunday Magazine section of the *Globe-Democrat*, a full page was devoted to a copyrighted article by Yost, headed, like the ad, "The Mystery of 'Patience Worth.'" The article was illustrated by an artist's sketch of two women seated at a ouija board, with a third woman sitting nearby and taking notes.

Beginning with the session on July 8, 1913, at which the "Many moons ago . . ." message was transmitted, the article described the coming of Patience Worth. The two women who were the main participants were identified only as Mrs. Jones and Mrs. Smith because "they . . . shrink from the publicity which may follow publication of these records."

Scattered about the impressive full-page layout were separate boxes headed: Prose Poem by Patience Worth, A Personal Message, Proverbs of Patience Worth, and Satire of Patience Worth. Generous samples of the ouija-board writings were given in the boxes.

Yost had no reluctance to admit publicly how impressed he was by the writings. They are, he said, "a series of communications that in intellectual vigor and literary quality are entirely without precedent in the chronicles of psychic phenomena."

After explaining the appearance and function of the ouija board, Yost briefly described the backgrounds of the two women, without revealing enough for them to be identified. He declared, "It will thus be at once apparent that the character of these people lifts them above any suspicion of charlatanism. Whatever may be the source of these communications, the persons receiving and recording them have no conscious complicity in their conception. The writer has known them for many years; he has been present at a number of the sittings and can testify to their genuineness."

Communications purportedly received via a ouija board are nothing new, Yost agreed. Such communications have been reported numerous times. But nothing of any importance, literary or otherwise, ever has resulted from such supposed communication. "It is the extraordinary—the amazing intellect revealed in the communications that come through the ouija board under consideration," he pointed out, "which makes them worthy of the notice and publicity that the *Globe-Democrat* intends to give them."

Just who did this so-called Patience Worth claim to be? Yost explained what his careful analysis of the already lengthy record had shown: "Patience claims to have lived in the first half of the seventeenth century and to have been of English birth. She is reticent as to her history, but her language gives evidence of Puritan or Quaker association and the inference is drawn from certain of her remarks that she came to the American colonies. She speaks the tongue of the period in which she claimed to have lived, a language strewn with obsolete and archaic words, but seldom does she use one that is not understood by the present generation.

"All of the objects that she refers to are things that existed in her time. In all of the great mass of manuscript that has come from her, there is not a single reference to an object of modern creation or development; not a single word, so far as the writer and others have been able to discern, that was not in use in the seventeenth century." In describing Patience's personality, Yost said, "She has a keen and instantaneous but caustic wit, sometimes tinged with the coarseness of the day in which she claims to have lived."

Yost went on in the article to discuss the poetry of Patience Worth, always unrhymed but frequently displaying startling powers of expression and a vivid, colorful mode of phrasing. "Some of the lines are obscure, but study reveals the meaning and the more one studies them, the more one must be impressed with the extraordinary intellectual power that is behind them . . . the intellect of Patience Worth justifies any man's respect. It is at once keen, swift, subtle, and profound and it is endowed with a marvelous knowledge of nature and nature's laws."

Then, alluding to the poem previously quoted ("Ah, God, I have drunk unto the dregs"), which was destined to become the most famous single creation of Patience Worth, Yost stated: "In the writer's opinion, there is nothing in literature that grips the mind with greater force, almost breath-stopping in its awfulness, than the first two lines of the brief poem . . . and there is nothing in literature more beautiful than its conclusion."

Ponder that for a moment. "Nothing in literature that grips the mind . . . ," "Nothing in literature more beautiful. . . ." A top editor of one of the country's major newspapers was making these statements about words produced by a device regarded by most people as a silly toy and operated by a woman with no apparent interest in writing and no perceptible knowledge of, or taste for, literature of excellence.

There is little doubt that Yost knew what he was getting himself into. He had placed his reputation, possibly his entire career, on the line. Apparently he regarded Patience Worth the risk.

The article created a sensation. As word spread, those who were not *Globe-Democrat* subscribers rushed out to buy copies. Yost was besieged with telephone calls and letters, asking the real names of the two mysterious ladies who were able to contact the spirits of the dead. Yost told his questioners to continue reading the articles to follow.

Recognizing a good thing, the newspaper ran a big promotional ad for the articles every day of the following week. On Sunday, February 14, the second article appeared, containing more Patience Worth poems, together with a more detailed analysis and discussion of the literary aspects of the work by Yost. Again, the real names of the two women were not given. On the following two Sundays, the third and fourth articles were run. The third was a discussion of the personality of Patience Worth, with numerous examples of her caustic humor and razor tongue. The fourth article was headed "The Prose of Patience Worth" and included two complete works, "The Fool and the Lady" and "The Stranger," a long Christmas story dictated during the previous December.

Public reaction to the articles continued to mount. Inquiries began to come in from other cities and a few psychologists requested more details and cautiously wondered if an investigation would be permitted.

On Sunday, March 7, the fifth and final article in the series was printed. In it, Yost revealed for the first time the names of Pearl Curran and Emily Grant Hutchings, as well as Mrs. Pollard and all the other major figures in the case. The story was illustrated with a large picture of Mrs. Curran. Titled "Is There Life After Death?" the article analyzed the many references in the Patience Worth writings to death, the foolishness of fearing death, and the strong inference—although usually couched in Patience's typical figurative style—that she was a resident of the spirit world.

The excited and enthusiastic reaction to the newspaper series and the widespread interest it aroused convinced Yost that a book should be written about the case. He began work on it immediately, using his five long articles as the framework for the full-length manuscript. Such a book had been planned months earlier by Mrs. Hutchings, but she apparently was dissuaded from the project by the feeling of the Currans that it would detract from the credibility of the account if the book was written by someone directly involved in the case. We can assume, also, that the indications of a growing coolness between Mrs. Curran and Mrs. Hutchings were a factor in the decision to have the book written by another writer.

So now, in early 1915, the case had become public knowledge. The word was soon to spread much farther. After Yost broke the story to the newspaper readers of St. Louis, another writer entered the picture. And while Yost gave the news to the man in the street, the second major chronicler of Patience Worth was to introduce her to the intellectual and literary circles of the world and, even more important, give her his coveted imprimatur.

3

Enter "Fatawide"

HE WAS A SLOPPY, fat man, a boozer. Two of his three wives had been operators of brothels. He was a non-believer, an excommunicated Catholic. After an erratic career as a newspaper reporter he had helped to start a disreputable gossip sheet in St. Louis. Yet this was hardly the whole picture. For he was also, wrote his biographer, "a humorist, a critic, and a discoverer. Pater, Yeats, and Emily Dickinson were among his early literary finds. Theodore Dreiser and Edgar Lee Masters were proud to count themselves among his later ones."[1]

This was William Marion Reedy, one of the most colorful and perceptive figures in American literary history, who regrettably has slipped into the obscurity of passing time. He was the editor of *Reedy's Mirror*, a St. Louis-based weekly journal of opinion and literature. The magazine covered the arts, politics, business and economics, sports, foreign affairs, and virtually any other topic that interested Reedy—and he was the most eclectic of men.

The son of a policeman, Reedy graduated from Saint Louis University at eighteen. After an up-and-down career in the newspaper business, he helped start a gossipy publication called the

Mirror in 1891. Reedy went into debt and began drinking heavily. He awoke one morning to find himself married to a brothel keeper. His magazine went bankrupt, but later a friend bought back the magazine at auction and gave it to Reedy as a gift. This time Reedy began to stamp his own unique intellect on the publication. He wrote thousands of words a week on topics of the day, reviewing books and discussing literature, analyzing the stock market, jousting with politicians, St. Louis newspapers and anyone else with whom he disagreed, and printing the works of new young authors that he deemed worthy of discovery.

The reputation of Reedy and his *Mirror* began to spread across the country and later to Europe. By the start of the Spanish-American War the *Mirror* had achieved a national circulation of more than 32,000.[2] The masthead of the magazine eventually noted that it was sold in London, Munich, Florence, Venice, Monte Carlo, Paris, Rome, Naples, Genoa, and Bologna. Also listed in the masthead were famous hotels in various European cities which kept a complete file of *Reedy's Mirror* in their reading rooms.

Despite his increasing fame and influence, however, Reedy never changed his appearance or his way of life.

One of his discoveries was Fannie Hurst, then an unknown young writer in St. Louis. In her autobiography she described her first meeting with Reedy: ". . . the open door revealed him practically reclining in a swivel chair, his feet high on an incredibly littered desk, his vast body seeming to run downhill in an avalanche of fat, mussed shirt crawling up out of his low-waisted trousers, a pair of cracked glasses low on his nose, dark graying hair pushed around on his head, eyeshade dangling from his neck like a bib. . . . Books, books, stacked on the floor, on chairs, overflowed the place."[3]

There was little question during the early years of the twentieth century that Reedy was one of this country's preeminent authorities on poetry. John T. Flanagan, writing of Reedy in the *Missouri Historical Review*, noted: "Each issue of the *Mirror* contained some poetry and some fiction. The verse was quite representative of the best being written in the United States. Among the more established poets whom Reedy printed were Bliss Carman, Richard Le Gallienne, Lizette Reese, Clinton Scollard, Paul

Laurence Dunbar, Percival Pollard. More important, he welcomed poets who had not yet won their spurs, native St. Louisans like Sara Teasdale and Orrick Johns, but also Edna St. Vincent Millay, Babette Deutsch, Witter Bynner, John Gould Fletcher, William Rose Benet, Carl Sandburg, Vachel Lindsay, and especially Edgar Lee Masters. Masters was his greatest find and not the least important date in American literary history is May 29, 1914, when under the pseudonym of Webster Ford, Masters published in the *Mirror* the first installment of his *Spoon River Anthology*."[4]

Reedy was a friend of the famous. "Alexander Harvey," it was written some years after Reedy's death, "called him 'America's supreme master of the intellectual life.' . . . 'He has stood for me.' wrote William Rose Benet, 'as, somehow, the symbol of native American genius.' . . . Frank Harris's first question, when he came to New York from London, was 'Where can I find Reedy?'. . . . Statesmen like Theodore Roosevelt and writers like Theodore Dreiser were proud of his acquaintance."[5]

In 1917 Reedy became one of the three judges appointed to select the recipient of the first Pulitzer Prize in Poetry.

After his death in 1920 the *New York Tribune* said: "The most appalling thing about William Marion Reedy was his lack of fame among his own countrymen. Here was a really great critical mind."[6]

William Marion Reedy—skeptic, free-thinker, non-believer. A sophisticated judge of poetry and art, quick to level his critical guns on writing he deemed inferior. It would seem most unlikely that he would take even a modicum of interest in words supposedly produced by a spirit through a ouija board. Reedy not only came and observed; he completely fell in love with Patience Worth. The conversion of Billy Reedy to an admirer of Patience Worth was perhaps the biggest single factor in her acceptance by national magazines and major newspapers, as well as many intellectuals and literary figures, as a phenomenon worthy of serious study and analysis.

Reedy first took notice of Patience Worth in February 1915 after the appearance of Yost's original articles in the *Globe-Democrat*. In the February 26 issue of the *Mirror* Reedy wrote a brief statement headed "Necromantic Poetry." It began: "Some competent authorities should investigate the poems of 'Patience Worth' printed in installments in the Sunday *Globe-Democrat*." He went on to say that "They are rather remarkable poems, though not great. Notably they are innocent of Latinism in language. The words are all Anglo-Saxon and therefore short. Where archaisms appear they are properly used. The thought is not modern save in so far as all real thought in the world, on the eternal subjects, is the same, ancient or modern."

Reedy added: "The blank verse has a fine vigor always though there are turns of phrase and uses of words that show, to the practiced writer, evidences of strain, as if someone were trying to write in the style of a past age. The language is certainly not fluently natural, to my thinking."

After this suggestion that someone might be straining to pose as something else, Reedy called for further study of the case: ". . . the work is in all respects extraordinary, in nothing mean or piddling. As a simple tour de force it is worthy of studious attention. The lady, the ladies, indeed, who handle the ouija board are of high repute. Neither of them is literary in any sense that would justify the suspicion of marked familiarity with the language about thirty years after Shakespeare. Both ladies say they could not do the work as it is done. They believe 'Patience Worth' is the spirit of a woman who once walked the earth and now revisits the glimpses of the ouija board illumination to convey a message. I don't see any message in her work, though it is better than any other that has come to us that way. I don't believe any person dead has ever come back to tell anybody anything. I believe someone with a special literary interest in the older English poetry is putting over something on the operators of the ouija board. Whoever it is certainly writes near-great poetry. The mystery of 'Patience Worth' is well deserving of exploration by the amateurs of psychology and necromancy."[7]

So the poems were "extraordinary" and "near-great" and worthy of study, Reedy said, but the idea that their creator was a spirit who had lived several hundred years before was obviously preposterous. Of his suggestions that someone appeared to be straining to write in a style not his own or that "someone . . . is putting over something on the operators of the ouija board," Reedy never again would offer them seriously.

After that initial mention, Patience Worth did not break into the *Mirror* again for many months. Then, in the fall of 1915, Reedy met Patience Worth—if not face to face, then at least face to board. Reedy had hardly been overjoyed at the prospect of getting entangled with the poetic wraith. He described later how it finally came about: "Well, I'd heard much of Patience Worth, had read her poems, her play *Red Wing*, her novel *Telka*. I had told those who talked to me about those performances that I was a doubter of communications from the dead. I suspected, somehow, a literary trick, a clever imposture. What I had seen of Patience Worth's work was infinitely better than anything I had seen before quoted as coming by any of the means of communication familiar to the student of or the ordinary reader about the spookishly occult. I had written a disdainfully negational paragraph about the validity and verity of the Patience Worth experiences. I had written so hastily that I had hurt Mrs. Curran, whom I did not know. Almost, I believe, I had angered Mr. Casper Yost. To me then came Mr. John H. Curran with some specimens of the poems. Would I read them? I would, and did. Would I come and witness and query the work of Patience Worth, and see and hear for myself? I would, and did. . . . I went with as open a mind as a man could have toward anything disputable. Indeed, I went with more of doubt than of hope or faith, with possibly a little contempt for myself for wasting an afternoon that I had intended to put in reading the exemplary *Tales* of George Crabbe. . . . 'Here I am,' said I to my wife, 'going out to put in an afternoon with a lot of daffy spook-spielers.' Anyhow, I went out to Mr. and Mrs. Curran's pretty home, 1363 Union Boulevard, Sunday afternoon, September 13th, 1915.[8]

"At the Curran residence we found, with Mr. and Mrs. Curran, Mrs. Curran's mother, Mrs. Pollard, Mrs. C. B. Rohland and Miss Hattie Dolbee of Alton, Ill. Later, Mr. Casper Yost came in. We talked of Patience Worth's poetry and some of her prose that I had read. I ventured the opinion that the poetry was not as splendid or as remarkable, aside from the conditions of its production, as Mr. Yost had maintained in the series of articles in the *Globe-Democrat*. Some specimens of the poetry were read by Mr. Curran and I still held that they were not, as poetry, unique and of so unsurpassable beauty and originality as to excite vast enthusiasm. Mr. Yost asserted that I couldn't recall anything like them, and I said that, as for likeness, they resembled, here and there, in thought and remotely in expression, dozens of poems that I remembered. My opinions seemed to shock Mrs. Curran very much as I developed them frankly, if not fully, even though I said that I did not see that it was necessary to the validity of the communications that the poems should surpass, or even equal, the old masters, the bards sublime. Probably there are as many fairly good, or even bad, poets in the realm of Patience Worth as there are in our own. Mrs. Curran, in no very joyous mood, got out the ouija board and I put my hands, with hers, on the pointer, which wavered about for a few seconds and then began rapidly to spell out this message:

> Hark, hark! Unto him who holdeth up unto the Earth the polished steel, I do speak. Yea, knowest thou that that showeth within the steel showeth not always as truth? Aye, it be awry atimes. He eateth not the loaf o' me, aye, but I do fashion on and on. Yea, for 'tis for the eat o' hungered. Set thou aweave.

"Here Patience gave about four hundred words of the 'Sorry Tale' under my and Mrs. Curran's hands. The writing was then discontinued and a long discussion of the writings ensued, after which Mrs. Reedy was urged to take the board.

"Patience: 'He' (that is I) 'hath not a love for the word o' me, but he hath a soft aneath the heart he hideth. Yea, and do I to touch the spot that be the soft, I do cast a beam unto her, ahere, o' loving. The men o' my day spake not out unto the dames and telled that they thought. Yea, but I do love thee none the less for thy putting. (Then to the company, of me) He loveth pottage and needeth not a wraith o' sweets. Hark ye, I do spin a tale.'

"Then with incredible rapidity the pointer spelled out the following lines, which we called 'The Parable of the Birds':"

> Lo, there wert a man, and he did plant him a tree. And it grew much and sent forth branches wide and thick. And lo, he saw the fowls of the air did seek out this tree, and they sang much, and more and more, until his day were full of musics.
> And lo, at a certain day, he went him forth, and there upon the tree did sit a bird who warbled loudly, and he loved not its song. Aye, but it sung on and on.

And lo, the man knew not this bird. And he spake that he would set him up a net and trap the host of fowls that sung, and from out o' them would steal that which did make the song, that he might choose that which did please him much, and cast awither that that did sound asorry unto his ear.

And lo, he did this thing. And 'twere for the stopping of the song of the bird he knew not. For the hosts did sing them mournful, and he knew their song, and not the song of the bird that had come unto him.

And he did slay the birds anetted and oped them up and lo, their song, he found, had been but the mourning of a sorry belly o'er a worm. And lo, he oped the bird he knew not, and naught wert within its paunch. And yet it sung and sung and sung.

And he loved not its song and yet it sung and sung and sung.

Reedy's report of the session continued:

"This parable was surely of direct application to the critical attitude to Patience's poems of the man who holdeth up the polished steel. Before the time of backed glass all mirrors were of polished steel. Then the ouija pointer, under Mrs. Curran's and Mrs. Reedy's hands, started off again:

"Patience: 'Lor' it taketh him o' soft heart to know a heart like hers ahere!' (This to Mrs. Reedy.) 'I'd seek a word to tickle o' the paunch o' him to shake. I'd put a song, but list thee, 'tis a sorry song, he sayeth! Yea, but here it be, a song.'"

At this point in his description of the visit to Patience Worth, Reedy quoted a five-stanza devotional poem which was given next. After this, someone suggested that Reedy ask a question of Patience. It is interesting and amusing to note that this skeptical man of letters began then to ask the kind of question that assumes that Patience really was the spirit of someone long dead and that she had knowledge of many of history's most vaunted mysteries. Virtually all of the famous men who came to visit Patience, many of them professing utter disbelief in her reality, wound up putting the same type of questions to her. Somewhere in even the most skeptical of men apparently lurks a tiny voice saying, Is it possible that this is really what it purports to be? If so, then perhaps she could tell me at long last . . . ?

In framing his question Reedy remembered reading that she had given a date somewhere about the time of Shakespeare, although she also had implied that she was of many times. He asked, "Who wrote the Shakespeare plays?"

PATIENCE: Aye, Lawk! He hath a taste o' the brew o' me and wisheth that I do deal o' my brother's brew! What hath Earth but stones for him who walketh shoon o' skins, sewn o' thong and crusts? Were words o' Him for such an one? Nay, 'twere better far they be dealt to one who held a measure polished much for hold o' them! Yea, and yet I do say unto thee, the word o' the skin-shoon man, who troddeth 'pon path o' sky and Earth, be his, e'en though they be o' thistledown.

Reedy analyzed the response this way: "I worked this out as referring, in 'shoon o' skins, sewn o' thong,' to Shakespeare's being an actor of 'sock and buskin,' and the phrase 'one who held a measure polished much for hold o' them' as a reference to Bacon, or it might be to Marlowe, and then I asked this oracle, 'Who wrote the letters of Junius?' "

PATIENCE: He who seekest world's pence, layeth up o' his brother's store, doth he find a loose o' store. Yea, 'tis a take and keep, by nay eye aseen. Yea, and I tell unto thee there be men o' Earth who digged up word o' them agone, and did cleanse o' rust and lo, coax out the shine, and beat the busom o' him and say: 'This abe mine own.' Set up thine own thought. Thou has eat the answering o' this.
REEDY: I am correct, then, in my surmise.
PATIENCE: Yea, yea, yea. Thou hast eat the loaves o' him and know the taste o' the bread. Thy head may lead thee astray, yea, but thy belly, never. Nay, it spatteth forth that awry.
REEDY: Was Marlowe murdered or did he escape to the Continent?
PATIENCE: Lor' I be my brother's keeper! He who fleeth ever leaveth trail and Time ever showeth it. If thou seest not the trail, then what think ye?

Reedy continued, "Now I remarked that these communications were cryptic, like the Delphic and other oracles, and while they were evidently replies to my questions, they could not be called answers to those questions. To this, thus: 'I say me yea, athin these words be the Yea and Nay.' Though I puzzled over the replies, I could not see the 'Yea' or 'Nay.' "[9]

The following Sunday, Reedy and his wife returned. Obviously the magazine editor was becoming intrigued with the shadowy conversationalist. No longer, apparently, was he complaining about spending time with "daffy spook-spielers."

Reedy gave the following account of his second encounter with Patience. I think it is worth quoting at length because it demonstrates Reedy's desire to challenge Patience with the most significant questions he could compose and also because it offers a rather comprehensive view of her religion and philosophy. Again I urge you to wend your way carefully through Patience's admittedly difficult language. It is slow going, sometimes tedious and laborious. But, once deciphered, it makes sense. This is a coherent system of ideas. It may or may not be objectively true, but it is, in my opinion, deserving of respect.

"On the next Sunday afternoon, September 20th, Mrs. Reedy and I went to the Currans' house again. Those present besides us were Mr. and Mrs. Curran and Mrs. Pollard. Patience was, of course, our theme. We talked somewhat of her identity and then passed on to some religious phases of some of her communications to others. I expressed some thoughts opposed to the theory of commerce between the dead and the living and said that I did not see why, if God had anything to say to anyone, it should not be said to that one direct and not through another being. I was infidel to the doctrine that there was proof of communication from God or from dead persons to living men. Mrs. Curran and Mrs. Reedy sat at the ouija board and this message came:

PATIENCE: Awoe is me! They seek o' my cloak and I tell to thee 'tis the cloak o' ye I do don. Yea and I do set it atatter till thou knowest not thy very own cloak and this cloak is thy tung. Hark ye, thou fat-awide [referring to my physical weight and width], unto thee I do speak, for hark, unto each and every man cometh He. Yea, as a bride, young and lovely. Yea, and she cometh unto thee at the fullness o' thy flesh and she hath not words. Nay, she be mute and man doth set upon her lips words. Yea, and some do set afilthed and others do set amusicked, and others do set agrinning 'pon the lips o' her. And lo, she goeth back unto Him at the leaving o' the Earth, and thou will see her decked with what thou hast put 'pon her lips. And hark! Ye men call this bride Muse, and lo, she be but the smile o' Him!

Yea, and more I speak unto thee, and this thou knowest not. Thou didst see not with thine eyes o' flesh afore thy coming. Aye, but at

thy bearing, thy mother oped up thine eyes and thee didst see and behold o' the Earth. Aye, now list thee! Death then, is thy mother, for, hark, at her bearing thou shalt shut up thy eyes o' flesh and see o' the land o' here.
Yea and yea and yea, and at hours thou knowest not there cometh that thou hast ne'er seen or heard. And yet it be and 'tis thine, and thou didst ne'er touch, aye, or see this thing. Then what think ye?
REEDY: Can man know anything, have any ideas, save such as come through his experience or the experience of others transmitted to him?
PATIENCE: Yea, and thou knowest much o' such.
REEDY: Must we not have either our own or others' experience?
PATIENCE: Ayea and anay. Thou hast much that hath come unto thee from Him. Thou knowest Him and ownest not thy sire. Even so thou knowest not his house.
REEDY: How is a man to know God?
PATIENCE: Alawk! Thy heart is packed afull o' Him, brother. Aye and thou knowest. Then speak so, and say 'tis well, for sure as sun shall rise, thy dust shall rise and blow unto new fields of new days. . . . Thou hast walled up thy heart o' words and yet it showeth athrough the patches o' thy words.
REEDY: These answers are not new, but are good; they are the correct answers according to the theologians.
PATIENCE: I bring ye not a new water o' a new well. Nay, nay, I bring but cooling drop o' the water Earth hath held for time and time, and yet I do step me thus so, and do me awry, that such as ye do to see a trick that shall set thee up upon thy scent to watch and wonder much. For hark ye, thou hast a trick o' tricks. I do ply then word e'en as do thou. Aye, but this be not thy path I do trod, and thou hast met a word that standeth top to bottom and thou wouldst know o' why. Yea, did it to stand o' thy day as thou wouldst set ashow upon thy polished steel [The *Mirror* again] then wouldst thou say, 'tis her ahere and not me.

"In other words," commented Reedy, "she spoke as she did, in her own 'tung,' because if she spoke in speech of today, I would say it was Mrs. Curran speaking and not she, Patience. Her word 'top to bottom' was her own, with no break into the language of today."

REEDY: Is there any Time over there?
PATIENCE: The yesterdays o' here o' thy day, are ahere this day, and days, and days o' what thou wouldst say were hours.

REEDY: How about Space?
PATIENCE: Thou wouldst drink ye full. Then hark! Look ye up and up and up and up and up and thou hast but stepped unto the border.
REEDY: Is Space infinite?
PATIENCE: Aye.
REEDY: How can there be two infinites?
PATIENCE: There be a two o' ye, thou shalt know. For the eye o' flesh there be for seeing, man builded wall and path. Unto the ye o' ye the eye o' flesh is closed. Yea, until the flesh o' ye hath gone. Then it opeth and thou shalt see and know the word o' me. Yea, there be 'pon Earth much thou seest not. Thou shouldst ope the eye o' the in-man. Then e'en thou canst know of this thing thou seekest, for did thy day to on and on till time wert not, e'en though thy reasoning had gone awry, thou still wouldst draw thee, from whence thou knowest not, much for the filling o' thy day. And this is as but the threading o' the spider's web for Him.
REEDY: Whose fault is it if one stray from the path through seeing not?
PATIENCE: Thy blind in-man.
REEDY: Whence cometh knowledge of the path?
PATIENCE: 'Tis athin thy very hands. Yea, thou knowest much and little. I do say this unto thee, and thee, and thee [meaning to the others about the board], and not alone unto him [Reedy]. Yea, flesh hath sorry and thou leavest not this thing thy very self but thy mother's mother o' thy tribe.
REEDY: Does it require any special grace to know God?
PATIENCE: Anay. He singeth e'en through the granites o' thy hills and mountains and e'en the dumb o' Earth sing out o' Him. And thou who hast much o' Him, art full o' his song up to thy filling and hear not the songs o' Earth. I tell thee thou shouldst list not unto thy songs alone o' Him, but unto him that singeth from out thy brothers and Earth that thou seest as but Earth and stones.
REEDY: How about predestination and free will?
PATIENCE: These o' Earth deal o' the word o' Him unto such as thou, and I tell thee they do take out the word o' Him and set it atween the palms o' their own hands and squeeze out the word until it fitteth the palms, and do offer unto thee. Thou hast to know 'tis He, the Him o'er him o' man, who smileth much o' this. For this be but the placing o' stones 'pon the path he hath builded up for thee. 'Tis nay awilled for thee. Nay, He hath afar more for thee than this path thou seekest out and deem thee art at doing thy task and oft at doing awry. Yea, for what seemeth awry oft buyeth,

aye ever buyeth, the thing he hath willed, buyeth mayhap not for thee, but for them o' him.

REEDY: This answers the question, except the last part, which is not clear to me.

PATIENCE: Thou art aright. 'Tis a muddle o' a put, yet it be ahere. List, this be a guilding up o' a vast, a vast, a vast o' loving, and this be not a place apart where thou shalt find the Earth-weary tasks. Nay, and what thou hast dreamed and waked to dream anew, thy dearest dreaming o' the fullness o' man, is the love o' Him. And thou art ever thee, for He is ever Him. Thou hast a sorry for a house o' Him that holdeth not a bigness o' man. I speak me now o' the ye o' ye. This, then, is the grow o' the rotting for this man o' man. Yea. Earth is fulled up o' tungs and gods and fools and men. Yea, but this ahere o' Him be afull o' God and men and men and men. Nay tung shall bar up the knowing o' thy brothers in-man, yet ye say I do speak unto thee with thy tung. This abe that you know the me o' me, the flesh aye should take in thereby. Athrough this flesh o' putting shall ye know the me o' me. This be not a need o' here.

Reedy continues: "There came, here, some discussion about the time of Patience's presence in this world, and her saying to another querist something implying that she knew many, many times."

PATIENCE: What think ye it meaneth that I do know the day o' me? Know ye not thy day? And those to come shall know thy day e'en though thou be not ahere. I tell thee this leadeth to a naught.

"Time was taken here for luncheon, after which Mrs. Curran and Mrs. Reedy again sat at the board. I spoke of the readiness, the pertinency, the fluency of Patience's utterances."

PATIENCE: Yea, I be aready o' the tung and did to bake me up the whole o' grain that he eat o' the loaf o' me. And though he hath spat up the song, he hath eat the loaf. Now do ye to weave o' the cloth o' me. Think ye I be a doler of wares without a price? Yea, and do ye work for the tale of me, I do for to fetch out sweets.

"She had been working for us long enough, now the folks at the board had to do some work for her and then she would tell something nice.... The pointer began to fly and soon there were spelled out about fifty words of the story 'Panda,' which Mrs. Curran has been taking for some weeks."

After giving the excerpt from *Panda*, Patience provided the "sweets" she had promised, a very complimentary tribute to Mrs. Reedy, followed by a short poem which the Currans interpreted as a statement of Patience's strong liking for Mr. and Mrs. Reedy. She had added, "I be atickle o' the heart that hath an iron bind," meaning that she would continue to jibe and tease Reedy, despite his strong set of mind (which by now was noticeably wavering) against her.

The session closed with a puzzling episode. It displayed Patience's lusty sense of humor and also represented one of her few forays (however clumsy) into another language. Here is Reedy's description of it:

"On leaving after our first visit, Mrs. Curran had given Mrs. Reedy a ouija board, and at home Mrs. Reedy had tried to work it. The pointer moved under her hands, but spelled out nothing intelligible, save, two or three times, the word 'Latin.' Many times the pointer, in reply to Mrs. Reedy's questions, 'Who wants to talk to me?' darted up to the word Patience Worth printed at the top of the board. The wandering maunderings of the succession of letters that spelled nothing tried our patience and we said, between ourselves, things not expressive of great respect for Patience. We had told about this experience, and the last saying started talk of it anew."

PATIENCE: I be ateeter for to tell. Shall it be put?
ALL: Sure, Patience, tell!
PATIENCE: I be a trickster. Yea and hie me unto thy hut and know thy word! Aye, and I tell unto thee 'tis this that set me at a telling! A war o' setting the word as me as the word. Yea, thou wouldst speak not o' the wraith o' thy grand-dam as thou speakest o' me!
MR. REEDY: Who wanted to talk to me at home, Patience?
PATIENCE: Thou hast much athin thy ear. Thou hast an eye unto him ayonder [Reedy] and an ear unto me! Yea, thou hast a heart ope, aye, but thou art in fearing the put o' me be ye.
MRS. REEDY: Patience, was it you at the house talking to me in Latin?
PATIENCE: Thou hast put aright. I tell thee I sat aside thy hearth. [Apologies from the Reedys.] Nay aneed, I telled thee o' thy grand-dam! Hold thou thy hand unto it.

"This meant that Mrs. Reedy should put her hand on the pointer with Mrs. Curran's, though as principal rather than as assistant. The first thing that was spelled out was: 'Hope has wings.' Then came a succession of words, which, as near as we could make them out, were as follows: 'O sic dominicus quante. Oporte regenia. Poste vigus—ursulis—sistus, donnus, dilegus omne. Jesu Christus Domine. Alawk, ye listed. Ursulis fidelio, Quantis, regenia, semper.'

"My Latin is very skimpily and fragmentarily reminiscential, but I had no difficulty in recognizing the above words as being a very poor brand of the speech of Virgil and Horace. The fact is, that it seems to be made up of misremembered scraps of monks' Latin and of what might be called hog-Latin. 'Jesus Christ our Lord' is plain, of course; and 'regenia' probably means 'regina,' or 'queen,' and 'semper' means 'always.' But the passage as a whole is what a Latinist would describe as 'hopelessly corrupt.' The words 'Alawk, ye listed!' were evidently an expression of merry mockery over my attempt to translate the gibberish into something intelligible. Mr. Curran began to be a little nervous and said we had better break off taking such stuff, as it might be some other intelligence butting in on the board, and that might possibly work an end of the 'putting' of the story 'Panda.' "

PATIENCE: Anay, 'tis a tracker, but hark! Much do ye learn ayet. Pontius Paillite genitus. This be a trick o' tricks. Ye make much I do tung as thou. Sistus Emanualus beatitudus. Ecce litus—padre.

"There are distorted echoes of Latin there, but nothing I could make head or tail of, and Patience plainly said in her own style of irony, 'It's a lot you are learning from me, I don't think.' Apparently she knew that what she was saying was Latin inexpressibly atrocious, and was, as the saying goes, having fun with us. It was just such 'Latin' as had come to Mrs. Reedy at her ouija board at home and had caused her and myself to say things to Patience that, as she said, we would not say of 'the wraith of our granddam.' That the lingo was meant to be Latin was plain, because after many spellings, to Mrs. Reedy utterly chaotic, for she has no Latin whatever, she had asked the board why it didn't speak English, and the reply came, 'Nay, Latin.' Of this we talked about it and about. Someone said, 'Maybe it was not Patience, but another who was talking by way of the board at the Reedy house.' "

PATIENCE: Nay, unto ye at thy hut I spaked. The tung o' me did put unto thee not as the tung o' me. . . . There a-be; 'tis done.

"Someone, taking this as dismissal, said, 'I wonder if Patience will not give us a word of goodbye,' and then came this:"

PATIENCE: Arest ye in the love o' me. 'Tis a robe o' the cloth o' Him. Yea, even as thine is o' the cloth o' Him.

"This ended the session."[10]

During the weeks that followed, Reedy and his wife paid more calls on the Currans and their ghostly writer. Patience always was glad to talk with him and usually addressed him as "Fatawide." During these visits Reedy bombarded Patience with questions about life over "there." And Patience was always ready with an answer in her usual elliptical style:

REEDY: Will I meet all those I want to see there—Homer, Virgil, Shakespeare?
PATIENCE: Alawk, where a-be the place they do set up o' him. I tell thee the cowled fool shall know thee as brother here. . . .
REEDY: What distinctive difference is there between Jesus Christ and any other man born of the flesh?
PATIENCE: Lor', this one o' Earth, the elder brother o' thee and me, be but the Son o' Him, like to thee, and ne'er hath spaked but this!
REEDY: Then each of us is divine as Christ?
PATIENCE: Aye, and Nay atimes. For lo, 'tis he who buyeth o' loving, love that be the love o' Him. . . .
REEDY: What becomes of the resurrection of the body?
PATIENCE: Aye, the dealers o' the Word tell o' this. This a-be not o' the flesh. Nay, but o' the fulling o' thy man o' man. The big o' men and men, and men o' Him that fill the Here.[11]

From a position of utter skepticism, Reedy had turned round to a feeling of deep, intensifying interest in this glib, provocative, amazingly literate personality—whoever she might be. He still refused to concede that she was a ghost, but whatever she was, he wanted to spend more time with her and talk with her of many things.

In the *Mirror* of October 1, 1915, Reedy told the world of his new involvement. In a front-page story headed "My Flirtation with Patience Worth," and running to several thousand words, Reedy told in detail how he was enticed, much against his will, to visit the Curran home and what had happened there. Explaining briefly the background of the participants, Reedy insisted, "There is absolutely no question of the integrity of any of the parties to the experience with the ouija board. When it is operated it is in a fully lighted room, without any of the usual concomitants of mystery and necromancy."

Of the poems, Reedy said, "They are poetry—no question of that. They have not rhyme, but they have rhythm, decidedly. They are more like blank verse than anything else, but they are not quite that. They are something like the much-discussed 'free verse,' but they are not that either. In a way they are of Biblical quality. The language is not contemporaneous. It is sometimes strongly reminiscent of the seventeenth century, but more often it is a still simpler English, without any French or Latin derivatives. . . . There are hundreds of words of strictly Anglo-Saxon origin, indeed more Anglo than Saxon. The speech is simpler than Chaucer, much simpler. . . . It is as near as anything I know to the very essence of folk-speech. Philologists find in the language words from the dialect of different counties in England, words now of an earlier, now of a later date in the dictionaries and glossaries. . . . The language is very figurative, abounds in similes, many very beautiful metaphors. In the poetry and in the drama and the novel there is much keen and clear descriptions of nature; in the play and novel, splendid characterizations, complicated plots, dialogue, witty, tender, forceful."

Then Reedy pronounced his judgment, undoubtedly knowing full well, as Casper Yost had, that it would bring him derision and ridicule from many of his intellectual friends:

"I think I know literature. Some people who know it have said I do. I say that these communications are literature, and literature of no mean order. They are wonderful, aside from their origin, for content and for form. They are thoroughly consistent in form, too. There runs through them all a sort of musical fugue and a fugue of spiritual suggestion, too. They contain passages of bewitching beauty, of rare high spirits, of pathos—and all in a language of an indescribable simplicity and felicity, though strange. . . .

"I do not think this poetry so great as Mr. Casper Yost thinks it. It does not equal Shakespeare or Spenser. It is not so great as Chaucer. But if there be any intelligences communicating poems by ouija board or otherwise it does not follow that they must be Shakespeares, Spensers, Tennysons, or Sapphos or Mrs. Brownings. But it is good poetry, better poetry than we find in our magazines as a rule—poetry with a quality utterly its own. I hope I make that plain, as to my judgment."

Reedy still would not accept the claim that Patience was the spirit of a woman long dead:

"I am no Spiritist. I do not believe that the souls of the dead set free come back to the souls that stay. I have never seen any purported spirit communication that seemed to me worth communicating. They have been all trivial or worthless. The cases set forth by the Society for Psychical Research mean nothing to me. Crookes and Lodge and all the rest of the necromancers have talked twaddle, as I thought, and think. . . .

"I do not believe in any human intermediary between God and me. I do not know if I believe in the immortality of the soul, but I do not say what the fool hath said in his heart. Practically, I am an agnostic . . . and I seriously doubt . . . if any man has any ideas other than those gained through the experience of himself or the transmitted experience of others. Therefore, when I read the Patience Worth poems in the *Globe-Democrat* I was inclined to think that they were a bit of clever literary fakery, even as I believed, and still believe, that such is the character of Elsa Barker's *Letters of a Living Dead Man* . . . W. T. Stead's familiar Julia and her communications strike me as ridiculous. Messages from Shakespeare and Darwin and George Washington and Lincoln are sorry stuff, and the conclusion of *Edwin Drood*, said to have been done by the spirit of Dickens, should be labeled 'Edwin Drool.' So I felt and feel. When I read the Patience Worth poems I found something better in its kind than I had ever seen before. Not better, considering its manner of coming into being, but better independent of any such consideration. They are poetry—indisputably they are that—good poetry—not egregiously original, yet not echolalian. This poetry has individuality and it has a quality of elsewhereness. Its tropes are not new. Its spiritual content is not unique—that is a kind of pantheism or universalism. It is an archaic Wordsworthianism, with a somewhat of Emersonism. But back of the pseudo-pantheism is an indubitable Deism."

Reedy went on to discuss a novel called *Panda* (it later would be titled *The Sorry Tale*), of which some twenty thousand words had so far been dictated, some of them at the sessions he had attended. It was a story of the time of Christ. Of it Reedy wrote, ". . . *Panda*, as far as I know of it, is of apparently as sound an antiquarian foundation as anything of Lew Wallace or Sienkiwiecz. Indeed, though I venture this very tentatively, it is truer than the works of those or of any fictionist dealing with that Event and those times, that I know anything about. I have read I know not how many stories of the Christ, from the Gospels down, but none of these has the quality of this *Panda*, so far as I am able to judge."

It was inevitable that Reedy would get around to discussing the core mystery of the affair: Could Mrs. Curran be the secret author of the writings attributed to Patience Worth?

"Now, Mrs. Curran is an educated woman, but not overwhelmingly so. She has read the usual novels, the usual poems that an educated woman reads. She is not familiar with early English literature. She is no philologist. She is simply a woman of agreeable intelligence, not at all, as we would say, a 'highbrow.' She knows nothing of the roots of language. Yet she has spelled out on the ouija board many hundreds of thousands of words in an English most primitive, with no Norman, Italian, Latin, Spanish, Danish, or other origins. Mrs. Curran is a musician and singer, but I doubt if she knows the dialect of the earliest known English song that has come down to us—'Summer is a cumin in.' She doesn't know Langland or Chaucer. She's read Shakespeare, of course, and the Bible. But she is not soaked in early English or, indeed, in later English literature. Often, indeed, she cannot understand the—argot, let us call it, of the questions put to the personality whose letter-by-letter dictation she spells out, and sometimes while she reads off the words of Patience Worth's answers she knows the words all right but the ideas conveyed by them utterly escape her. I've seen her and heard her cry out over responses, to questions put by myself, 'What is this stuff? What does it mean?' Mrs. Hutchings might, as a literary woman, know many of the things I refer to, but Mrs. Hutchings is not always or, indeed, often present. Mr. Casper Yost is a man of wide reading and deep and accurate knowledge, but the communications do not come through him, and he is not often present. Mr. Curran is an intelligent and clever man, but no pundit. He can write well, and make a good speech, but he couldn't make a speech of ten minutes in one and two syllable words to save his life, no more than I can.

"A well-known professor of English literature, an authority, indeed, upon the growth and use of the language, has read all, has seen and heard delivered much of the matter purporting to come from Patience Worth.[12] He has studied it carefully in the light of all his knowledge. He has looked up the language used in all the glossaries. There is no man, not even W. W. Skeat, whose opinion upon a point of early English linguistics I would more unhesitatingly accept than this professor's. He finds the language wonderful. He finds words used in senses to our tongue and mind and time most recondite. All the words are not of any given period, nor are they all from one early English locality. They are from almost all the counties and shires and many of them peculiar locutions to those subdivisions of England. They are always used in their exact original sense. The language, as a whole, is of such a consistency of word-texture as no mere student could use through hundreds and hundreds of thousands of words without an occasional break into the speech of today. He says the speech of Patience Worth has no modernisms and that is a miracle, for not the most practiced writer of the speech of any special period, except one's very own period, can keep out of his writings the words in which he does his ordinary thinking. Patience Worth's language is no special speech like that invented by Chatterton, the marvelous boy, in those inimitable forgeries, the Rowley poems. It is a speech that is living and living only in such use as is made of it in, on and by Mrs. Curran's ouija board. Mrs. Curran herself is no more mistress of this speech than I am of the forms of speech of, let us say, the writings of Walter Scott."

Through these communications of extraordinary length, Reedy said, "there is one thoroughly consistent character manifest—the character of a woman. This woman, Patience Worth, does not date herself. She does not locate herself otherwise than 'here,' meaning to her auditors 'there'—wherever that may be. She is supposed to have knowledge of Plymouth settlement and to dislike the Indians. It is not clear that she was married. She was asked that, and intimated it were well to let by-gones be by-gones, or words to that effect. She has seemed to intimate, a time or two, that she has never lived as her interlocutors live. Once or twice, in dictating the novel *Panda*, which goes in a sort of imitation Oriental style, she has fallen into the locutions characteristic of her style in *Red Wing* and *Telka* and on such occasions she always checks and corrects herself with some evidence of amused annoyance. This personality, Patience Worth, is piquant in the extreme. She is witty and aphoristic in a homely way. She is saucy, but never rude. She will not answer personal questions about herself or tell you the usual stock things of so many spirit communications, about lost jack-knives in the distant past, or when your wealthy grandmother is going to die, or whether you're going to inherit money or take a profit or loss on a speculation. None of that stuff goes with Patience. She doesn't like big words. She is ready with repartee and she says things that probe the character of her questioners. Often she will comment upon an unspoken thought of one in the party when she is communicating. She can say sweet things prettily, as well as sharp. Indeed, she is a wholly charming personality, much beloved by all who have come under her influence—a womanly woman, with mind and heart and a wee bit of temper at times. And always she has her insistent, her iterated and reiterated message. A beautiful message...."

After describing in detail his visit with Patience Worth and his conversation with her, as we already have reported, Reedy concluded his lengthy report this way:

"What of it all? I don't know. But will anybody say that the narrative is not remarkable, particularly in the way there came from the board a reduction to small words of the philosophic conceptions usually expressed in sequipedalian verbiage? The 'me o' me,' for the essence of individuality; 'the in-man' for the soul, or the fundamental personality. That the language is a consistent and unvarying form of our root speech, with no glaring anachronisms, is clear. Moreover, taking the expression as a whole, it certainly indicates a personality of strong fiber, colorful, sprightly, percipient, pungent and fragrant. The quality of femininity informs every line of these sayings. The words seem to convey, somehow, gestures and facial expressions as accompaniment. Patience Worth, be she whom she may, is arch and coquettish, with a mind of no small power, and altogether loveable. . . .

"But, comes the question, does what she tells add anything to the sum of human knowledge, does she tell us anything new? Frankly, she does not; but why should she? For my part, if there be a Patience Worth, I find myself wondering if there's anything to tell about what we all want to know—about all that is connoted in my questions about Time and Space. Witty, wise, eloquent, poetic though she be, I fear me that this dulcet oracle, too, is dumb, and I say it, who, reading her, have learned to love her as a person more real than many whose hands I grasp and who have speculation in their eyes."[13]

Patience Worth now had been formally introduced to Reedy's worldwide circle of friends. Her name now was known to and her message pondered over by poets, novelists, critics and fanciers of the arts in many cities. In short, as far as the "right" people were concerned, Patience had arrived.

Reedy's long article in the October 1 *Mirror* brought him a flood of letters. Many expressed a desire for more information on Patience, some were skeptical, others were seething with faith in her reality. In the next issue, a week later, Reedy wrote another article—equally long—headed "More Parleys With Patience Worth." Beginning the article was a twelve-line poem by Patience titled simply "Lullaby," which also has become one of her best known creations.

The second article included another lengthy analysis of the Patience Worth writings, and Reedy continued to marvel over the "quality of the language in its simplicity of word and phrase." He said further, "It requires the highest form of intelligence and literary skill to put things simply in the ordinary speech of one's own day, but Patience Worth speaks to us in the simplicity of an earlier form of our speech. She speaks with an antique, an archaic figurativeness and about the subtlest concepts of the human mind. She comes nearer than any of the philosophers I know of to using the most elemental language in a way to express the *Ding an Sich*."

In this article, Reedy gave one of the first hints that the ouija board was rather incidental to the production of the Patience Worth materials. "I asked Mrs. Curran how the communications came to her—did they come to her from the board, or did they come down to the board through her? The latter, she intimated.

That is, she said as soon as the pointer began moving on the board, picking out the letters, she began at once to see what was coming. She did not see it exactly before the pointer indicated the words, but as the words came."

Reedy went on then to report in detail another of the sessions at the Curran home which he had witnessed. During that sitting there was some discussion as to whether the communications were the expression of another personality speaking or writing through Mrs. Curran. Patience seemed determined to make it clear that she and Mrs. Curran were two separate entities, Patience: "They seek o' me athin her ahere, and I do say me so, though she be a dame o' worth, yet I speak me unto thee, she be a measure far less the hold o' me. Earth seeketh o' roads unto the Here and seeketh amid flesh, yea, then hark ye unto me. The road thou seekest unto the Here showeth not in the flesh or 'pon the Earth, but athin thy heart it showest. The voice speaketh unto the man o' man o' ye, and this be the voice that hath spoke ahere. She be but she and I be me."

What conclusions can be reached about this strange affair? Reedy wrote this: "If Patience Worth be an invention, the inventor is a genius of no mean order. If she be a second personality of Mrs. Curran, then that lady is miraculously blessed with two personalities of most ingratiating and respect-compelling qualities." Anyway, Reedy says, "to say 'dual personality' is to state something, but not to explain it."

With all this, Reedy again makes clear that he still flatly refuses to accept the spiritualist explanation for the manifestation of Patience Worth. "I have no explanation. I seek one. I do not believe the dead can or do speak to the living . . . no reported message . . . has ever told us anything new or even of an importance commensurate with the importance of converse with the dead. No word has come to us in this fashion that imparts to us any idea that we cannot find in the words of those who wrote or spoke in the flesh as we know it."[14]

Reedy's continuing fascination with Patience Worth was to produce torrents of copy in the *Mirror* for the next few months. Articles about Patience appeared in twelve straight issues, along with letters commenting on the phenomenon and expressing various shades of belief and opinion.

The introduction of Patience to the world had come about entirely, so far, through the written word—through the descriptions and interpretations of Yost and Reedy. On November 2, 1915, however, Patience was presented "in person" to an influential group of St. Louisans.

The Papyrus Club of St. Louis (formerly the Authors Club) was an organization of writers, composers, and artists formed about ten years earlier. It is not too surprising that Patience Worth soon became a topic of discussion for the club—both Casper Yost and C. Edwin Hutchings were past presidents and past chairmen of the program committee and John Curran and Mrs. Hutchings were current members of the program committee. On November 2 the club held a dinner meeting and a "Patience Worth Program." Speakers on the subject of the mysterious visitor included club president Richard Spamer of the *Globe-Democrat*, Yost, Mrs. Curran, and Dr. E. George Payne ("Psychology and Patience Worth"), plus a vocal rendition by Mrs. Payne of "Spinner, Spinner o' the Sky," words by Patience Worth, music by Ernest R. Kroeger, a well-known St. Louis musician and composer.[15]

Mrs. Curran brought her ouija board along and Patience briefly addressed the audience:

"Good dames and sirrahs:

"At the board thou hast sat and eat o' earth's grow. Aye, and now do ye to eat o' the grow that knowest not the rooting place o'. Yea, thou shalt hark unto the word o' Men and yet they do to prate o' Dame. Ayea, and me thinks 'tis a word aspoke amany, that be not the word that hid 'pon the tung, lest the Dame be offended!

"Aye, then come thou and sit 'bout the board and thine ears shall hark unto the words o' me and thou shalt see the cloth the hands o' the loves o' me did to fashion out for me. Ayea, I then shall sit me meek, and thread me up a bobbin's full for the next o' put.

"Ayea, and 'tis frocked that I shall to be, and nay dame shall see! Awoe! Nay, this be a piddle putting, good folk!

"Athin thy heart shall set the me o' me at thy go ahence. And 'tis ahope I be 'tis a loving warmth 'twill find. And so dost thou to smile, 'tis sweets and love I cast thee. And doth thy heart to shut it up, lo, then shall I to knock till thou dost leave me in.

"Anight o' cheer! A heart o' love! A God's wish o' loving 'pon thy day. Anight! Anight!"

Capping off the evening was a talk by William Marion Reedy on "My Friend from There." It was reported at length later in St. Louis newspapers.

Patience Worth, he said, is "surely, the sweetest, dearest, kindliest spirit that ever visited the 'pale glimpses of the moon.'" Admitting his natural predilection against the supernatural, Reedy said he felt at first that "if this manifestation was not a fake, it was at least worthless." He had read hundreds, perhaps thousands, of so-called spirit communications, he said, and "no one of them that I can now recall was worthy of any designation other than that of unutterable rot."

Only the day before, he noted, he had "received from Kansas a package, not prepaid, containing a stack of manuscripts including a communication from the spirit land from each of three people— Robert Burns, Elbert Hubbard, and Boccaccio. You can imagine what Boccaccio would write in the atmosphere of Kansas! . . . These communications were simply inexecrable."

But then he had encountered Patience. After briefly describing his impressions of what she looked like and her personality, Reedy went on, "As to her worth, her writings . . . speak for themselves. And they speak, with a voice of as definite and characteristic a quality as ever came from the tongue or the pen of man. The writings of Patience Worth, and her speakings, are unlike anything that I know of in literature, at least in English literature, and I have dabbled in that in its best examples from the time of Beowulf to O. Henry. She speaks an English almost undefiled. She has no relationship with Chaucer or Spenser. She is herself, and herself alone."

Reedy asserted again that he did not claim Patience to be a Sappho or George Eliot or a Sara Teasdale. He did not value her poetry as highly as some others did. "But there can be no question in any mind at all inclined to justice that these poems constitute a consistent body of thought, surrounded, embellished and glamored by a singularly spiritual quality of emotion and feeling."[16]

Yost and Reedy had done their work well. From all over the world, letters were now coming into the Curran house. People wanting an audience with Patience, people wanting a poem written for them, people wanting solace in their bereavement, people wanting advice on their investments. Additional psychologists were inquiring about undertaking detailed studies of the case. Newspaper reporters and magazine writers from all over the country were requesting interviews.

Patience Worth and the attractive young housewife she referred to as her "harp" or her "lyre" or her "hands" had become international celebrities. And their fame was just beginning.

4

Patience vs. the Scientific Man

SOME MONTHS BEFORE Reedy's dramatic presentation of the Patience Worth mystery in the pages of his *Mirror*, other literary experts had heard of the strange happenings in St. Louis and had undertaken their own investigations.

One of the first of them was John Livingston Lowes, a distinguished scholar and noted authority on English literature. Lowes, at the time, was Professor of English at nearby Washington University, where he also had served as dean of the College of Liberal Arts in 1913–14. A few years later, in 1918, he was to move to Harvard University, where he became internationally known as a literary scholar. One of his books, *Road to Xanadu*, is generally considered one of the critical masterpieces of this century.

On March 4, 1915, the record indicates Lowes's presence for the first time. Like almost everyone else exposed to Patience, Lowes obviously was fascinated and returned numerous times in the months following.

At that first session, Lowes joined Mrs. Curran at the board and helped produce a segment of *Telka*, a medieval drama that Patience had begun dictating on February 7 and that was to be one of her major long works. Following that, Lowes asked permission to put some questions to Patience, and he first asked her how it was that she used the language of so many different periods.

Patience responded: "Do I then tung from mouth awide, I then do put questions at awide, or do I prate through mouth aslant, 'tis then aslant, and crooked tale I spin. 'Tis so, eh? Brother, thy tung doth hang atilt and straight upon its middle."

The record doesn't show Lowes's reaction to that illuminating passage, but it does placidly note: "This not being an entirely lucid answer to the question, the Dr. put it in another form, this time very carefully and completely."

Patience apparently was angered that the question had been repeated and grumbled, " 'Tis put. List ye! Did I not tell thee o' the mouth aslant? I do plod a twist o' a path and it hath run from then till now." The last part of this response often has been cited by followers of Patience as a particularly meaningful remark. It is interpreted to mean that she has walked a long, winding road through history and has become familiar with many different periods and their tongues.

Lowes then asked why Patience used so many words that were not used in her time, or any other time.

PATIENCE: Atwist ye put it then! Yea, atruth. Did he who fashioned o' the letters buy the right to tung as I do choose?

Another visitor at the session, a Professor Wallen, had been persistent with demanding questions of an obvious skeptical nature. At this point he broke in sharply and asked, "How many people are in this room?"

PATIENCE: Thee hast an eye!

Her response to other questions put by Wallen were in the same irritable mood. She made no secret of her dislike for the man.

Lowes then resumed his own interrogation: "How does it happen that in the poetry you write there are echoes of poets who wrote since you lived!"

PATIENCE: There be aneath the every stone a hidden voice. I but loose the stone, and lo, the voice!

LOWES: Do you feel the things you write now as if they were your own experience?
PATIENCE: Yea, and thine, and thy neighbor's.[1]

About ten days later Lowes returned to talk further with Patience and brought his wife with him. The courtly professor, perhaps embarrassed by the belligerent probing of his colleague Wallen during the previous visit, was careful to get off on the right foot with the quick-tempered lady of the ouija board.

"Please understand," he said to Patience, "that any question is put in a spirit of high regard and with no frivolous intent."

PATIENCE: Think ye I be no friend and doth thee not then trust?
LOWES: Are these plays and poems thought out between the sittings?
PATIENCE: Doth the spider think o' web?
LOWES: Have you been silent through all the years till now?
PATIENCE: Yea, as North Wind atie about the crest o' earth; ever round and ne'er aloosed—well-a-day—till now.
LOWES: What did you mean the other night when you spoke of a path atwist from then till now?
PATIENCE: Didst e'er to crack a stone and lo, a worm aharded? 'Tis so, for list ye, I speak, like ye, since time began.[2]

A few days later Lowes and his wife came back once again. The professor tried hard to extract information from Patience about her own life, but as usual with such queries, he had little success. The following exchange from that session is amusing because Lowes begins to take on some of Patience's speech quality as he asks his questions and finds the track seem to go warm and then quickly cold again.

LOWES: You said to me that I did but pluck the grass, not gather o' the blossoms of the world. 'Tis so. Will you be patient and let me pluck a little grass just now and pin the tale to word once more? (He quotes a passage from Patience's play *Red Wing*.) Wilt spell to me your meaning? How many ladies' blood did the king spill?
PATIENCE: I take it ye would drink blood. There be 'nuff. A twain aspill and 'twere not astruck aright.
LOWES: I think I am on the right trail. What kind of a bugle do you mean?
PATIENCE: A cup 'pon a stem, blast aye a blast. Thee art 'pon the road but at a branching o' its long.
LOWES: I must be on the wrong trail.[3]

Occasionally Lowes tried to take Patience by surprise. At a later session he suddenly asked her, "Who are you?" Just as quickly Patience responded, "I be Him—alike to thee. Ye be o' Him."[4]

During the spring and early summer of 1915, the sessions continued regularly. A great variety of visitors came to the Curran home and talked with Patience. They constantly peppered her with questions about herself and her present form of existence. She evaded such questions or responded with impatience. On April 7 Yost asked her again to confirm the date when she supposedly had lived:

PATIENCE: I be liken to the wind. And yea, like to it do blow me ever, yea, since time. Do ye to tether me unto today, I blow me then tomorrow and do ye to tether me unto tomorrow, I blow me then today.[5]

A few weeks later a Mrs. Richardson blithely asked, "When I heard curious bells ringing, was that you trying to communicate with me?"

PATIENCE: Ye list at straining, aye, I be athin thy heart at quiet. Think ye I be a tinkler o' brass? Nay, I be a putter o' words. There be nay need o' knocker, nay, thy heart be oped.
MRS. RICHARDSON: On your plane, is there any difference between Christ and Jesus?
PATIENCE: Why put ye such a word? There be but a here. Aye, ye prate o' plane. I be me.[6]

Additional portions of *Telka* were being given at almost all of the two or three weekly sessions at the board. They were interspersed with short poems, parables, or just conversation with the visitors. Sometimes Patience expressed indecision over whether to "sing" and "give sweets"—that is, dictate poems and comments for the enjoyment of the guests, or rather to "weave," her phrase for work on a novel or play, something she obviously considered to be more difficult, precise activity. Sometimes she asked the guests which they would prefer and let them decide.

On July 5, in a final burst of activity, Patience dictated some 7,000 words in two sittings of three hours each and thus completed *Telka*. The record noted that this was the greatest amount of material produced in a single session to that time.

Telka was the second long work completed by Patience. The first had been *Red Wing*, a six-act medieval play of some 20,000 words. It was never published separately, although it did appear in *Patience Worth's Magazine*, about which we'll have more to say later. *Telka* also was medieval in tone, or seemed to be; one was never completely sure of the time or setting in the Patience Worth works. But the general feeling was medieval; the language was the strange Old English amalgam that typified the writings being transmitted by Mrs. Curran. Generally called a "medieval idyll," *Telka* was some 60,000 words in length. Although it was published some years later, it never stirred the same interest as several of the other long works by Patience Worth.

Casper Yost, however, found *Telka* of great interest—apart from literary considerations of plot or characterization—because of its linguistic peculiarities. He subjected the text of the play to a careful analysis and began to study various reference and scholarly works pertaining to the literary uses of the English language.

In an essay titled "The Evidence in *Telka*," which is carried as an appendix to a 1928 edition of *Telka*,[7] Yost declared flatly that the work was "a literary miracle."

About nine-tenths of *Telka* is dialogue, Yost noted, and from beginning to end it is rhythmical dialogue. More important, according to Yost, is the fact that about 90 percent of the language in the play is of Anglo-Saxon origin or use. The remaining 10 percent, he wrote, is composed of Old French, with an occasional Scandinavian word and, rarely, one of Celtic or direct Latin origin.

Yost frankly admitted that he was as bewildered as anyone else about the source of the language: "It seems not to be the language of any period of England or of any locality of England. I am unable to find that, in the form she gives it, it was ever written or ever spoken. It has words of various periods as well as of various localities."[8]

It perhaps should be mentioned here that Patience never denied that her language was a composite. She once said, "Yea, yet look ye into the words o' me. Ye shall find whits o' this and that ta'en from here and there—yet foundationed upon the salt which flavours it o' my ain land."[9]

Yost's judgment that *Telka* was a literary miracle was based on its amazingly high proportion of Anglo-Saxon words according to his analysis: "I believe it is safe to say that no book since the days of Layamon, with the exception of Wickliffe's Bible, is as exclusively Anglo-Saxon as this work of Patience Worth's. . . . With a single exception, there is not one word of later entry into the language than the year sixteen hundred." After making that rather sweeping statement, however, Yost qualified it by admitting that he could not prove the declaration; there might be a few such late-originating words that he overlooked.

He went on: ". . . upward of four hundred thousand words [are] to be found in a dictionary of the present day, only a few thousand of which are Anglo-Saxon. It is true that Anglo-Saxon is the essential framework of our language, and it is difficult to write a single sentence of length without using Anglo-Saxon words, but it is also somewhat difficult to write a single sentence wholly in words of Anglo-Saxon origin that would not be commonplace, and I do not believe that any one could write and speak rapidly, fluently, and beautifully, as Patience does, so restricted."

To prove his assertion that this work had no equal for several hundreds of years in terms of its overwhelmingly Anglo-Saxon content, Yost quoted a study by Dr. John H. Weisse of English writings from the fifth to the nineteenth centuries, in which Weisse analyzed the relative proportions of words of different racial origins. The Weisse study, reported Yost, showed that the average percentage of Anglo-Saxon words in writings of the twelfth century was 88, for the thirteen century it was 74, for the fourteenth century it was 60, for the fifteenth century it was only 53 percent. From 1600 to 1878, the average fell all the way down to 28 percent. Chaucer's average was 64 percent, the King James Bible was 77 percent, Shakespeare's was 59 percent, and the U.S. Declaration of Independence contained only 42 percent Anglo-Saxon words. And the percentage in *Telka*, Yost declared, was an incredible 90 percent. Since the thirteenth century, he wrote, the percentage of Anglo-Saxon words in *Telka* has been matched only once—in Wickliffe's Bible.

Despite the Anglo-Saxon cast of the language, Yost felt that the play was modern in the form of most of its words: "There are not a dozen words in it that are obsolete as a whole. There are many words that are obsolete in the forms she gives them, but their stems are in constant use today. For example, athin for within, afore for before, becracked for cracked, are but common words in archaic dress."

And he added: "And it is her construction, more even than her vocabulary, that is peculiar and individual. She has no reverence for the parts of speech, and little respect for the holiest rules of syntax. 'I be dame,' she says, and therefore not amenable to rule. If it suits her to make a noun, an adjective, or even a preposition do service as a verb, it is done."[10] Yost noted later in the essay that, during the period (sixteenth, seventeenth centuries) generally associated with Patience Worth, "there was in all the leading writers . . . a striking disregard of the precise functions of the parts of speech, and this was especially characteristic of Shakespeare."[11]

His own reaction to *Telka*, Yost proclaimed, was "That she has in this work proven herself, proven the independence and separateness of her personality, in the achievement of a literary composition of a character quite beyond the probable conception or execution of a finite mind, I am thoroughly convinced. . . ."[12]

It should be mentioned here, for the sake of accuracy, that some aspects of the Patience Worth case have tended to take on mythic proportions, with the story being exaggerated as it is passed down. For example, Kenneth Walker in his book *The Extra-Sensory Mind* attributes the textual analysis of *Telka* to a "philologist" and later quotes a "classical scholar" as attesting to the historical accuracy of another Patience Worth work. Similar references have appeared in magazine articles about the case. Both references, my study revealed, were really to Casper Yost. Although a learned man, Yost was neither a philologist nor a professional scholar and could hardly be considered a disinterested expert, as the two references seem to imply.

As the sessions continued into the summer of 1915, more and more of the philosophy of Patience Worth became apparent. One of the dominant themes was her dislike of excessive verbalizing and theorizing and her displeasure with intellectuals for what she deemed their overindulgence in such activity. On July 7 she gave this rather bitterly ironic parable:

THE PARABLE OF THE CLOAK

There wert a man, and lo, he did to seek and quest o' sages, that which he did mouthe o'ermuch. And lo, he did to weave o' such, an robe, and did to clothe himself therein. And lo, 'twere sun ashut away and cool and heat and bright and shade.

And lo, still did he to draw 'bout him the cloak, and 'twere o' the mouthings o' the sage. And lo, at a day 'twere sent abroad, that Truth should stalk 'pon Earth, and man, were he to look him close, shouldst see.

And lo, the man did draw 'bout him the cloak, and did to wag him "nay" and "Nay, 'twere truth the sages did to mouthe and I did weave athin the cloak o' me."

And then 'twere that Truth did seek o' Earth, and she wert clad o' naught, and seeked the man, and begged that he would cast the cloak and clothe o' her therein. And lo, he did to draw him close the cloak, and hid his face therein, and wag him "Nay." He did to know her not.

And lo, she did to fetch her unto him athrice, and then did he to wag him still a Nay, Nay, Nay! And lo, she toucheth o' the cloth o' sages mouths and it doth fall atattered and leave him clothed o' naught and at awishing. And he did seek o' Truth, aye, ever and when he did to find, lo, she wagged him nay and nay and nay.[13]

In early July 1915 Patience began to hint that something momentous was going to take place, something that she was approaching with trepidation. She seemed uncertain over whether she could do justice to it. She would soon begin dictating, she told them, a "sorry story." It began to seem very clear that Patience deemed this coming work of much greater importance than anything she had done so far.

At one of those sessions, when she again brought up the forthcoming task, Patience gave this striking poem, which her listeners interpreted as being a "prayer for material to weave it with":

Wind o' the days and nights,
Aye, thou the searchers o' the night,
Lend thou to me of thee.

Sun of the Day, abath o'er the Earth,
Lend thou of thee to me.

Rains o' the storm, awash
O' Earth's dust to anaught,
Lend thou of thee to me.

Sweets o' the Earth, the glad o' Day
Lend thou of thee to me.

Prayers o' the soul, the heart's own breath,
Lend thou to me of thee.

Fields o' the Earth, agold o' harvest-ripe
Lend thou to me of thee.

Dark o' the Night, strip o' thy robe
And lend o' thee to me.

For I do to weave and wash, and soothe and coo
And cloak o' one who needeth thee,
A one o' His, astricken
A one whose soul hath bathed o' crime,
And Earth hath turned and wagged a Nay to him.[14]

At the sitting on July 14, 1915, Patience began the writing of the "sorry story" that had caused her so much concern and foreboding. This was the beginning of *The Sorry Tale*, Patience's massive novel of the time of Christ. It was the work that was to become her most famous and the one that, to her followers, solidified forever her stature as a literary creator of such genius as to burst past the boundary of the explainable.

In his preface to the published version of *The Sorry Tale*, Casper Yost tells how the writing of the novel began. He explains that two people, in addition to the Curran family, were present on the evening of July 14, two people "under whose hands Patience had expressed a wish to begin the tale."[15] It is assumed, based on the description that follows, that Yost was one of the two guests for, strangely, the record of the July 14 session is missing from the Patience Worth Record.

"There was a certain solemnity to the occasion," Yost noted, "a feeling that something of profound significance was to be inaugurated. Solemnity is quite unusual in the meetings with Patience, whose exuberant humor is one of her most charming qualities, and who, however serious she may be, loves not a long face. But on this night, there were no flashes of wit. On the contrary, it was for a while a tremorous, hesitating, faltering Patience, almost overcome by the task upon which she was entering.

" 'Loth, loth I be,' she cried. 'Yea, thy handmaid's hands do tremble. Wait thou! Wait! Yet do I to set.' (to write). For a moment, the pointer circled slowly about the board recording nothing until it picked up the murmur: 'Loth, loth I be that I do for to set the grind' (the circling motion of the pointer). And then, for the first and only time in the long experience with her, she asked for a period of quiet. 'Wait ye stilled,' she said. 'Ah, thy handmaid's hands do tremble!'

"For three or four minutes, there was no sound in the room, and then, as if in reality from out the silence of twenty centuries, as if actually from out the darkness of the greatest night in all history came the plaintive cry of Theia, 'Panda, Panda, tellest thou a truth?'

"There was no further hesitation in the delivery. Without another pause, except by Mrs. Curran for rest and discussion, the story proceeded rapidly and about two thousand words were received on that evening. The first thing noticed was the great difference in the language and the atmosphere from anything previously written by Patience. Next was the knowledge displayed of the people and the time and of the topography of the country. The language retained some of the verbal and syntactical peculiarities of Patience, the same freedom from grammatical restraints, but it was not the language of her other works, nor that which she used in her conversation."[16]

The writing of *The Sorry Tale* was to continue for twenty months. Parts of it were dictated at almost every session with the ouija board during that period. At first the segments mostly were brief, perhaps 500 words, sometimes less. Later, they lengthened to 2,000 and 3,000 words at a time, and eventually a segment of 5,000 words was dictated in one evening, with the ouija board churning out letters as fast as they could be noted down.

Mrs. Curran was to have many partners in the project. "As in all her work," Yost pointed out, "it mattered not who was present or who sat at the board with Mrs. Curran. Whether the vis-a-vis was man or woman, old or young, learned or unlettered, the speed and the quality of the production were the same. From start to finish, some 260 persons contributed in this way to the composition. . . . Each time the story was picked up at the point where work was stopped at the previous sitting, without a break in the continuity of the narrative, without the slightest hesitation, and without the necessity of a reference to the closing words of the last preceding installment. These words were often read for the benefit of those present, but Patience repeatedly proved that it was not required by her."[17]

Throughout 1915 Yost had been working diligently on his book about Patience. It was based on the five original articles in the *Globe-Democrat* but incorporated a good deal of additional poetry by Patience and some further discussion of her personality and general philosophy. Periodically, Yost would ask Patience to clarify a particular statement or poetic phrase and the ouija board would respond with the desired clarification. Yost also asked a time or two whether Patience was satisfied with the direction his book was taking and was gratified to receive her encouragement.

In the fall of 1915 the book—which Yost had titled *Patience Worth: A Psychic Mystery*—was accepted for publication by the prominent New York publishing house of Henry Holt and Company. Holt himself was deeply interested in psychic phenomena and spiritualism; a couple of years earlier he himself had written a book on the subject called *On the Cosmic Relations*.

During that same period in 1915 the Patience Worth case had been brought to the attention of Dr. Morton Prince, a noted Boston medical man and a leading expert on cases of personality dissociation. A mutual friend (there is some evidence it was Professor Lowes) asked Dr. Prince to look into the case and then urged Mr. and Mrs. Curran to submit themselves to such an investigation, in the interest of determining the true origin of Patience Worth. Because they had been planning a trip East to meet Henry Holt and consult with him about the plans for Yost's book, Mr. and Mrs. Curran agreed to meet Dr. Prince and to allow him to interrogate them about the coming of Patience.

It suddenly occurred to someone, however, that perhaps Patience was not inclined to be a tourist and would not leave St. Louis. On November 10, 1915, the *St. Louis Post-Dispatch* carried a front-page story headlined: "PATIENCE WORTH" TO RISK TRIP EAST IN A PULLMAN CAR.

"Until last night," the newspaper story read, "there was uncertainty whether 'Patience Worth' would go along. The plan is to introduce her to psychics of Boston and select circles in other cities and have her present via the ouija board at a conference of the Currans with a New York publisher, who is preparing to print the 'Patience Worth' output.

"It can readily be seen that if 'Patience' should be averse to travel there would be predicament.

"So last night the ouija board was produced and she was asked point-blank if she was going East with Mr. and Mrs. Curran. This reply was spelled out on the board:

"'E'en as doth the breath o' thee to hug, so shall I, to follow thee. Think ye I'd build me a cup and leave it dry?'

"There was some discussion of time and space, and the question as to whether 'Patience' was amenable to these, and Patience said: 'I be ahere, ayea and there. Yea, athin (within) the hearts of thee bideth the me o' me. So 'tis, be ye athin the hearts o' loved, e'en though they be amany, thou art there, where'er thou be'st.'"

The article added that Mr. and Mrs. Curran, while in the East, would seek to find the grave of Patience Worth. They planned to spend two days in Washington, four in Boston, two in New York, one in Buffalo, and two in Chicago.[18]

Just before leaving on her journey to the East, Patience had a bit of a public wrangle with one Arthur Delroy, described by local newspapers variously as "president of the Psychic Society of New York" and as an "English psychic entertainer." Delroy addressed an audience of 700 St. Louisans at a civic luncheon and was quoted by reporters as declaring that the ouija board had no more psychic value than a doorknob. As to Patience Worth, Delroy said that her language was not archaic English, but the type of language learned at Sunday school. "It would not surprise me," he remarked, "to learn that Mrs. Curran had attended Sunday school quite faithfully when she was a girl."[19]

Her followers lost little time in presenting Delroy's comments to Patience. She responded: "'Tis fools that smite the lute and set at awhir o' folly song, when sage's hand do be at loth to touch."

An eager reporter hustled back downtown with Patience's remark and brought it to Delroy. The "psychic entertainer" made this statement in what was intended to be a hilarious parody of Patience-style: "Nay, thou puttest me among the nobles. I be not the wise man from the East who wouldst prithee never be the last word, but wouldsy patiently wait, yea, t'll'st the millionth Patient utterance. This eve I lay on my lowly couch, yea, my veriest lowly couch—and, Prithee, verily, Selah, wav'st my psychic waves—yea, my uttermost psychic waves—in contrite woe. But Patience neared me not. Sure fools rush in where angels fear to tread."[20]

Very little record exists of the trip East by the Currans, except for some significant meetings in Boston and New York. (Obviously the Currans did not find Patience's grave, for, had they done so, it would have been triumphantly announced.) Some information is provided in the record about a session in Washington's New Willard Hotel. No date is given, but Washington was the first stop on the trip, around November 13.

On November 14 Mr. and Mrs. Curran, accompanied by their ouija board and presumably their mysterious literary friend as well, arrived in Boston for the great confrontation with Dr. Morton Prince. (So far as we know, he was not related to Walter Franklin Prince, who became involved in the case several years later.) The Currans were greeted by newspaper reporters, and Mrs. Curran told them: "The man we have come to see is one of the most noted psychologists and we have come to him because we are puzzled. I suddenly found myself with a wonderful gift and did not know how it came. He, I believe, can explain it."[21]

Morton Prince, a distinguished-looking man in his early sixties, was a specialist in neurology and abnormal psychology, one of the world's leading authorities on the pathology of mental disorders. Some ten years earlier he had published *The Dissociation of a Personality,* considered a landmark in its field. He had founded and was the editor until his death (in 1929) of the *Journal of Abnormal Psychology.*

The Currans came to Dr. Prince's home for the first interview and set up their ouija board. What follows is, to me, one of the most delightful episodes in the entire chronicle of Patience Worth. Imagine this noted scientist, obviously skeptical and suspicious of fraud, determined to get at the truth of the matter by assiduous, aggressive interrogation, coming up against the will-o'-the-wisp Patience Worth, who had successfully evaded the questions of many other intelligent men and who obviously had no intention of being pinned down to the bedrock of solid fact by this insolent knave, scientist or no. Dr. Prince was soon to discover that trying to nail Patience was like trying to grab a handful of mist.

The following report of the interview is pieced together from newspaper accounts and from the Patience Worth Record. For the newspaper story, the Currans supplied an interpretation (or, if you will, a translation) of Patience's comments, and this appears in parentheses.

DR. PRINCE: Do you mind having this investigation made, Patience?
PATIENCE: Ye be at a seek o' a measure o' smoke's put. It slippeth it athin the measure-pot and slippeth it out at each and every corner that be aloosed. Aye and doth to slip it then awhither e'en from thy very hands. (You are trying to measure smoke. It slips into the pot with which you measure, and out again at every crevice; yes, and it floats away out of thy hands. In other words, you are attempting the impossible.)
DR. PRINCE: But do you mind the investigation?
PATIENCE: Ye turn ye up a stone, ayea and aneath there be a toad, aye and he blinketh him at the light. So be it. Be ye then aseek, he uppeth and doth to flee aneath a hedge bush. (If you seek, you may find a homely thing. But if you try to catch it, he will dodge away beneath a hedge.)

Dr. Prince's temper already was starting to fray:

DR. PRINCE: I want to know whether you object to this investigation, yes or no?
PATIENCE: Here be a one who hath o' a ball o' twine and be not asatisfied with the ball, but doth to awish that I do awind it out. List thee, Brother, at thy poke aneath the stone! 'Tis well and alike unto me.
DR. PRINCE: Well then, answer my question!
PATIENCE: Alor'! A heart that be atrue, e'en though it doth stab thee, 'tis loved!
DR. PRINCE: Will you help and cooperate?
PATIENCE: What think ye, that I builded me up o' a path and do to trod not 'pon its way?
DR. PRINCE: Have you ever tried to write with a pencil?
PATIENCE: He wisheth that the bloom be stripped, then it shall be so. Nay, Brother, nay quill did I to seek.
DR. PRINCE: Will you try to write with a pencil?

PATIENCE: She ahere be nay aput o' quill.
DR. PRINCE: How did you come to choose the ouija board?
PATIENCE: I telled unto the Puller (her name for Dr. Lowes) o' the path atwist, and the put o' time and time. 'Tis so, Brother.
DR. PRINCE: How did you come to use Old English?
PATIENCE: It be o' the day and tide o' the tung o' me. Yea, Brother, but unto its put do I to add the take o' this and that.
DR. PRINCE: Can you use modern tongue?
PATIENCE: Yea, but do I to fashion me o' loaf that be alike unto the loaf o' her ahere, then thou sayest 'tis her. (If I speak in her language, you will say that it is she speaking.)
DR. PRINCE: You say you can talk modern English. Will you?
PATIENCE: Thou art aseek that I be not me. Then list; e'en though thou sayest that I then should to cast the cloak o' me, I be not at this thing. Nay, I speak me out aclear, let man then eat the loaf!
DR. PRINCE: How about this word "put"?
PATIENCE: Nay, 'tis a word afew that wert mine o' the day o' me. Aye and some do I to put that she ahere knoweth not. Then 'tis that she doth to list unto that she knoweth and I do to set me a one she knoweth. "Put" hath ever been to set aplaced. So 'tis, a quill doth to set aplaced.
DR. PRINCE: How did you get it?
PATIENCE: Atwist I set it so.
DR. PRINCE: How did you get "neckabout"?
PATIENCE: Nay, Brother, 'twere a put o' a one who telled the give unto a nobled o' a jewel. Aye and did to put it neckabout.

The session ended and it was agreed by all parties that another meeting was indicated. Two days later the Currans returned to Dr. Prince's home and the interview resumed:

DR. PRINCE: Do you see me?
PATIENCE: Alor'! An old un!
DR. PRINCE: Do you hear me?
PATIENCE: Thinkest thou that thou mayest send for a loud o' a put and I be amuted o' the ear?
DR. PRINCE: No, darned if I do!
PATIENCE: Thou art o' a put o' word that thou knowest, man, be not afitting o' a sirrah o' the day o' me!
DR. PRINCE: What would they have said in your day?
PATIENCE: A dang.
DR. PRINCE: Can you feel me touch you? (He touches Mrs. Curran on the hand.)
PATIENCE: Nay, thou art atickle o' flesh and I be as smoke, that

setteth it awhither aneath thy very hand. (No, you are touching flesh and I am immaterial and drift away under your very hand.)
DR. PRINCE: Well, you say you hear and see, how do you do it?
PATIENCE: Athrough the throb o' her do I to do o' this and that.
DR. PRINCE: Have you yourself the actual sensations of the senses?
PATIENCE: See ye, sirrah, there be unto thee but the flesh eye. Aye but athin thy in-man be an eye, yea and through this do I to see me.
DR. PRINCE: Can you write with Mrs. Curran's eyes closed?
PATIENCE: I be aset athin the throb o' her. Aye, and doth thee to take then the lute awhither that she see not, think ye then she may to set up musics for the hear o' thee? (I am in the very essence of her; if you take away the lute, and prevent her from singing, how can she make music for you to hear?)
DR. PRINCE: Try it anyhow.
PATIENCE: 'Twould be but the aset agrind o' naught.
DR. PRINCE: What period did you live in?
PATIENCE: 'Tis aput.
DR. PRINCE: What decade?
PATIENCE: Lor', I be as the Puller telleth, o' the russets. (Lord, I am as the Puller—Dr. Lowes—says. I was one of the Roundheads, of Cromwell's time. It has been written down already.)
DR. PRINCE: What year were you born in, and where?
PATIENCE: 'Tis apry ye be. I be atrothed unto the Puller.
DR. PRINCE: Answer my question! You said you would cooperate.
PATIENCE: Yea, thou wouldst to shed o' the blood o' me and then hand unto the wraith o' me the blood-blade to wipe.
DR. PRINCE: That's dodging!
PATIENCE: 'Tis a merry put thou settest o' a wraith at, sirrah, that she doth to duck o' thy throw!
DR. PRINCE: Oh, go away!
PATIENCE: Welladay, wert so, then how wouldst find the put o' me?
DR. PRINCE: Who was the King in *Red Wing*?
PATIENCE: Lor', did I not to pettiskirt 'bout the blood o' him?
DR. PRINCE: What town were you born in?
PATIENCE: The Puller hath the put o' me.
DR. PRINCE: Who was governor of the state when you arrived?
PATIENCE: There were naught but sands and weary. Thou art aseek and I be not o' the town's spot that did to tell o' this.
DR. PRINCE: Why don't you tell about yourself frankly?
PATIENCE: Thou art athrow awhither o' the loaf o' me I did to fashion out o' love, and 'tis ne'er o' the earth's care what I be.
DR. PRINCE: This is not so.

PATIENCE: Set thee aweave. A piffle for the measure o' smoke, fetch ye o' bread! (Let us get to work on the novel. It is useless to measure smoke; let us work on more meaningful things.)
DR. PRINCE: Now be good, Patience, and tell us what town.
PATIENCE: 'Tis ne'er a sweet that trappeth.
DR. PRINCE: I've got some gumdrops over there.
PATIENCE: Then seal ye up thy put. (Why don't you shut up?)
DR. PRINCE: Tell me the name of the town you lived in.
PATIENCE: Look ye, there be o' me nuff, e'en now 'pon thy earth. Yea, thou art aseek and I be not atell.
DR. PRINCE: Tell me your father's name.
PATIENCE: Think ye he be aWorth much and I aWorth little?
DR. PRINCE: Tell me your father's first name.
PATIENCE: 'Twere John.
DR. PRINCE: Your mother's name.
PATIENCE: Lor, sirrah, she wert a dame. Good Anne.
DR. PRINCE: What was her maiden name?
PATIENCE: Amore he pryeth. Yea, I be not aput ahind the hut since I do leave ye not athin its walls.
DR. PRINCE: What was the name of the ship in which you came over?
PATIENCE: Amore he seeketh ahind the hut. Since I be not atelling o' the me o' me, he seeketh neath the cloak o' me that he see and I do know not! (Still hunting behind the hut. Since I will not talk of myself, you are trying to look beneath my cloak without my knowledge.)
DR. PRINCE: What kind of a vessel was it?
PATIENCE: A masted.
DR. PRINCE: How many masts?
PATIENCE: Lor', 'tis a step adeed he be ahind!
DR. PRINCE: How old were you when you came over?
PATIENCE: A goodly dame.
DR. PRINCE: Again, how old were you? You can't get me off the trail.
PATIENCE: Set thee a look unto the tale o' the ass o' the Puller. (This referred to a parable, dictated some time previously in St. Louis, in which a wise man and a teacher could not get an ass to move, despite angry words and blows, until a child came along and moved the animal just by whistling gently and stroking its nose.)
DR. PRINCE: How about this word "kit"?
PATIENCE: O' the russets there be them that have o' the curds that they do feed 'pon them e'en as thou and thou dost eat as breads and in the kit did they to stow the curd. And it smelled o' mould and

reeked o' sweat and looked ablacked o' the stain o' the curd's drop and 'twere the tide o' me.
DR. PRINCE: What sort of a thing was it?
PATIENCE: O' woods, binded.
DR. PRINCE: Box, keg, or barrel?
PATIENCE: 'Twere e'en as thy bowl, amany o' a kind. Good night![22]

So, abruptly, Patience brought the interrogation to a close. According to newspaper accounts, the meeting ended with Dr. Prince telling the Currans that the questioning of Patience Worth had been utterly inconclusive and unproductive. The only way he could get to the bottom of the affair, he said, was to put Mrs. Curran in hypnosis. This was flatly rejected by the Currans. They stated later that they were afraid that submission to hypnosis might permanently impair Mrs. Curran's ability to communicate with Patience.

St. Louis newspapers the next day headlined the results of the much-discussed Boston meeting: PATIENCE WORTH NOT SO PATIENT IN BOSTON SEANCE. . . . "PATIENCE WORTH" AND CURRANS QUIT BOSTON; TEST FAILS. . . . MRS. CURRAN REFUSES TO BE HYPNOTIZED AND PSYCHOLOGIST IS DISAPPOINTED. . . . MRS. CURRAN HALTS SCIENTIST QUIZZING "PATIENCE WORTH."[23]

The newspaper stories also indicated that Dr. Prince was extremely upset because the Currans had given the press an account of his interviews with Patience. "I considered the interviews entirely private and confidential," he said. "I have not read the story, but I am very much surprised that any statement has been given out to the press by Mr. Curran, who came to me with an introduction from a St. Louis friend." The eminent scientist also told reporters: "Nothing of scientific importance or interest developed from the interview. I consider the results inconsequential and of no scientific value whatever."[24]

Dr. Prince said he had telephoned the Currans to protest their statements to the press. "I do not believe, after what I have said to the Currans, that they will give out anything about our interviews. It is a shame to think that these people may make public a lot of stuff that will hurt me all over the world. I consider the thing of no consequence whatever, and I would rather say nothing about it."[25]

John Curran told newsmen later that he had refused Dr.

Prince's request that he keep silent. He told reporters that he and his wife had nothing to conceal.

From Boston the Currans traveled with their ouija board to New York City in order to meet with Henry Holt and other executives of his publishing firm. In a magazine article a few months later Holt described his first meeting with Patience Worth on November 19, 1915. Present in addition to Holt and his wife were Alfred Harcourt, a member of the firm, a Miss Pilsbury, and the Currans.[26] There was no trance, Holt wrote, and the conversation was entirely natural.

Holt described it this way: "With Mrs. Curran, my hands . . . were on the planchette part of the time, but I had no agency in moving it. Mrs. Curran supposed the hands of a companion to be necessary as a counterweight to prevent movement too rapid to be recorded. That was not her impression at the beginning of her experiments years ago when the movements were slower. I doubt if there was then any definite reason beyond sociability, or any real necessity for a cooperator.

"The pointer was moved so fast that I got but vague impressions of the letters to which it pointed, but Mrs. Curran named them and pronounced each word as it was finished, and Mr. Curran took it all down in longhand.

"Mrs. Curran did not appear to be making any effort, but her face, which is generally very mobile, gradually took on an intense, fixed expression, and the eyes got a little out of focus, which I do not think they do when she is not at the board. There was nothing like an assumption of the seeress, but an unconscious earnestness and, as I said, a fixity, much in contrast with her jolly, humorous self before and after the board. It did not lead, however, to any signs of fatigue. It has, I understand, in some other sittings.

"I asked Mrs. Curran why she did not persistently try to substitute the pencil for the board. She said (I think that Patience told her) that there were so many habits connected with the pencil that Patience's influence on it could not be as complete as on the board."[27]

After a few introductory comments by Holt and Patience, the ouija board began transmitting another segment of *The Sorry Tale*, with Holt and Mrs. Curran manning the planchette, and some 400 words were produced.

Holt wanted to know why it was necessary for him to place both hands on the board when one would do as well and be much more convenient. Patience, ever ready to sermonize, responded: "Then dost thou to choose thee for to tuck thy leg even as doth the crane, do then this thing. I be nay sit o' one leg. Nay, Brother-sage, list thee: If then thy brother thou lovest better far than thy very heart, doth offer unto thee one hand at thy greet, 'tis there a cold heart that be thine. Yea, but doth thee seek thy brother with love o'erflowing thee, then thou dost offer unto him both thy hands that they be afulled o' love and thereby shalt thy love flow it unto him."

At this point Harcourt took Holt's place at the board and asked Patience if she was aware of the change in personnel.

Patience replied: "Yea. Here be a one who holdeth o' the grams [scales]. Yea he holdeth athin his hand word and doth to look unto the put o' these words, and doth to set him up then a pot o' brew and set ahotted till the brew doth to smell it at afinished and areadied for the eat o' hungered. Then doth he to taste thereof and wag him 'yea' or 'nay.'"

The publishing executives in the room were startled at this accurate portrayal of Harcourt's work in evaluating manuscripts and his custom of preparing and sipping a hot beverage as he made his editorial decisions. Mrs. Curran, so far as they knew, had no way of knowing these things about Harcourt's duties and work habits.

In the minutes that followed, these sophisticated leaders of the New York publishing world began discussing mundane details of book production with the unseen personality whose work they were preparing to put on the market. It is somewhat difficult to imagine these well-known publishers carrying on such a conversation with a ouija board, but here's what the record shows:

Harcourt asked if she would be interested in the colors in which Yost's book would be bound. Patience answered: "Yea, I be! 'Tis Lady Lisa's colors. 'Tis blue and gold." (This referred to a character in one of Patience's first long works, the play called *The Fool and the Lady*.)

Harcourt then asked what kind of design she would like to have on the book. Patience answered: "'Tis a sunrise."

Holt had another design in mind and asked for her reaction to it. "I had thought of a brazier with a rising cloud of smoke trailing into a question mark."

Patience responded, "This abe a goodly put. Yea, Brother, but 'tis smoke that soon doth vanish and 'tis sun that ever riseth."

Holt pointed out that another recent book was decorated with a sunrise and asked whether Patience could suggest something to make her sunrise design original. She said, "Yea, from out the clouds'-hug doth this sun to climb."

Holt then drew a sketch of what he thought the decoration should be and Patience responded, "'Twere a hand adear that set atraced thereon and athin the heart o' him doth the me o' me to rest and rest."

If you find a copy of *Patience Worth: A Psychic Mystery* on your library's shelves, assuming that the original binding is still present, you'll discover that Patience got her way: The book is colored blue and gold and the front cover is emblazoned with a large sunrise. The sun is coming out of a thick bank of clouds.

Harcourt then wanted to know whether Mrs. Curran's picture should be in the book. Patience, typically, responded, "Think ye that I be awish o' flesh? She be but the pot."[28]

5

The Verdict of the Critics

THE PUBLICATION DATE of Casper Yost's book was set for February 1916. Meanwhile, Patience was never out of the news for long.

On November 21, 1915, Mrs. Charles P. Johnson, wife of a prominent St. Louis attorney and herself a well-known local writer, wrote a long analytic piece for the *St. Louis Republic* in which she recapitulated in some detail the activities of Mrs. Curran and speculated over the possible origins of Patience Worth. It was one of the earliest of many such speculations over the next half century.

In her article Mrs. Johnson quickly asserted that she was completely skeptical of the supernatural explanation of Patience Worth and intended to seek a rational answer. Yet: "I am fully convinced that Mrs. John Curran is honest in her belief as to the source of this writing."

One of the readiest explanations that had been suggested, Mrs. Johnson noted, was that of dual personality and yet, she pointed out, such cases on record offer evidence that "the person does not remember, when in one state, what occurred in the other. Now there is positively nothing of this in Mrs. Curran; she remembers everything all the time, nor is there any manifestation of any change in personality or appearance. When using the 'ouija' board, Mrs. Curran says she moves the pointer herself, and she does this to express or describe by spelling a ribbon of pictures that passes before her mind's eye. As she explained this, she drew her thumb and forefinger slowly from temple to temple, saying this picture is as if the characters were acting, and at the same time without any effort whatever the words form and she spells them out as quickly as one writes on a typewriter, making the punctuating and end of a line understood by pauses in the dictating."

As further evidence of her contention that Mrs. Curran does not alternate between two separate realms of consciousness, Mrs. Johnson went on: "Sometimes she looks over to a guest while writing and asks some question entirely foreign to what she is spelling out; again answers the telephone, or inquires what the message was; exchanges a few words of greeting to late visitors as they enter, and goes on with the work without a moment's hesitation."

The article pointed out that Mrs. Curran writes huge amounts of material, does so at various times with many different people at hand, seems not to care whether she is in the right mood or humor and, with all this, she shows no fatigue. "An ordinary writer accomplishing so much every day would be brain-fagged."[1]

Mrs. Johnson made some very delicate, ladylike speculations about the state of Mrs. Curran's nerves: "There are times, neurologists say, when one is more susceptible to suggestion, and during special states of disease the mind develops powers such as it does not possess when the body is in full health. This is especially true in such ailments as are said in unscientific language to lower the tone of the nervous system." Later, she added: "Mrs. Curran for some years previous to this experience had been treated by physicians for various ailments—from a prospective visit of the stork, a tumor, consumption—all of which failed to materialize. The tone of her nervous system evidently was reduced."

Mrs. Johnson's suggested answer to the riddle of Patience Worth was a theory that a genius for writing had been developed in Mrs. Curran's ancestors, had been transmitted to her through heredity, and had lain dormant in her until "awakened from its dormancy by the concentration given by Mrs. Curran using this board as a means."

She concluded: "The neurologists and psychologists and alienists and literatists will be obliged to explain this phenomenon. The neurologists will say it is nerves, the spiritualist will say spirits and the literatists will differ as to whether it is Bible or archaic English—and perhaps it never will be explained, but likely a new line of investigation will be opened up that will prove of benefit."[2]

During those last months of 1915 and the early part of 1916, Billy Reedy also was merrily keeping the pot boiling in his *Mirror*. An article about Patience appeared in every weekly issue for three months, accompanied also by some of the numerous letters from readers that came in concerning the strange writings and their creator.

In his issue of October 15 Reedy printed Patience's Christmas story called "The Stranger," which had been dictated before Christmas the previous year. In his introduction to the story, Reedy commented: "For the descriptive merit of the story, for its distinctness and deftness of characterization, for its swift economy of words, for its dramatic quality—for its beauty and mysticism—let the story speak for itself. . . . The idea of the story is not original, but it is utilized with regard to a particular time and place with perfect fitness and, so far as I can judge, without a single anachronism of speech or detail of life of the place or time."[3]

The following week, October 22, Reedy did another of his own long discussions of Patience, headed "Chat of a Charming Spook." Reedy reiterated that he had always shied away from so-called psychic phenomena, "but here I've been hobnobbing over Mrs. John H. Curran's ouija board with Patience Worth, who seems to have lived at least two hundred and maybe more years ago and now inhabits eternity, and it's a quite ordinary thing. It doesn't interfere with one's ordinary way of life at all. It's quite amazingly and amusingly natural. One understands how the mystics, the saints who had visions, were generally such cheerful and indeed common sense, often practical, hard-headed folks."

Reedy then complained about something that was to plague

him throughout his friendship with Patience Worth: He was being deluged with other examples of so-called spirit communications. "Many persons have written me that they have had wonderful converse with the dead. Many matter-of-fact men have met me on the street and told me of strange things that had been told them by mediums through the ouija board and by clairaudients and clairvoyants."

Reedy still insisted, however, that all of this so-called spirit literature was utter junk—with the blazing exception of Patience Worth. "The poems, parables, stories, novels, plays of Patience Worth are done in a language that is all her own. Her figures of speech are not trite. All her 'properties' are achronistic with her period. She tells a story of Charles I and makes him stutter. 'Why do you make the king stutter?' she was asked by a scholar. 'The blood-taint,' she replied. And the lady who takes down or takes up the words of Patience from the ouija board had never heard of the blood-taint of the Stuarts. In a narrative she calls *The Sorry Tale*, there is a description of a night in the Arabian desert which not Robert Hichens himself could surpass in detail, down even to the camel's nose hanging out and down over his mouth. And such descriptions in other stories of other places and times are similarly true to conditions and situations."

Reedy then described another long session with Patience, during which he questioned her closely about such matters as gravitation, the validity of Newton's theory, the origin of the moon, and any writing she might have done before she "left the earth." To all of which Patience provided her usual allusive responses. She did make clear, however, that she flatly refused to assume the role of seer, thus setting her far apart from many others (in 1971, as well as 1915) who claim psychic powers. Reedy asked, "Paticnce, you speak of things past; can you see into the future?"

And Patience answered: "Nay, Brother, nay. That that man seeketh layeth close to Him, yea, e'en as doth the sun's light climb it up o'er the earth's curve at morn, afore he showeth him on the sky's arch. So doth the day o' Him to hold 'bout Him that that shall be asoon, and were he not ablind, he might see o' this athout the eye o' man or me. Yea, thy day o' yesterday hath set upon thy track asomething that showeth 'pon this day."

Reedy: "Can He set aside His laws at the prayer of His creatures?"

Patience: "Brother, brother, I be aprate to thee! Yea, and hark, much word o' Prayer be but words, and He doth list not unto word. Nay, he knoweth e'en the mite whose wings-whirr be all o' its voice."[4]

The following week Reedy declared that he was receiving letters from all over the country demanding more news of Patience Worth. Yes, he would talk about her a bit more this week, but then he hoped to give the subject a rest for a while.

Once again, Reedy made clear that he found nothing especially new in Patience's message; it was, he said, a type of pantheism which was uttered a thousand years ago. And again he refused to say that Patience was a spirit: "I say nothing about her save that she displays a lovely, loving, a loveable spirit in all that she imparts. I don't say that she is supernatural but I do say she is spiritual, and while I deny the supernatural, I proclaim the spiritual. She says nothing that is foolish, nothing that insults the intelligence, nothing that wounds the human heart. She may be a subconscious personality of Mrs. Curran, she may be a reflection of something of the personality of her inquisitor; I do not know. All I know is that I have had high, rare, keen pleasure in my conversations with her. She is as good company as I have ever known, and I have had converse with many of the prophets, priests and kings and queens of thought and talk."

In that same (October 29) issue of the *Mirror* Reedy printed a letter from a professor of English, one of the first public statements of approval of Patience from a professional scholar. The letter was from Robert T. Kerlin of the faculty of Virginia Military Institute. Professor Kerlin expressed deep interest in the Patience Worth articles and called Reedy's attention to the regular, iambic rhythm of her writing. "The Stranger," he said, "may be scanned from beginning to end, and will be found to be more regular than Shakespeare's blank verse. Test it anywhere, the result will be surprising and, I will add, delighting."

Referring to a work of Patience called "Leta's Prayer," Professor Kerlin cited its "marvelous beauty" and his letter concluded: "But the poetry of it! It seems impertinent to prate of metrical feet when 'Leta's Prayer' is under consideration. There is only one prayer known to me that has more beauty and more sublimity in it. No, Mr. Editor, with all respect for your literary judgment, I affirm that not Chaucer, not Spenser, not Shakespeare ever reached this altitude of poetry."[5]

In another of his articles on Patience, in the November 12 issue of the *Mirror*, Reedy raised a question that was to come up repeatedly. A letter from a reader had pointed out that a minor character in a novel called *To Have and to Hold* had been named Patience Worth. Startled at this report, Reedy had quickly looked up the novel, which had been written by Mary Johnston and published in 1900. He found that the book took place in the early seventeenth century and that the name Patience Worth appeared only fleetingly—the heroine of the story took the name from her maid and used it when she fled to Virginia in a consignment of wives for the colonists there. In addition, Reedy pointed out, "there is nothing in the language of *To Have and to Hold* that acutely resembles the language of Patience Worth. Most of the speech in the novel is euphuistic, formal, stately, very much of the plume and gauntlet and sword. Patience talks a more vulgar speech, in the true sense of vulgar. Her hints of her experience and fate are not drawn from the book."

Apparently still troubled by the coincidence, Reedy questioned Mrs. Curran about it. "That's old," she said. "We read the novel about a year after our Patience Worth began communication through the ouija board. . . . There's nothing of our Patience in the novel but the name. We have tried to find out from Miss Johnston something about the name Patience Worth, how she came to select that particular name, if she knew of any such person in the history of the Virginia colony, and so forth . . . we have never received an answer. The only thing we can say, in the absence of any exact knowledge, is that the name in the novel is a coincidence."[6]

In spite of Reedy's publicizing of the duplication of names and Mrs. Curran's explanation, questions about the apparent coincidence kept coming up during the next few years. Individuals would discover the duplication on their own and proclaim it to be an important clue. Yet, there is no indication that the Mary Johnston novel was connected with the Currans' Patience Worth.

Reedy continued to be bombarded with letters about Patience from his readers. When he announced at one point that he would suspend any further discussion of the case for the time being, many readers wrote in to protest. Typical of the letters was one printed in the November 12 issue. It was signed only with the letter "C.," but Reedy, in an editor's note, declared that the writer of the letter was "a distinguished woman scientist, artist, and novelist."

Whoever she was, the versatile letter writer obviously was captivated by Patience Worth. "Patience may add nothing new in what she says," the letter stated, "but if she is real, she adds a tremendous amount, by *being* what she is. And with all my heart I hope she is real. My heart believes in her, even though my mind is awaiting a possible explanation—from the unknown realm of the subconscious." The letter ended: "I shall be heart-broken if Patience is ever explained away."[7]

After the Currans' ill-fated meeting with Dr. Prince in Boston and the scientist's public criticism of them for refusing to submit to hypnosis, Reedy came strongly to their defense. In the *Mirror* of November 26, commenting on Mrs. Curran's refusal to be hypnotized, Reedy declared, "She did right. No one should submit to being hypnotized, to the surrender of that person's will into the control of another person. Dr. Prince's idea was evidently that in hypnosis a second personality, a subconscious Mrs. Curran would come to the surface and reveal itself as the intelligence calling itself Patience Worth. But if it had, the mystery would not have been solved. For myself the mystery would remain—the mystery of genius. The Patience Worth communications are true literature of an unique order. . . . If Patience Worth is a subconscious self in Mrs. Curran the explanation is no more explanatory than saying Patience Worth is a spirit. Regardless of explanations, the literature stands, a charming expression of personality, a contribution of beauty to the world."[8]

In the *Mirror* for December 3, Casper Yost wrote a lengthy analysis of "The Religion of Patience Worth." He had been attracted first by the beauty of the language, Yost wrote, but "as the productions of Patience continued, I began to perceive building up within them a system of religion more attractive to me than the beauty of the dress in which it was clothed."

Yost disagreed with Reedy's description of Patience's theology as pantheistic. ". . . the common understanding of pantheism is the materialistic philosophy that denies the existence of a supreme reasoning being, holding that nature is the sum and substance of all things, that nature itself is God, and that only in man does it rise to consciousness. To that pantheism Patience is distinctly opposed . . . the God of Patience is a personal, creating, directing God, one who lives, and moves, and has a being."

Yost also stated that, despite some statements apparently to the contrary in her writings, Patience affirmed the divine origin of Jesus and his resurrection.[9]

Also heard from during those weeks of constant discussion of Patience Worth in *Reedy's Mirror* was the eminent Professor John Livingston Lowes. In a letter to the *Mirror,* Lowes protested that he kept hearing reports of his views on the case but that such reports were without foundation. He had not made any statements about the case, Lowes wrote, because he felt much more would have to be known before he would feel qualified to make any comment. "I believe the phenomenon to be worthy of serious scientific investigation. That is, as I see it, the case is one for expert judgment. Since I am not an expert in the field which is primarily involved—that of the subconscious personality—I prefer to suspend my own judgment until the recognized authorities in that field have had a hearing. The linguistic and literary problem, about which alone I should have any right to speak, is too closely bound up with the other to be separated from it."[10]

As the time drew near for the publication of Casper Yost's book, all of those closely involved with Patience Worth grew tense in their anticipation. The reaction of literary critics and readers to the Yost book, they knew, would very largely determine whether Patience would become a major influence upon thousands of persons or whether she would subside, after a brief sunburst of fame, into a local curiosity—a skyrocket that had had a moment of glory, then sputtered into silence.

If the nation's critics and literary commentators failed to take the case seriously, if they rejected Yost's contention that the writings had real literary merit, then there would seem to be little chance of bringing her writings to the wider audience that Patience's followers believed, with great intensity, she merited.

Some advance heralding of the Yost book was provided by its publisher, Henry Holt. He edited a widely read magazine called *The Unpopular Review* and in the January 1916 issue—a month prior to the publication of the book—Holt wrote a twenty-seven-page article about Patience. Much of it was excerpts from the Yost manuscript and long samples of Patience's writings. He quoted Yost's analysis of the language used and the religious thoughts expressed, along with a description of the personality presented by Patience, with copious quotes to illustrate her changing moods. Then Holt gave a detailed report of the sitting in New York on the previous November 19 when Patience gave instructions concerning the physical appearance of the forthcoming book.

In his discussion of the case, Holt brought up the much publicized interview with Dr. Morton Prince and indicated that the well-known doctor had seemingly made up his mind about the case before ever talking to Patience. "Some ten days before [the interview with Patience in Boston], we had had a long talk with the gentleman [Prince], who happens to be a valued personal friend. We said: 'Of course you'll promptly send anything you find?' He replied: 'I don't expect to find anything,' and we answered: 'Then you won't.' And he didn't. Considerable familiarity with the records concerning the involuntary writers long ago led us to say that persons approaching them in an unsympathetic spirit seldom get any interesting results . . . hostile influences generally stop the functions." Holt also defended Mrs. Curran in her refusal to be hypnotized and denied that this was due to any fear of exposure on her part.[11]

As to the suggestion by some critics that Mrs. Curran got into the whole thing for notoriety, Holt made a very logical objection: ". . . how utterly unsupposable it is that a woman capable of composing work of which some specimens are declared by competent critics to be close to masterpieces, should, loving notoriety, try to throw upon another intelligence the credit of her work, and smother it under a language that nobody uses, and that it requires some effort to understand."[12]

Was there an answer? Holt had little more to offer than anyone else, except for this comment: "Pretty much every philosopher big enough to attract attention has taken for at least his second guess, a cosmic soul as the source of all psychic phenomena, those of individual souls of course included: for we know no others; and in the sources of that nearly universal guess, we suspect the solution of the mystery to lurk."[13]

Finally, in February 1916, some thirty-two months after Patience first introduced herself, Casper Yost's *Patience Worth: A Psychic Mystery* was published. The book, building and expanding on Yost's original series of newspaper articles, told of the first coming of Patience Worth, gave liberal samples of her work, and analyzed her philosophy and personality, as well as the origin of her language.

Before beginning his account of the unusual happenings in St. Louis, Yost explained his own position: "The compiler of this book is not a spiritualist, nor a psychologist, nor a member of the Society for Psychical Research; nor has he ever had anything more than a transitory and skeptical interest in psychic phenomena of any character. He is a newspaper man whose privilege and pleasure it is to present the facts in relation to some phenomena which he does not attempt to classify nor to explain, but which are virtually without precedent in the record of occult manifestations. The mystery of Patience Worth is one which every reader may endeavor to solve for himself."[14]

The story then was related of the first (identified) appearance of Patience on July 8, 1913. Since then, Yost wrote, the ouija board has produced writings that include "conversations, maxims, epigrams, allegories, tales, dramas, poems, all the way from sportive to religious, and even prayers, most of them of no little beauty and of a character that may reasonably be considered unique in literature."[15]

Most alleged spiritual communications have displayed an obvious lack of intelligence, Yost admitted, but he claimed that Patience "reveals an intellect that is worthy of any man's respect. It is at once keen, swift, subtle, and profound."[16]

The author expressed strong doubt that Patience was simply a role assumed by Mrs. Curran. He based this mainly on the difficulty of maintaining a steady flow of archaic English in impromptu conversations and in answering questions put to her without warning, without letting modern expressions or words often creep in.[17]

Also, Yost declared, Patience "is surprisingly familiar with the trees and flowers, the birds and beasts of England. She knows the manners and customs of its people as they were two or three centuries ago, the people of the fields or the people of the palace. Her speech is filled with references to the furniture, utensils, and mechanical contrivances of the household of that time, and to its articles of dress, musical instruments, and tools of agriculture and the mechanical arts."[18]

"No one not growing up with the language used," Yost wrote in another section of the book, "could have acquired facility in it without years of patient study. No one could become so familiar with English nature without long residence in England; for the knowledge revealed is not of the character that can be obtained from books. Mrs. Curran has had none of these experiences. She has never been in England. . . . She has never been a student of literature, ancient or modern, and has never attempted any form of literary work. She has had no particular interest in English history, English literature, or English life."[19]

Yost took pains to emphasize that the sittings with Patience are not surrounded by the spooky, mysterious atmosphere that usually pervades seances. "There is no ceremony about the sitting, no dimmed lights, no compelled silences. . . . The assistance is of the ordinary, fun-loving, somewhat irreverent American type. The board is brought into the living-room under the full glare of the electric lamps. The men perhaps smoke their cigars."[20]

Mrs. Curran does not go into a trance when the communications are being received, Yost noted, and she may even talk to other people while the board is in operation. She makes no apparent effort at mental concentration.

Yost admitted the possibility that the writings could come from Mrs. Curran's unconscious, but how could this be, he asked, if the knowledge never had been acquired by her through conscious means? "No one, for example, who had never seen or heard a word of Chinese, could speak the language subconsciously."[21]

As he had in his newspaper articles, Yost again maintained that the reputation and social position of the Currans put them above any suspicion of fraud (a rather naïve opinion, I would think, to be held by a veteran newspaperman). He also emphasized that Mrs. Curran did not give public exhibitions and did not receive any pay for the sittings held in her home; that only specially invited guests had been in attendance.

A major portion of the Yost book was given to samples of the Patience Worth writings and to Yost's analysis of the language. He cited several examples of words given by Patience which were unknown to anyone in the group and which, upon careful checking, were found to be authentically archaic English words. One of these was the word "cockshut." His research revealed, said Yost, "that cockshut was a term anciently applied to a net used for catching woodcock and it was spread at nightfall, hence cockshut acquired also the meaning of early evening. Shakespeare uses the term once, in *Richard III*, in the phrase 'Much about cockshut time,' but it is a very rare word in literature and probably has not been used, even colloquially, for centuries."[22]

The evenings with Patience, the book reported, are vastly diverse in nature. "She may devote the evening largely to poetry, possibly varying the themes, as on one evening when she gave a nature poem, one of a religious character, a lullaby, a humorous verse and a prayer, interspersed with discussion. She may talk didactically with little or no interruption. She may submit to a catechism upon religion, philosophy, philology, or any subject that may arise. She may devote an evening to a series of little personal talks to a succession of sitters, or she may elect just to gossip."[23]

What is Patience's purpose? Yost said: "She gives the impression that she is a messenger. 'Do eat that which I offer thee,' she says, ' 'Tis o' Him. I but bear the pack apacked for the carry o' me by Him.' "[24]

Her message, Yost wrote, is simply Love. "Love, going out to fellow man, to all nature and overflowing toward God. . . . Love for everything is the essence of her thought and of her song."[25]

There was no doubt in his mind, Yost wrote, that Patience strongly affirmed the immortality of the human soul, but she persistently refused to give concrete details of life after death.

Now the die was cast. The book was out at last, and the little group of devoted followers in St. Louis waited nervously for the critical and public reaction. So much depended on it. The response to the book was everything they had hoped. With only scattered exceptions, the reviewers reacted very favorably to the quality of the Patience Worth literature and even to the possibility of the author being a voice from the dead as the Currans and Yost had come to believe. At least, if the critics were not willing flatly to accept the spiritualist interpretation of her origin, few of them opposed it with hostility or ridicule.

Heading the list of favorable reviews was that of the highly influential *New York Times*. The unsigned review in the *Times* appeared on February 27, 1916, under a four-column headline: "PATIENCE WORTH" A PSYCHIC MYSTERY. The subhead read: 'Remarkable Plays, Poems, and Stories With an Early 17th Century Flavor Produced Through a Ouija Board."

The lengthy review got right to the point: "Amazing enough, whatever be its explanation, is this 'psychic mystery' of 'Patience Worth,' whose messages out of the darkness never sink to the commonplace level, but always show high intelligence and sometimes are even tipped with the flame of genius."

Two short tales given in the book, the review said, "show vivid picturing of scenes, clear-cut characterization, the ability to express keen emotion in action. And they have spiritual and intellectual as well as dramatic value." The poems of Patience "have dignity, remarkable beauty, sustained imagination, and profound spiritual significance."

The review concluded: "It is evident that 'Patience Worth' has given to psychologists, psychists, psychiatrics [sic], skeptics, and the merely curious the hardest and most interesting nut they have ever had to crack. The immense mass of the communications, their high level of literary quality, their flashes of genius, the distinct and interesting personality revealed, arrest attention and put the whole affair immeasurably beyond any other communication which has ever pretended to come from the other side of the grave."[26]

The *Book Review Digest* for 1916 included quotes from three reviews of the book, all favorable: "Patience Worth can write real poetry and has a sense of humor that is rare in ghosts or secondary personalities."—*Independent*, July 10, 1916. "What makes the problem significant is the quality of Patience Worth's utterance. That she is sensitive, witty, keenly metaphysical in her poetry and finely graphic in her drama, no one can deny. As one reads Mr. Yost's narrative, one comes to delight in her. Whoever or whatever she is, she meets the test that human beings meet. Mr. Yost has done his part admirably. He has respected rich data. He has had sufficient humility to postulate a mystery."—F.H. in *The New Republic*, March 25, 1916. "The transparent and palpable genuineness of the entire case, in all its aspects, is the chief impression you bear away with you from an unbiased study of it."—Lawrence Gilman in the *North American Review*, June 1916.

In March the *St. Louis Globe-Democrat*, Yost's newspaper, proudly carried a roundup of national press reaction to the book. It began: "The *Globe-Democrat*, having been the first to present 'Patience Worth' to the public, quite naturally takes an interest in the spread of her fame, and now that her works have been given a permanent place within the covers of a book, it is pleased to observe the unanimity of approval of the literary merits of her productions among its contemporaries in other cities. With but a single exception, the newspapers of the country that have commented upon the phenomenon, and they are many, speak in terms of high praise of the quality of the literature and of admiration of the personality."

Here is a sampling of the reviews reprinted by the St. Louis newspaper:

New York Evening Sun: "The unusual distinction about this Patience Worth is her exceptional and consistent intelligence. She shows in all her messages every sign of a vigorous, keen mentality . . . she reveals a large creative gift . . . an output of original prose and verse that would do more than credit to any literary modern . . . [she dictates] a play in pure Elizabethan, a fanciful, imaginative play, the atmosphere and characters of which are so true to the Elizabethan period that it might almost be produced as part of the Shakespearean tercentenary. . . . Patience Worth, with her baffling consistency of intellect and personality, will not be banished by laughter or exposed by an investigating professor who has an eye for secret strings."

Chicago Evening Post: "Whatever psychological or spiritistic mystery be back of 'Patience Worth,' the product of the ouija board in this instance is not merely curious, it is both entertainingly humorous and beautiful. . . . Patience Worth discloses herself as a wit, a poet, a dramatist, and a philosopher. Her poetry is instinct with religious feeling and love of nature."

Elia W. Peattie in the *Chicago Tribune*: "Patience Worth is a powerful, unique, but impalpable personality . . . she has produced literature of extraordinary beauty and significance. . . . It is really impossible in the close limits of this review to give an indication of this rare, elusive spirit and the strange combination of sympathy, homely knowledge, mirth, and spiritual elation which pervades it. To quote the poetry without first giving some evidence of its peculiarities would be to do an injustice to a rare and beautiful thing."

Kansas City Star: "Her poetry is irregular and the earlier verse is rather fragmentary. It shows tenderness, is graceful in its imagery and has real depth of feeling. . . . A lullaby in blank verse, a lullaby sung to an imaginary child, is one of the most charming things in the whole book. . . . Her appreciation of the out-of-doors is keen and heartfelt—the appreciation of one who has lived close to the things she sings. . . . Striking figures are in much of the verse. . . . There is a solemnity, an earnestness about the ideas upon immortality that is very striking. Whether as a psychological study or as literature, it is intensively interesting and totally unlike anything that has ever come before the medium of the mysterious board."

Even the witty and sophisticated Franklin P. Adams, writing in the *New York Tribune,* was impressed: "We wish we had a ouija board and that Patience Worth would contribute." Of the short poem previously mentioned which begins "Ah, God, I have drunk unto the dregs and flung the cup at Thee!", Adams declared: "Perhaps somebody we know all about has done something as good as the appended verse by the somebody we know nothing of, but today's conductor has not seen it."

Also chiming in with his own felicitations on the book was Billy Reedy. In the *Mirror* for February 25 Reedy reported to the many readers who had been eagerly awaiting Yost's volume that it was now in the bookstores. Reedy declared that Yost tells the story of Patience Worth "with admirable clearness. . . . The writings are edited with marvelously meticulous care for the clearing up of the slightest obscurities. The result is a fascinating story with charming lyric and dramatic and comedic interludes."

Reedy stated once again his enthusiasm for the literature: "The expression is of literary force, sweep, fineness, delicacy. The works are works of creation—their literary value is indisputable. They are original. . . . They are like no other writings in the world. They are as wonderful to the well-read person as to the less literate."

The famous editor and critic renewed his defense of the Currans: "As for the absence of all deceit and trickery in the production of the Patience Worth writings, I am willing to stake my head upon the honesty of Mr. and Mrs. John H. Curran. Neither of them, nor anyone in any way associated with them, could write the things that come from Patience over the ouija board. No living writer could simulate such a style, nor, more than that, such a quality and turn of thought as these writings reveal. Style and thought are the same in variation through the 500,000 words of the works that I have read. Patience Worth is a personality, strongly individualized, and that personality is the personality of a rare, beautiful, loving genius. If my own experiences with the communications of this personality had not so convinced me, Mr. Yost's narrative would. It is a thrilling story of a spiritual adventure. I accept the Patience Worth personality as a fact. I say her work is of the substance of genius."

Yet, Reedy would not make the ultimate concession. He ended the piece by saying: "But I do not believe that Patience Worth is one of what we call the dead."[27]

And so the returns were finally in from all over the country. Patience Worth was a resounding hit!

There was rejoicing in St. Louis as one favorable review after another came to the attention of Patience's loyal fans. They were convinced now that the wraith of the ouija board was destined to become a significant spiritual and moral force in the world. Whether or not it could be proven that she was the spirit of a woman long dead, it now seemed certain that her message of hope and love would resonate far and wide. Helped by the plentiful publicity and favorable reviews, Yost's book was selling briskly across the nation, and within weeks the publisher had ordered a second printing. By 1918 the book had gone through four printings.

During those exciting early months of 1916 the news of Patience and her message was spread to a still wider audience by various national magazines which devoted considerable attention to the case. For example, in the June issue of *Harper's Magazine*, Henry Mills Alden wrote in his "Editor's Study" column that he was generally skeptical of so-called psychic phenomena because "the 'illuminations' thus mysteriously derived, in the automatic deliverances that have taken a written form, have been obvious and, on the whole, boresomely tedious, suggesting no alliance with genius in either the special or generic application of the term." But, he went on, "these writings attributed to Patience Worth are exceptional—especially the poems. Notwithstanding an intolerable deal of chaff and the extravagantly overdone archaism, we find gleams of genius."

And the popular *Literary Digest*, in its issue of May 6, carried a long article headed "What Is Patience Worth?" The article began: "It is difficult not to take 'Patience Worth' seriously. Quotations from her writings in the newspapers have been brief and fleeting, but even these scattered specimens have indicated a wit, wisdom, and grace of phrase that would be distinctive in any flesh-and-blood writer of today."

The article went on to quote lengthy excerpts from Yost's accounts of the sittings with Patience and examples of her wit and vivid personality. It also related the curious episode in Holt's New York office when Patience gave instructions concerning the color and design of the book cover.[28]

A sudden, jarringly unexpected development in April 1916 brought dismay and anger to the followers of Patience Worth and smashed like a bulldozer into their mood of rejoicing. The country's best known and most respected investigator of psychic mysteries launched a savage attack on the Currans and those who had helped them to spread the word about the strange case. The assault came without warning and was a stunning blow to the St. Louisans.

James H. Hyslop had been a college professor of philosophy, ethics, and psychology for more than twenty years, serving for the last seven of those years as Professor of Logic and Ethics at Columbia University. In 1903 he had given up his university post to organize and direct the American Institute for Scientific Research, which in 1907 became the American Society for Psychical Research, the most prestigious American organization for the investigation of psychic phenomena. Hyslop served as director of the A.S.P.R. from 1907 until his death in 1920 and wrote seven books on psychical research. In 1916, at the age of sixty-two, Hyslop was the preeminent United States authority on psychic matters, a demanding investigator who spent much of his time putting reputed supernatural happenings under rigorous scientific examination.

In the April 1916 issue of the A.S.P.R. *Journal*, Hyslop reviewed Yost's book and turned the review into a denunciation of the Patience Worth case and all those involved in it.

He wrote: "It is curious to see how a superficial respectability [of Yost and Holt] will give vogue to a product that will not stand a moment's scientific scrutiny, even though it be or contain much that is genuine.

"The ground on which they try to excite our interest is not its excellence as literature, but on the ground that the phenomena are ordinarily inexplicable.... But it is right at this point that the book marks an entire failure. It has not a scientific note in it. There is no evidence whatever that a scientific man would regard as conclusive regarding the origin of the material. We are asked to swallow without hesitation the superficial statements and beliefs of a newspaper editor who boasts his ignorance of psychic research and of a publisher who desires to sell his wares...."

Hyslop demanded more information about Mrs. Curran's background and especially her early reading: "There is not a word in the volume about this fundamental question!" He really didn't blame Yost too much, Hyslop declared, because he (Yost) just didn't understand the need for proper scientific information regarding the origin of the data. "He seems to have been entirely ignorant of the resources of sub-conscious memory in such cases."

Hyslop went on: "Mr. and Mrs. Curran should have taken the scientific man [presumably Dr. Morton Prince] into entire confidence and offered every opportunity to investigate it to the uttermost. But that course they evaded in the interest of pseudo-miracles and the result is a book that must pass into history as a fool adventure to influence the public in behalf of ideas which have no adequate credentials whatever between its covers."

The review grudgingly admitted that Patience's works had some literary value: "There can be no doubt that the poetry is good, far above the usual product of automatism, and the same is true of the other literary material. It is all good literature and deserves reading on that account alone."

The importance of the ouija board itself was flatly rejected by

Hyslop—and later developments in the case were to prove him quite right on this point. Referring to the implication that the board is a major factor, he wrote: "Such a conception is worthy only of children and savages." But the most damning part of the attack was Hyslop's implication that fraud was involved and that profit was the motive. He accused Mr. Curran of seeking out scientific men only to advertise the book and not to investigate genuinely. "Notoriety and making a fortune out of the book were the primary influences acting on the parties concerned."

He charged that the language of Patience Worth was not really archaic, that it was couched in an archaic style, but contained many new words. He also claimed that Mrs. Curran had known Ozarks people who spoke an archaic tongue and that Mr. Curran had read Chaucer and had discussed the style with his wife.

Finally, Hyslop accused Holt and Yost of concealing such facts from the public. The case of Patience Worth, he declared, was "a fraud and delusion for any person who wishes to treat it seriously."[29]

Ironically, the same A.S.P.R. *Journal* would, twenty-two years later, offer almost a point-by-point rebuttal of Hyslop's accusations. An unsigned article, written shortly after Mrs. Curran's death, brought up Hyslop's charges and noted that the dialect of the Ozarks people in no way resembles the English of Patience Worth. As to the alleged reading of Chaucer, said the *Journal*, it is very unlikely that Mr. Curran could have imparted an enormous vocabulary to Mrs. Curran through conversation. In addition, the Patience Worth dialect bears little relation to Chaucer. ". . . there is no known language exactly like Patience Worth's. Hers is a mixture of centuries of English colloquial expression." As to Mrs. Curran's early reading, the article said, it was well established that Mrs. Curran never "got much beyond the poem 'Hiawatha' in her formal literary education and . . . exhibited little interest in literature from that time on." Hyslop was to contend later with great self-assurance that Mrs. Curran's subconscious was obviously the origin of the writings. But the *Journal* argued in 1938 that, on the contrary, "the remarkable erudition exhibited by Patience Worth, which it has been well-established was quite beyond the normal mind of Mrs. Curran, would seem to disprove the theory of dissociated personality."[30]

Immediately after Hyslop's attack became known in St. Louis, the followers of Patience rushed into battle to defend her. And their comments unleashed a running war of letters with Hyslop and others that was to last well into the summer. In the June 2 issue of the *Mirror* Reedy analyzed the Hyslop article and proceeded to challenge it at length, after expressing surprise that the attack came not from "orthodox religionists" as had been expected but from "one who is known everywhere as a believer not only in the possibility, but in the actuality of communications between the dead and the living."

The editor agreed that his main interest in the case was literary, not spiritistic, and that he felt Yost tended to accept too easily the spirit theory of the communications. But most of Hyslop's arguments, he said, were not well sustained by the evidence, including the "ugly" ones. As to the Chaucer question, Reedy said, familiarity with Chaucer would not equip anyone to do the Patience Worth writing. "There is no more Chaucer in Patience Worth than there is Patience Worth in Chaucer.'"

Reedy added: "Professor Hyslop writes himself down no philologist when he conveys the impression that the Patience Worth writings are a mosaic of archaisms. This is not true. The archaisms, the obsolete and obsolescent words in the writings are very few in number. What Professor Hyslop does not understand is that the language in which Patience Worth writes is a language which she has constructed for herself out of simple Saxon root-words."

As to Mrs. Curran's refusal to be hypnotized by Dr. Prince, Reedy said, "Mrs. Curran very frankly stated her reason for this refusal; that she did not care to submit herself to a condition, one of the consequences of which might be her loss of a power from which she obtains so much mental and spiritual gratification."

Concerning the accusations made by Hyslop against Yost and Holt, Reedy wrote: "It seems to me that when Professor Hyslop uses such language as this: 'the publisher has only joined with the original parties to perpetrate a fraud on the community,' he goes beyond the license of either literary criticism or scientific analysis."

His own belief, Reedy said, was that the writings came from Mrs. Curran's subconscious or telepathically from those around her. He did not agree that Patience Worth was a spirit and he realized that the Currans and Yost felt differently.

Reedy summed up his case: "I am as uncompromisingly antispiritistic as Professor Hyslop is comprehensively credulous in that respect. I say this only to indicate that it is from no prejudice in favor of the position taken by Mr. Yost or the Currans that I express my faith in their good faith as against the insinuations of Professor Hyslop. . . . Nothing true that Professor Hyslop says openly or by insinuation concerning Mrs. Curran and her relation to the Patience Worth phenomenon has been concealed by Mr. or Mrs. Curran. The facts of Mrs. Curran's reading, of her residence in the Ozark region where archaic seventeenth-century words still live, of her association in early life with spiritist preachers, of the occurrence of modern neologisms in the writings have never been concealed. Her refusal to submit to hypnosis by Professor Prince was widely published at the time it occurred. No person who has made any study of the Patience Worth words and works has been put off, no matter what line of investigation his inquiries took. So far as I have knowledge of the Patience Worth 'mystery' and those immediately connected therewith, I feel justified in saying that Professor Hyslop's review of the book . . . is a wanton and only too probably a malicious attack unjustified by the facts of the case . . . everybody identified with the communications and the publication has dealt fairly, openly, and above board with everybody who has made any pretense of investigating the phenomenon."[31]

Two weeks later the *Mirror* carried Hyslop's reply. (Reedy was careful to point out that the letter, apparently inadvertently, carried no signature, but was on the letterhead of Hyslop's organization and quite obviously had been written by him.) In the letter Hyslop argued that he would have been pleased to defend the "super-normal character" of the phenomena in question, "but there was no disposition on the part of the author and the publishers to reveal the full facts which would give the book a scientific interest, either for subconscious fabrication or for spiritistic interpretations." He added, "I have a good deal of evidence on hand to sustain my position, but did not care to print it at the time."

He could judge the validity of any case only by the evidence presented in that case, Hyslop declared, and "I offered the opportunity for the kind of experiment that would have settled the case, before the book was published, but it was refused. . . . There would have been no danger whatever in Mrs. Curran's being hypnotized by Dr. Morton Prince. It is silly for anyone to look at it in that light. . . . I had an entirely distinct method which would have settled the question of subconscious production. . . .

"What I desire to see in all such cases is that people put all their cards on the table. The scientific man can learn something then. I know scientific men who refused absolutely to have anything to do with it because there was no proper effort made to get at the facts. The publisher and those from whom the facts were obtained did not desire either to run down the subconscious theory scientifically, or to find out the facts which might make it spiritistic. They kept away from the public everything that would solve the problem and simply desired to mystify the reader by supposing the ouija board has some mystery about it. It was impossible for me to avoid scientific method in the criticism of such a procedure.

"I do not care particularly about the philological question," Hyslop's statement continued. "I would be no judge of that. I have the testimony of two philologists in regard to it, which take out of it most of the mystery which the publisher is willing to inculcate."

Hyslop went on to say that Reedy had covered some points in the *Mirror* which were not mentioned in Yost's book and that he (Hyslop) knew the information to be correct. ". . . if that matter had been properly threshed out by the scientific man first, the publication of such a book would not have been open to criticism."[32]

Also carried in the same issue was an angry letter from Professor Robert T. Kerlin, the teacher of English literature who just a few months earlier had proclaimed that Patience's poetry had achieved heights never reached by Shakespeare, Chaucer, or Spenser. With all the shrillness of a man betrayed, Kerlin berated Reedy for his criticism of Hyslop: "How can you nonchalantly—no, not that, but hotly, rather—set aside as unimportant, if not impertinent, the two items in the said review pertaining to Mrs. Curran's acquaintance with earlier English—the English of

Chaucer and the archaic survivals in the Ozarks—is to me incomprehensible. Surely, readers of Mr. Yost's book were warranted in assuming that he had given all the facts in Mrs. Curran's life that might have a bearing on the problem...."

Kerlin blamed Reedy as well: "Nor can you escape your responsibility in the case. Unless it has been in some issue of the *Mirror* that has failed to reach me, you have nowhere intimated that Mrs. Curran had such an experience as living in the Ozarks and such a schooling as the reading of Chaucer with her husband. This has the appearance of knowing concealment; otherwise it is incomprehensible failure to appreciate evidential facts, so egregious as to render both reporters of the case incompetent."

In the midst of his accusations, however, Kerlin paused to defend his own critical acumen: ". . . the wonder in my mind at the beauty and fervor and freshness of these Patience Worth effusions is, as it has been from the first, at the highest pitch—wonder and very much admiration. It is genius, nothing less (nothing more, either) manifested under the most extraordinary circumstances. . . ."[33]

The bitter exchange of verbal fire continued in the following issue of the *Mirror* as vigorous defenses were argued by Yost and Emily Grant Hutchings, the erstwhile midwife at the birth of Patience. "We who have worked with Patience Worth," Mrs. Hutchings loftily announced, ". . . cannot lie supine while the skeptic annihilates her with so absurd a bludgeon as the Chaucer-and-Ozark theory.

"I have known Mrs. Curran long and intimately," she said, "and I know to an ultimate certainty that she never read Chaucer in her life. I know, too, that the only reading of Chaucer that her husband did was in my home, fully a year after the Patience Worth dialect had been coming . . . their argument has not a leg to stand on."

Mrs. Hutchings also said that she had visited the girlhood Missouri homes of Mrs. Curran and had talked to the people there. "Their English offers no foundation for the fabric of speech that Patience Worth uses."

Yost wrote a longer and more carefully reasoned reply to Hyslop, although the mild-mannered, courtly newspaper editor could not conceal his anger at the Hyslop implications. Hyslop's criticism, wrote Yost, "is neither fair nor truthful. It is singularly lacking in the calm dispassionateness and the scrupulous exactitude of science. It makes charges without investigation and presents allegations that are disproved by the book itself. It is from beginning to end a tirade of abuse, unworthy of a scientist, unworthy of the cause which he represents."

Yost pointed out that, of all the "hard-headed and, perhaps, inherently skeptical critics" who had reviewed his book, none except Hyslop had questioned the genuineness of the case. The book, Yost insisted, "is . . . a fair, frank and straightforward presentation of facts, without conscious concealment of anything essential. . . ."

He refuted Hyslop's charge that the author and publishers were not content to sell the book on the ground of its literary value, but capitalized on the mystery of the origin of the writings. On the contrary, said Yost, he had minimized the mystery of the case and had devoted fully 90 percent of the book to the presentation and discussion of the literature. He had also stated, contrary to Hyslop, that the ouija board was an insignificant factor.

As to the two chief accusations, the "Chaucer-and-Ozark theory," Yost pointed out that the language spoken in the Ozarks does contain an occasional divergence from standard English, as does the language of almost every rural area, but "a residence in the Ozarks would no more account for Patience Worth's language than one in any rural region of the United States where English blood has long been dominant. . . . I have not been able to discover a single instance of the use by Patience Worth of a word or idiom peculiar to the Ozarks."

As to Mr. Curran's knowledge of Chaucer, Yost wrote, "it was not mentioned in the book because it does not exist. He has never read Chaucer, either to himself or to Mrs. Curran. . . . And, anyway, the language of Patience Worth bears not the slightest resemblance to that of Chaucer."

Yost concluded his argument: "The 'omission' of these two points is the burden of Professor Hyslop's complaints against the publishers, the author, and the Currans. It is quite evident that he has collected, or been given, considerable misinformation about Patience Worth and the persons associated with this personality. He has made no attempt to get the facts from first hands. He has not communicated with me at any time. He did write repeatedly to the Currans, entreating them to put the matter in his charge. This they declined to do, for most excellent reasons. The entire correspondence upon this point is in Mr. Curran's possession and may make interesting reading at some future time, if circumstances justify it. But Professor Hyslop did not attempt to get any of the information upon which he now lays so much stress. All of the information of that nature that was to be had was at his disposal, but that was not what he wanted . . . there is no disposition to withhold the minutiae of detail in which the scientists delight, but which the public abhors. Mrs. Curran will quite willingly tell the full story of her life to any reputable scientist who cares to inquire, but she quite properly refuses to lay her body and mind on the altar of science."[34]

Completing the war of words were two final communications. A contrite Professor Kerlin wrote in again on June 30 and announced: "I wish to set myself right toward Mr. Yost, the Currans, and the entire subject of the Patience Worth mystery." He had misunderstood, the professor said, and thought that Reedy had admitted the truth of Hyslop's Chaucer-and-Ozark claims. The Ozark point he now regarded as negligible. The Chaucer question was more important: "But now it appears that Mrs. Curran never read Chaucer at all! Very well. My complaint against Mr. Yost is gladly withdrawn. . . . Let me reassert with the greatest emphasis my feeling of respect for this mystery, my feeling of almost awe and reverence for Patience Worth. . . . I am a solicitous student of the facts, and above all of the wonderful utterances of Patience Worth—her maxims, the equal of which I never have found elsewhere, her little dramatic stories and her poems, both of which are unapproached in their beauty and their spirit by any writer of our time, unless it is Tagore. And Mr. Yost's book is admirable. . . ."[35]

And the last word in the debate was granted to Hyslop, whose letter appeared in the *Mirror* on July 7. In regard to the Chaucer incident, he wrote, "I received my information from a scientific man to whom Mr. Curran told it himself. The incident must rest between Mr. Curran and that man. . . . Science requires us to put all our cards on the table. No facts can be concealed. . . . I was not disputing the integrity of the Currans or anyone else within their lights, when criticising the book. I had no animus against Mr. Yost for his part in it. He displayed admirable courage in standing for the facts and probably many scientific people were not willing to stand for them as fearlessly as he did."

Although his attitude was now much more temperate, Hyslop could not resist closing his letter with a new charge: that the publisher had edited some of Yost's statements in the book so as to color the facts. "The duty of the publisher was to see that the whole of the facts were on record with the scientific man and then he would have abbreviated for the public without inviting scientific criticism for garbling the evidence."

For most of 1916 James H. Hyslop was the prime villain for all the loyal followers of Patience Worth, and by now their numbers had multiplied. Strangely, however, the caustic Patience herself was the least bothered by Hyslop and his charges. She once commented, as the Currans and their guests angrily condemned Hyslop: "Ye art yet for to learn there ne'er wert a bloomed field, greened and sweet o' grasses deep, but some ass seeked to browse therein."[36]

During the late months of 1915 and then into 1916, as the publication of Yost's book was first awaited and then took place, the sessions with Patience continued two or three evenings a week. Friends and their guests continued to throng the Curran home, and the ouija board hummed with conversation, retorts, poems, and comments, in addition to almost continuous work on the book of Christ, *The Sorry Tale*. During this period Patience also began dictating another long work, a happy, robust medieval story which she dubbed *The Merry Tale* and which, she said, was offered as a kind of mood balance for the somber, complex tale of the Holy Land which was her main concern. At most of the sessions in 1916 she would intermix short poems and other statements with segments, of varying length, of the two books. She also was kept busy, after Yost's book was published, writing personalized inscriptions for the book that were requested by virtually all of those who came to call upon her.

Many of the social leaders of St. Louis were among the guests. One of them noted in the record during this period was Mrs. David R. Francis, whose husband had been Mayor of St. Louis, Governor of Missouri, and Secretary of the Interior, and during this same year was named Ambassador to Russia. He had been, as well, the leading figure in the organization of St. Louis's near-legendary World's Fair of 1904.

In the spring of 1916 Patience intensified her work on *The Sorry Tale*. A part of it was given at almost every session, segments ranging from a few hundred words to as many as 3,500 words in one evening. The record for this period indicates for the first time that Mrs. Curran was seeing scenes from the book in her head and was hearing dialogue at the same time the ouija board was spelling out words. Sometimes, as John Curran noted in the record, there were problems:

"We again discussed the things Mrs. Curran saw, the Jews bartering in the market place. . . . The tale of Paul to Panda presented great difficulties to Mrs. Curran. Paul used a boy's language in speaking and over his words came the words of Patience's narrative. Mrs. Curran saw Paul and Panda and heard them talk. This confused the language that Patience was giving her as the story. Added to this trouble was the fact that Mrs. Curran saw not the picture of Christ and the Jews that Paul was telling of, which would have helped her, but saw only the scene in the hut with Paul and Panda."[37]

The guests at the sessions asked Patience a bewildering variety of questions about religion, about love, about current politics, about war and evil and death and life. A Miss Hurd once inquired, "How can we see and know God?" And Patience responded with her oft-repeated call to look around you, at children, at nature, and inside yourself: "Ope up thy heart, dame, and look unto the babe's palm, yea and unto the deep o' the sky's arch. Yea, and feel athin thy heart the throb that telleth thee He hath smote thy lute."[38]

In the summer of 1916 Yost went to New York and conferred with Henry Holt about plans for the next book—this time to consist solely of the writings of Patience Worth. *Telka* had been completed for some time and the Currans and Yost wanted it to be issued next, but Holt preferred *The Sorry Tale* to come out first, and this was agreed to. They consulted Patience, and she promised to work hard: "There be a waggin' o'er the puttin's. Look ye, dost thee set thee wished that thou deal the Sorry Put, thy handmaid shall weave, weave, weave. Up and at the weave, weave, weave, until the done, that thou mayst do this thing."[39]

She kept her promise. During one two-week period five sittings produced 16,000 words of the book. At one sitting, 5,800 words were dictated, the most productive session up to that time. On two occasions 3,000 words were given in a ninety-minute period.

Early in 1916 there was another development attesting to the spreading fame of Patience Worth, a development that seemed to insure that, long after the books bearing Patience's words had crumbled into dust, her name and her utterance cast in sturdier stock still would survive.

Mr. Curran was called upon by A. A. Speer, an old friend, who reported that he and an Edward Stephens had been appointed as a committee to select certain inscriptions to be placed in and about the new Missouri State Capitol in Jefferson City. Both men were members of the commission planning the beautiful new structure. They had decided to ask Patience Worth to contribute an inscription for the capitol. There was only one stipulation: It must be limited to 120 letters.

Patience was asked whether she was willing to supply such an inscription and she answered, "At thy next o' sit this thing shall be done."

At the next session Patience was asked if she was ready with her contribution for the new capitol. She responded that she had two and was undecided which to offer. She asked, "What wouldst thou, a word unto man, or wouldst thou a word unto a man?" The Currans suggested that the inscription had better be addressed to *men*, but Patience objected, "Yea, but he who seeketh goeth unto the 'laws hut' loned and needeth o' a word!" This was interpreted as meaning that she preferred to speak to one man at a time.

The record continued: "After some circling at the board, she said, 'I be nay at loving o' a put aset in a measure.' We were all aware of this and of the difficulty also of making a suitable quotation, which would be new and like Patience Worth and yet would be strong enough and pungent enough to be worth a place in the new capitol. However, after some circling, the following inscription was given: " 'Tis the grain o' Him that be athin thy hand.

Scatter thee nay grain awhither. E'en the chaff is His and the dust, thy brother's."

The record (that is, John Curran) went on to note: "This figures out just 120 letters counting the spaces between the words, which is in itself a very remarkable feat.[40] As was said by one of St. Louis's greatest literary men, the next day, this inscription contains 'all the law and the gospel and the highest possible conception of man's relation to his brother and to God.'

"We then asked her if she would like to give us the other quotation which she had in mind and she answered, 'Nay, waste o' grain! Be this alonged, 'tis the dame thou lovest that shall snip its tail.'

"This evidently means that if this quotation should be found too long, then she could shorten it, but preferred to leave it stand as it was."[41]

On a warm June day in 1970 I visited the imposing Missouri State Capitol, which sits regally on a high bluff over the Missouri River in Jefferson City, in an effort to find Patience's inscription. I searched the length and breadth of the building without success. Several capitol staff members with whom I talked had no knowledge of the inscription or of Patience Worth. There are a couple of books about the building, but they make no mention of Patience.

Whether the inscription requested by Messrs. Speer and Stephens and supplied by Patience ever was actually installed in the capitol, I could not determine. Possibly it was there for a while in the form of a plaque or framed scroll and later was taken down, to rest now in some dusty storeroom. Possibly someone had a change of heart or someone became apprehensive over the mystery of the inscription's origin and decided to leave it out of the massive building. In any case, my own inspection of the four capitol floors indicates that the inscription is not now in evidence.

6

Patience's Blessed Event

DURING THE LATE SUMMER of 1916 there began one of the most bizarre episodes in the entire strange history of Patience Worth. To put it quite bluntly: Patience became a mother. And the act created new headlines in newspapers and magazines across the land.

Although she did not physically bear the child, there was no doubt from the very first that Patience regarded the baby as her own and that she expected everyone else to have the same attitude. Which, sometimes, was exceedingly difficult for those involved, in the circumstances.

It all began on August 16, at one of the regular sessions with Patience. Those at the sitting expected her to begin work on another segment of *The Sorry Tale*. Instead, she declared that she was going to tell them something "close, yea close." She continued: "Ye see, I be a weaver of cloths. And this cloth be not for him who hath. Yea, and thee and thee and thee [indicating those sitting around the ouija board] do have o' a fullsome measure. Look, look, a time a-later the purse shall fatten [meaning that money from the sale of her works would be more plentiful] and ye shall seek ye a one, a wee bit, one who hath not. Aye, this be close, close."

At first there was confusion about the meaning. Then they suddenly realized that Patience wanted the Currans to adopt a baby. The Currans had never had a child of their own, but they insisted that they had given no thought to adoption until this night. They asked for further information and the ouija board responded: "Thou shalt deliver o' the goods o' me [meaning the income from publishing her books] unto the hands o' this one, and shall speak its name, 'Patience Worth.'"

This caused great surprise. The child must be a girl—and she wanted to bestow her own name upon the baby!

Patience went on: "Look, look ye, this one shall be a one that needeth sore, mind ye! And look ye, look ye. For all this wee hand plucketh from out thy heart, even so shall it be filled."

And Patience ordered that the child be told of her: "Ye shall whisper sweets unto this bit; e'en at in the sma' ear that heareth not the full wordin'. Yea, and unto this one thou shalt speak o' a fairie damie who ministereth; and o' Him who hath sent her."

Although the child would be adopted by the Currans, Patience made it clear that the baby would be the joint responsibility of all those in the group who came to talk with Patience and partake of her words: "Nay one shall take unto him the all. Nay, this one shall be the flesh o' all who love o' me, and shall smile sweets unto them."

How, Mrs. Curran inquired, did Patience intend for them to find such a child to adopt? Patience replied, "Ye shall seek the path. Out the first grain's shellin' [first money received] ye shall shoon o' it. See ye, e'en now the wee be awaitin'. Wait ye, when thine eyes fall 'pon it, thy heart shall leap."

The ouija board even provided some directions on clothing the child: "Ye shall set her spinster-prim. Look ye, look ye, and bonneted o' white like unto thy damie [herself]. Yea and a wee, wee kerchief; and ye shall set it gray caped. Yea, and ye shall see that about the wee neck hangeth the sign o' Him." The instructions about clothing conformed to a description of her own attire that Patience had given some time previously.

The Currans and their friends obviously took the unusual request quite seriously. They began visiting orphan homes and hospitals, seeking a qualified infant. They claimed, however, that whenever they discovered a baby girl eligible for adoption, there was some circumstance inconsistent, they felt, with the instructions that Patience had given.

Some of the followers of Patience thought that she would mysteriously provide the baby, possibly by having one left on the Currans' doorstep. After all, it frequently happened that way in fiction. But Patience objected, "Thinkest thou that the sheep cometh unto the shepherd without the callin'? Nay. Ye shall seek, and thine handmaid shall leap thee at thy heart, and thee and thee and thee, the loves o' me, shall for to set thee warm o' lovin'."

Periodically during the days that followed, Patience informed her listeners that she was "merryin'," but refused to say why she was happy. She also warned them that they must not seek a baby that was "whole," which was interpreted to mean a baby born into good circumstances: "Nay, for look, be it but a broked one, 'tis His and fit that it bear the name o' thy handmaid. And nay man suffereth."

They wondered whether the child might turn out badly, but Patience said flatly that this would never be. This was the first time she had issued a prediction about any individual.

As the search for the baby continued, Patience told them: "'Tis creepin' 'pon thee." Finally, Mrs. Curran discovered, by what the record termed "the merest accident," the baby to be selected. The child was not yet born. The mother was the impoverished widow of a mill worker who had been killed in an accident. She was living with and dependent on the charity of a friend. It was determined that she was willing to offer her child for adoption. (There is no indication in the records whether the mother was offered any financial inducement for her consent.)

The group referred to by the newspapers as the "Patience Worth clan" eagerly awaited the coming of the baby. Many of the women set to work sewing clothes for the child. (The size of the "clan" is not known with exactness. But the record during this period indicates the names of perhaps twenty to thirty people, friends of the Currans and friends of their friends, who attended the sessions with great frequency. It is these people who presumably made up the inner circle, although of course there were many others who came to the Curran home on occasion and a much larger number who eagerly kept informed of Patience's activities through frequent newspaper and magazine articles about her.)

Early in October Patience was busily writing a segment of *The Sorry Tale* when, at nine o'clock in the evening, the ouija board suddenly stopped, according to the compilers of the record. Patience said only, "This be 'nuff," and refused to say more. An hour later, word came that the woman had given birth to a baby girl at exactly nine o'clock. Patience, asked about this later, said, "Think ye I be astirring o' brew [working on a story] and this thing bein'?"

A short time later (apparently within a few hours of the baby's birth), Mr. and Mrs. Curran brought the infant to their home. Those who ascribed supernatural qualities to the Patience Worth case often cited this moment as providing powerful evidence of the para-normal. The baby was found to have red hair and brown eyes, which fit the description that Patience Worth previously had given of herself. And it was also found that the child's father was English and her mother Scotch, which also conformed to the heredity that Patience had announced for herself. (Admittedly, if fraud had been involved, one reason for the long delay in locating a child would have been to enable them to find parents with the proper nationality to fit the case.)

Henry Holt, writing about the incident in his magazine, said that the congruities seemed to suggest something more than mere coincidence: "The chances were but one in two that the unseen baby would be a girl, and probably about one in a hundred that she would be a redhead. The chance of her having in America an English father was, according to the last census, about one in one hundred and fifteen. Finally the chance of a Scotch mother would of itself be one in three hundred and eighty-five. We figure the chances against the whole thing being coincidence at about nine million to one, but we are stale in such calculations, and never were proficient. And we have known coincidences against which the chances were bigger than that."

Asked about her reaction to the blessed event, Patience burst forth with this: "See ye, I did for to say me that thy handmaid was at the merryin'; for look, she hath ta'en a tinder-top [redhead]! More, look ye, He hath lo'ed this one so that He hath left the gold o' His mightiest work, the glitter o' the flaming sun, to shed upon her and it sheweth unto a riched treasure o' gold."

The birth of the baby, which the Currans legally adopted a few days later, produced instant headlines in the local press. The *St. Louis Republic* headlined its article PATIENCE WORTH APPEARS IN THE FLESH . . . OUIJA BOARD SPIRIT ORDERS ADOPTION . . . GIRL BABY IS LEGAL CHILD OF CURRANS. A photo of Mrs. Curran accompanied the article.

Interestingly, a subhead on the article indicated that the followers of Patience Worth believed that the baby was a reincarnation of Patience. This is curious because Patience repeatedly denied the validity of doctrines of reincarnation and always affirmed that a single human spirit, once uttered by God, is uttered forever. On one such occasion, sometime later, Patience declared:

> *Who would become a child*
> *If heaven were a rebirth to infancy?*
> *What then the game? To become*
> *A child again with no heritage*
> *Of memory? Then life is vain.*[1]

The baby was legally named Patience Worth Curran and became a member of the family. During the years that followed, Patience frequently gave advice and instructions concerning care of the child and incessantly directed the Currans to give the child an abundance of love: "Nay pity-lovin' but lovin' lovin'!"[2]

Poems by the dozen were dedicated by Patience to the baby, which she often called "mine own bairn [baby]." This one was typical of her fervent love for the child:

HEAVEN IN MY BABY'S EYES

Two eyelids oped, and lo, the heavens' ope I saw,
And, like a twinklin' star God's smile reflected there.

Two lips did part and through their curve,
I breathed the breath o' heaven.
Two wee arms raised and circled me
With wondrous love; an armor, oh my God.

Two hands, rose-tipped, like winged things
Seem beckoning me, back back close to Thee.
Two feet have trod the newsome day.
Oh lovin' God, keep watch!

The earth is mine! Two dimple hands have given me
   the key
And Heaven is mine! but for the touching of its
   magic gold
The gates would ope and I might see, but why?
Oh why? when these two eyes be oped to me?[3]

The importance and significance of the baby always were strongly emphasized by Patience. On one occasion when Mrs. Curran referred to the child as a sign, Patience responded: "Who hath spoken that the babe of the flesh o' me be but a sign for the face o' men? I say me that she be e'en more than this thing, for she hath the key athin her sma' hand that openeth the heart e'en o' the great God, and this be the key o' love."[4]

Though she apparently had been a spinster herself, Patience wanted it known that this child was to be considered hers. Some years later, when the child criticized Patience for some upbraiding of Mrs. Curran, Patience responded angrily, in effect, "Who do you think you're talking to like that? I am your mother and she is just the person taking care of you and providing love for you." And when the day eventually came that Patience Wee, as she was called, was married, Patience Worth sent her a tender blessing, which was signed, "Thy Mither."

The reaction to the much publicized coming of the baby was rather predictable. It excited new furor in the breasts of those who believed implicitly in the reality of Patience as a discarnate spirit; it produced fresh laughter and ammunition for those who ridiculed the entire affair as a hoax or an exercise in credulity.

One of the few publicly negative reactions came in a letter published in the *Mirror* and signed by "A Poor Laborer." The writer said his skepticism about the case had almost been overcome until he read Reedy's account of the baby. The story, he said, proves "the other world (?) just as unjust and cruel as the world we are living in right now." The victims of the case, he declared, are the parents of the child, the father now dead and the mother "forced to give away the fruit of her heart and sufferings to wealthy strangers whose entire life is one continuous holiday of ease and pleasure." He went on, "Indeed, the robbing of the poor stops at nothing, not even at the cradles of their babies. If the

'Patience Worth clan' wants to do something real generous and whole-hearted, let them adopt and take good care of the baby's mother, also. Do not separate the mother from her child."[5]

There was no response to the letter from Reedy or any of the "clan."

During those months, as the sessions with Patience continued regularly, Mrs. Curran continued frequently to report seeing pictures in her mind as the ouija board ground out the language. On one occasion, in August 1916, she saw a vision of Patience herself, apparently during the last moments of her life. Patience often had given strong indications that she had been killed by Indians after coming to this country from England. (Once Patience was asked about the tribe to which the Indians belonged. She answered stonily, in effect, "Would you, with a blade at your throat, seek to determine the identity of your assassin?")

The record gives this account of the vision of Patience as seen by Mrs. Curran: ". . . the picture showed Patience, a small, wee figure in gray, come out of the copse of pine on the bluff-top, speeding, speeding to the bluff, then half-running, half-falling, down, down to the beach where the waters seethed. Within her breast an arrow stood and the small hands held it as she ran and fell, and half raised to her knees."

Patience then said, "And then, and then, when the tide had come unto—Look. Look. Ye know! See. See. 'Twere sunk deep."

Mrs. Curran continued her description of the scene: "The dear eyes looked across the sea, straining to find the dear home-land afar. But all grew misty and the yearning eyes grew dim, and she sunk on the sand by the sea's waters like a wounded swallow, a mere bit of gray along the vasty shore."

And Patience added: "And thy damie went her speeded unto a new land nay man knew. And the far curve o' all the sea that shut all awhither faded, faded. And the wakin'. Ah, that I might tell thee all, all the joyin', unto all brothers, unto all men."[6]

The Currans, like all the others involved with Patience Worth and the thousands of people who had read and wondered about it, continued during those months to speculate on the real origin of the writer, although they had come rather firmly to believe by this time that she was truly a spirit.

In November 1916 something happened that startled both Pearl Curran and her husband and mystified them even more.

Heretofore, all of the Patience Worth utterances had come from the ouija board, although, as mentioned, they often were accompanied by vivid pictures that Mrs. Curran saw in her mind. On a November evening, however, as the Currans sat in the small room in their home which had been set aside for the Patience Worth readings, Mrs. Curran suddenly put aside a newspaper she had been idly perusing and walked over to a desk. She took out a pencil and sheet of paper and began writing. Nothing was said. After a few minutes her husband asked what she was doing, but she asked him to wait a moment and be quiet. A short time later she handed him the paper on which this was written:

THE WONDER BABE

Ye wee wonder-babe,
Wi' heaven still aclingin' ye!
The angels fashioned ye
And gaed ye o' their gracin's.

Ye tiny hands, sae helpless sma',
Ye buddie bloe sweet lips,
Ye haloed headie, golden crowned,
And e'es sae wonder-knowin'!

They fashioned ye and left ye flee
Prae out the heaven's hame fair,
Back to the woed earth's sorries deep,
To make me know and lo'e Him.

John Curran wrote in the record of this night that he was "stumped, thoroughly frightened and full of questions as to why. After all that had been said about the possibility of Mrs. Curran writing the matter herself, and in view of many antagonistic theories about the work, it looked as though, if Patience Worth was what she claimed to be, that she had placed within Mrs. Curran's hand a blade and bared her breast. And why, why?"

Utterly confused by what had occurred, the first time that Mrs. Curran had written material in the style of Patience without resort to the ouija board, the Currans turned back to the board and asked for guidance.

Patience answered: "See, I did for to chide thee 'gainst the scatter o' grains. But look ye, 'tis ne'er a deal o' sweets unto the lender o' hands, and thy handmaid did set her but for this dealin'. See, hath she not ta'en unto her breast the wee flesh o' me? This song be o' this thing and be dealt unto her."[7] It is hardly clear in meaning, but seems to indicate that Mrs. Curran, who lent her hands to Patience and had taken her into her heart, seldom got any sweets of her own. And this was intended as a special gift of Patience, to be given directly, without any intermediary, to Mrs. Curran

They continued to hammer Patience with questions about herself and her purpose in coming to them. A few weeks later, when such questions again were asked, she replied: "Look ye upon this thing. I be abuildin' up a span that shall be a safe footin' for them that seek. Their feet shall not mire and they shall be ta'en o'er safely."[8]

In the January 1917 issue of *The Unpopular Review*, publisher Henry Holt told in detail the story of the adoption of Patience Wee in an article titled "That Patience Worth Baby." And he also reproduced portions of a letter Mrs. Curran had written to him which give some additional insight into her state of mind in those months and her attitude toward the great puzzle which had brought her, within three and a half years, from an unknown housewife to a controversial personality discussed by people throughout the world.

Holt noted that the letter from Mrs. Curran was very well written and tended to bolster the suggestion that the Patience Worth writings were the product of the involuntary exercise of literary capacities possessed by Mrs. Curran. "She is," Holt noted, "by no means as devoid of literary faculty as thought by her and some others who believe Patience Worth to be a separate intelligence."

In her letter, Mrs. Curran told of her continued work on *The Sorry Tale*, which she wished could be speeded up and finished. She told of the baby's progress and the love she was getting from all the friends of the Currans, and added: "I shall take my compensation out of her love and shall only hope that she will love us. Nor shall I entertain even a faint desire that she should be either a freak or a genius. I haven't decided which I am yet, and it is mighty uncomfortable not to know which. After all it is a mighty faint line that divides a freak from a genius, isn't it?"

The letter went on: "As to how much of the stuff that I am producing is voluntary and how much involuntary, it is my honest opinion (and I have particularly watched to see if any events during the day have any effect on what is produced; and try to view it from every side) that none of the work in all the nine hundred thousand words . . . was consciously or voluntarily produced by me.

"At times my own mind acts while delivering for Patience Worth. For instance, at one point in *The Sorry Tale*, I saw a very rocky path in the small visions that seem to relate the tale to me, and immediately *my* mind remarked to itself 'what a rocky place' and my hands recorded on the board 'the rattle of rocks.' Immediately Patience Worth broke in and asked me why I put my own tongue in her 'brew' and corrected the 'rocks' to 'stones,' thus making the phrase consistent with the book, in which the word 'rock' doesn't appear.

"Outside of such small intrusions of myself, there is no voluntary intrusion. And when I do think and am conscious, or should I try to put into words myself what I am seeing, the whole vision vanishes.

"Everything is as spontaneous to me as it is to those about me. The plot is in the dark, the characters spring up new and strange, even the names are hard for me to get. At times the plot and characters become so involved that my conscious mind is worrying over them, and yet Patience Worth will go steadily on. I feel as though I were in a strange land, and even smell smells that I have never smelled before, and am conscious of the atmosphere of foreign lands."

She also told in the letter of sometimes having brief, lightning-like visions when at the very beginning of a story or novel and later, in the course of writing the book, the vision materializes as a scene in it. Occasionally she would get a flash of a single character, then would think no more about him until, sometimes weeks later, he would show up in the story.

"Now tell me this," Mrs. Curran asked Holt. "If I can do these things, and it is a part of me, if it is voluntary or conscious in even a measure, why are none of these scenes, none of these stories, none of Patience Worth's works of today; and why is it that I don't have visions of this time and day? It is very hard for me to write in the ordinary way. I have been almost all afternoon writing this letter to you, while if it had been *The Sorry Tale* or a big poem, I would have done three thousand words in an hour and three quarters, and forgotten it."

How did Mrs. Curran herself view the answer to the riddle? Her letter to Holt concluded with this: ". . . I feel that I should say that after three years and six months of close acquaintance with Patience Worth and after receiving over nine hundred thousand words of her dictation, I have come to believe, from out as clear a mind as the average among a rather high class acquaintance, that Patience Worth is a discarnate spirit, speaking to me and through me to others, from a state of actual existence outside, beyond or different from, the ordinary life of mortals.

"The influence of the personality is for the highest good, as witness hundreds of letters from the heart hungry and the lonely; and the best of it all is that they come from people of the highest intellectuality."

Holt, although he was the publisher of the Patience Worth books and stood to profit from continued speculation that she was, as Mrs. Curran suggested, the spirit of a dead woman, stated frankly that he doubted this. He rejected the possibility of a hoax, arguing again that Mrs. Curran—if she wanted literary fame and had the talent to achieve it—would hardly have chosen a language that no one speaks and probably no one ever did. And he doubted that a hoax would have fooled the many persons of high intelligence who believed in Patience Worth.

"A much more probable [solution]," he wrote, "is that she possesses in an unprecedented degree a faculty recorded of many others, of building up from trifles of observation, often unconscious, great structures entirely out of proportion to the known material, and doing this in day dreams, just as nearly all of us do in our dreams at night. But how that faculty gets into us, and where it comes from, are perhaps the hardest questions, and perhaps even in these days, the most important questions engaging the minds of men."[9]

As 1916 drew to a close, the monumental work which Patience called *The Sorry Tale* was nearing its conclusion after months of work. On December 15 *Reedy's Mirror* printed the first sample of the epic-length book to be made public. In his introduction to the segment Reedy wrote: "It is a long story . . . but there is not a dull page in it. It is a tale of sorrow . . . that reaches the point of anguish at times. . . . It is no milk-and-water tale; red blood runs through it, blood that is frequently shed by violence. There is love in it and hate, tenderness and cruelty, devotion and treachery, poetry, passion, humor, philosophy, religion—thickly studded with glowing epigrams and wise aphorisms."

In February 1917 the dictation of the book was finished. The activities of Mrs. Curran were by this time of such interest that her mere announcement that *The Sorry Tale* was completed rated a lengthy story in the *St. Louis Globe-Democrat*. What part Casper Yost played in the extensive coverage by his own newspaper cannot now be determined, but we do know that his responsibilities normally were confined to the editorial page and were not concerned with local news coverage.

During the previous twenty months, according to the news stories, Patience had dictated the awesome total of 600,000 words, and her total output since her first appearance in July 1913 had passed the million-word mark.

The conclusion of *The Sorry Tale*, dictated on February 17, 1917, brought great happiness and a sense of profound accomplishment to all those who had taken part in the project of twenty months' duration.

After the closing words of the book were given, Patience said, "It is thine in His goodness." She went on, in great exultation: "These hands have upped and downed in His weavin'. Oh, the joyousness athin me that it be a fullsomeness! Give ear! Give hark! Give thy hearts unto it. It shall write upon the earth's sides His love. Weary ye not. Beat thy hands one upon the other and speak: 'It shall be!' Leave folly the path's ways. 'Tis well. The star beams! In subdued tones thy handmaid hath lifted up her voice. Yea, out silence. Oh, did ye know the waiting, waiting! Ye shall eat more o' bread for it is His will. What would I sing? My voice is heavy still, of sorrow. Yet, would I make the echoes o' all earth's dins joy, joy, joy, joy!"[10]

The next few months, as the Currans and their friends excitedly awaited the publication of *The Sorry Tale*, were busy and happy ones. Patience, along with her usual output of conversation, random poems, and religious dissertations, periodically gave new portions of *The Merry Tale*. And just two weeks after the harrowing work on *The Sorry Tale* had been completed, she began the dictation of a major new novel. It was to be called *Hope Trueblood* and was a story of Victorian England.

The first few words of *Hope Trueblood* provided a major shock for the Currans. For the language was utterly different from the previous Patience Worth materials. Unlike the archaic, sometimes barely decipherable argot that had been Patience's trademark, the language of the new book was decidedly modern, rather old-fashioned and prolix in style, but modern nonetheless.

The new book began with these lines: "The glass had slipped thrice and the sands stood midway through, and still the bird hopped within its wicker. I think the glass had slipped through a score of years, rightfully set at each turning, and the bird had sung through some of these and mourned through others. The hearth's arch yawned sleepily upon the black woolen table cover, where yellow fruits cut of some cloth were sewn. It may have been that I fancied this, but nevertheless it yawned.

"The wick had been lighted, as it had been the score of years, at the first coming of darkness. The kettle had been hung within the yawning hearth, and sent its steaming mists up the dark of the chimney's pit, for it had so often climbed the way. The fire seemed fitful, sleeping almost to ash, then suddenly flaming up as though to see the trinkets upon the what-all or read the woolen sampler that told unto the coming guest: 'God is Love.' "[11]

How did Patience account for this radical transformation of her writings into language of a more recent time? As usual, she was enigmatic and gave no clear reason for the change. Her own comments and conversation were still in the original archaic tongue.

Those in Patience's immediate circle were busy during those early months of 1917 making enthusiastic plans for the future. They were, of course, looking toward the publication of the two new books currently being dictated, plus additional works that undoubtedly were to come. In addition, Casper Yost was making plans for a new book analyzing the religion and philosophy of Patience Worth in much greater depth than had heretofore been possible. He had given it the tentative title of *The Task*. And Yost and the Currans also had decided to publish a monthly magazine devoted to the works of Patience Worth and those who followed her.

Meanwhile, the two and three sessions a week with Patience were continuing and guests kept flocking to the Curran home to meet the invisible author. The record shows that among the visitors during the early months of 1917 were poetess Amy Lowell, budding novelist and short-story writer Fannie Hurst, a Countess Kingston of Great Britain, and numerous faculty members from Washington University and other educational institutions.

One of the guests, a composer from New York, asked Patience one night "if she could explain how a couple of friends of his at Battle Creek, Michigan, had been awakened by a cool wind blowing over them at night and, raising up, they had both seen a white figure."

Patience answered, with a snarl that she reserved for this type of haunted-house question, "Look ye, I be nay dealer in wraiths!"[12]

In June 1917 Henry Holt published Patience's magnum opus, *The Sorry Tale*. It was a massive work: 325,000 words. Subdivided into three sections, it totaled 640 closely packed pages of type. The book began with a preface by Yost, who summarized the history of the case to that time. Concerning *The Sorry Tale*, Yost wrote:

> ... the knowledge shown was and is most puzzling. I do not undertake to say that there are no errors of fact or condition, no anachronisms. I merely assert that after much study and research I have been unable to find anything that I could so term with certainty. There are some things upon which no authority accessible to me gives any information. There are some variances from history, profane and sacred, but these are quite evidently intentional and with definite purpose. From the beginning to the end of the story Patience seemed to be absolutely sure of herself. Discussion of mooted points brought no comment from her and no modification of the statements. Several times she condescended to clear a doubt by later putting an explanation into the text, but in doing so she emphasized the original assertion.[13]

The novel is of the time of Jesus and Jesus is a major figure in it, but the main character is called Hatte.. He is the son of Tiberius Caesar and a Greek dancing girl of noble birth who is discarded by Tiberius and sent away to die. Hatte is born in a hut outside Bethlehem on the same night that Jesus is born. Their paths cross only a few times in the book until Calvary, when Hatte is the thief crucified alongside Jesus. The novel takes place mostly in Bethlehem, Jerusalem, and Nazareth, but there are additional scenes in Rome. All of the locations are described in prose that is redolent with atmosphere. Here, taken at random from the book, are several excerpts from *The Sorry Tale* which give some idea of the style and form of the work:

Page 24:
And it was night and dark. And storms arose, and lightnings licked the skies with fiery tongues. And waters washed the hills. Then did storm break and still fell o'er and about Bethlehem. Sheep, storm-lost, bleated, where, out upon the hills, they lost them. And Simeon slept, and waked with crashing, and sought the hills. And he brought back unto the hut sheep of Simeon and sheep of men. And he met upon his way a man, a fisher, one Peter, who offered of fish that he might eat of lamb's meat. And Peter spake of the casting of the morn, and dragged a net and leaned upon a staff.

And Simeon said unto him: "How have you come unto Bethlehem?"

And Peter answered: "Much word hath come from out the walls of Bethlehem. Anna of Jerusalem hath had visions that she sayeth come from scripts; and sayeth within Bethlehem the Christ is born. And Bethlehem murmureth much 'mong her people. The fishermen sent me unto her that I bear back that which she sayeth."

Page 109:
The morn spread forth, the golded tresses of the sun, and lo, a star still rested upon a cloud bar. And Jerusalem slept. The temples stood whited, and the market's place shewed emptied. Upon the temple's pool the morn-sky shewed, and doves bathed within the waters at its edge.

Beside the market's way camels lay, sunk upon their folded legs, and chewed, their mouths slipping o'er the straw, and tongues thrust forth to pluck up more for chewing. The hides shewed like unto a beggar's skull, hair fallen off o'er sores.

The day had waked the tribes, and narrowed streets shewed bearded men, and asses, packed. The temple priests stood forth upon the stoned steps and blew upon the shell that tribesmen come. From out the pillared place the smoke of incense curled, and within the stone made echo of the chants and sandals-fall of foot.

And tribes sought out the place, and lo, like unto ants they swarmed up and o'er the steps, to sit and make wisdom of the working of the priests.
Page 523:
And he caused that Simon bring up the net. And Simon fell upon his face and cried out:
"I am a wicked man! Behold, before thee have I set my doubt. Aye, and how may a man's doubt become greater than his God, save that he put his doubt before his God?"
And Jesus said: "Thou hast acknowledged thy doubt and fallen down before it. Cast thou the nets!"
And Simon let fall the net unto the waters, and behold, the waters stirred and the boats swayed, even so that it seemed that storms lay beneath the water. And they made to draw forth the nets, and behold, the fish leaped high and the silver shewed glisted within the light. And within the boat the men were not enough that they draw forth the nets. And they that watched saw, and men sprang unto the waters and swam to the spot and lended aid that they bring forth the nets. And they marveled and said: "What is this man?" And they cried: "Master! Master!"

Now, once again, came the agonizing wait for the reviews. Once again the little group in St. Louis, augmented by the devoted followers of Patience across the country—many of whom had made a pilgrimage to St. Louis to talk with her—waited for the judgment of, first, the book critics and later of the larger jury, the reading public.

Once again their waiting was, for the most part, rewarded. The reviews began coming in and the majority of them were good, a few ecstatic. The response was more mixed than it had been for Yost's book. In retrospect, however, this seems understandable. Yost's book had been an intriguing account of a mystery and could be favorably judged on that score alone. The new work, however, was a gigantic novel, awesome in its scope and ambitions. Very few such works, in any age, are unanimously praised by reviewers and a majority vote in favor, even today, is considered by publishers as a thoroughly acceptable verdict.

The *Book Review Digest* for 1917 lists excerpts from ten newspaper and magazine reviews of the book. In the plus and minus coding utilized by the *Digest*, four of the reviews are rated as favorable, four others as leaning to the favorable side, and two as negative.

As was the case with Yost's book, one of the most respected critical voices, *The New York Times*, uttered a fervent "yes" vote for the book. Said the *Times*: "It is a tale of Bethlehem and Jerusalem and Rome in the days of Jesus Christ and its theme is the interaction of the love and hate incarnated in the bodies of the Christ and of the thief who died on the cross with Him. . . . A great crowd of characters, there must be more than a hundred, carry on the action of the drama, and every one is individualized, full of its own tang of humanity, human and live. . . . 'Patience' works her own will with the gospels. She invents new miracles, she retells the old ones, she fills out with incidents the lives of Christ and His disciples; but the touching beauty and simple dignity of the figure of Christ are treated always with reverence and there is nothing in the tale to which the most orthodox could object."

The *Times* reviewer summarized his opinion this way: "The long and intricate tale is constructed with the precision and the accuracy of a master hand. It is a wonderful, a beautiful, and a noble book, but is not easy to read. Its archaic language and its frequently indirect modes of expression make necessary constantly the closest attention. The meaning is often so obscure that only considerable study will make it clear. Whoever would read it through will need to be well supplied with time and patience. But if he appreciate the noble and the beautiful in literature he will be well repaid. And he will marvel more deeply than ever over the mystery of 'Patience Worth.' "

Here are brief excerpts from other reviews as they appeared in the *Book Review Digest* for 1917:

Boston Transcript: "If, however, on account of its psychic claims, one approaches the story with unbelief or scoffing, one is instantly rebuffed by its quality. Especially is one impressed with that strongly marked individuality, that touch of a unique personality pervading the book, which we call style."

Dial: "The plot, stripped of verbiage, is consistent and straightforward; many of the incidents are amazingly dramatic or poetic; and the presentation of the life then extant in Palestine is accurate and full."

The Nation: "Certainly this book deserves to be weighed not merely as a 'psychic phenomenon,' but as a piece of creative fiction."

Clement Wood in the *New York Call:* "But it is a wonderful book, a more astonishing and sustained work than the earlier Patience Worth volume, and unquestionably the most remarkable product of the so-called spirit world, whether it be a sub-conscious achievement, or due to some unnamed psychic manifestation."

Review of Reviews: "Laying aside all questions of the actual authorship the novel has beauty and extraordinary power."

The two negative reviews were excerpted by the *Book Review Digest* as follows:

Catholic World: "This tale of the Christ is not in the least impressive. Its sole interest lies in its much advertised and to our mind spurious origin."

Outlook: "We are sorry that we cannot join in the praise which has been given to these two books by some critics that take them seriously and find that the literary ghost, so to speak, who communicates under the pseudonym of 'Patience Worth' is 'sensitive, witty, keenly metaphysical.' We will admit that 'Patience' has better qualifications as a writer of fiction than most 'controls,' but we find her writing feverish, high-flown, and terribly prolix."[14]

And, no longer unexpectedly, the comparatively faint negative chorus was belatedly joined by Professor Hyslop. In a brief review printed almost two years after *The Sorry Tale* was published, Hyslop wrote in the A.S.P.R. *Journal* that "The contents may have a spiritistic source, but there is no evidence for this view either in the book, or in anything published under the name of Patience Worth." Hyslop again suggested that the material came from Mrs. Curran's subconscious. Admitting that he was not competent to judge the book as literature, Hyslop said, "I could find no interest whatever in it."[15]

Some months earlier in the same publication, Hyslop—losing his academic cool—had referred to the "lying literary productions" of Patience Worth.[16]

To those who had taken the lead in proclaiming Patience Worth's existence to the world, there was no doubt in their minds: The new book was a masterpiece, the consummate evidence that Patience was unlike any other automatic writer that ever had been reported and, in fact, perhaps was unlike *any* writer ever before.

In the *St. Louis Globe-Democrat*, Casper Yost reviewed *The Sorry Tale*, and his review was carried under a headline which proclaimed: THE GREATEST STORY EVER WRITTEN. Yost gave a detailed résumé of the book's plot, interspersing it with such comments as "a most remarkable book . . . simply as a story, it is truly wonderful. The plot is tremendous . . . the threads of the great plot are woven with consummate skill. . . ."

Yost concluded his review this way: "The headline of this review declares this to be 'the greatest story ever written.' The assertion is made deliberately, with full realization of the risk of a claim so sweeping. Yet the test is not very difficult. Let any person of competent and unbiased judgment put it by the side of any one of the masterpieces of fictional or narrative literature and compare their literary, intellectual, and spiritual qualities. It does not matter what book is selected. If the glamour that hangs about a work of long accepted greatness is dissipated, and the comparison made upon absolute values, *The Sorry Tale* will rise superior in one or all of these qualities. It is the supreme masterpiece of narrative literature. The world has never seen such a book."[17]

Admittedly, Yost hardly was a disinterested critic. In a sense, it is hard to understand why his newspaper would permit him to review the book, since he was so deeply involved in the entire Patience Worth affair. Yet there certainly was nothing undercover about it. Everyone was quite familiar with Yost's tie to the Currans and undoubtedly took this into account when reading his report. Rereading his words, I still cannot help but marvel at the strength of his conviction. Knowing full well that the Patience Worth case was highly controversial and—on the part of Hyslop, at least—had been made the target of allegations of dishonesty, Yost nevertheless was willing to stake his reputation as a newspaperman and as a student of literature and the classics on the greatness of *The Sorry Tale*.

"It is the supreme masterpiece of narrative literature. The

world has never seen such a book." How many other books have ever received such an encomium from someone of the stature and acknowledged honesty of Casper S. Yost? Striking new books often have received high praise, but seldom, if ever, have they received this kind of praise—this designation of an importance so manifest as to be almost unearthly.

There are many who perhaps would challenge Yost's credentials as a literary critic, but few of them would dare to raise such a challenge against William Marion Reedy. And Reedy, too, made it very clear that he considered *The Sorry Tale* to be a new classic of world literature.

In his *Mirror* for March 30, 1917, Reedy reported that he had just read the complete manuscript of *The Sorry Tale*. He wasted no time in giving his judgment:

"This is the most remarkable piece of literature I have ever read. It has no fellow that I know of. It is written in a language that is its own and no other's—not a language in imitation of old or middle-English, but a language of locutions and turns of phrase and formation of words peculiar to Patience Worth. The story is a fifth gospel. The narrative of the accepted four gospels is rewritten in a form bold and unique. The mere story is a marvel of intricate construction, without discoverable flaw. It has the local color of Palestine and of Rome. There are one hundred characters in it—real characters expressed in action, not superficially described. It is full of incident of passion, humor, tragedy, meanness and moral splendor—aside from the personality of Christ that forms its focus. The theme is tremendous."

Reedy went on with much more in this vein, using such phrases as: "beautiful in form and spirit . . . anguishing irony . . . an exquisite piece of writing . . . the book is full of the writing that biblical scholars call wisdom. It is beautiful and deep when one has mastered the difficulties of its form . . . original in every aspect in which it can be considered and it appeals to all the emotions with the sureness of literary artistry."

Reedy's review ended with this: "I have no hesitation in saying that this production—I ignore any religious claims for it and I discount the adventitious interest of the manner of its presentation—is a world's literary marvel. It is a new gospel shaped out of the old gospels and it has claims entitling it to the highest consideration of critics of creative fiction, independent of the psychological mystery surrounding its coming into being."[18]

As respected as was Reedy's critical opinion, and there were few literary critics of his time more highly regarded, there undoubtedly were some who still would not unequivocally accept his verdict on the Patience Worth literature because they considered him to be a party to the affair. Like Yost, he had—at least in the minds of some—surrendered some of his critical objectivity by becoming personally involved with the Currans and their friends. But another judgment was soon to be given on the new Patience Worth book—a decision rendered by someone who never before had spoken out on the case, someone whose scholarly credentials could hardly be questioned. And when this new verdict was published, it provided for the devoted admirers of Patience Worth new and infinitely more powerful evidence as to the literary talents of the shadowy author in the Curran household.

Roland Greene Usher was a brilliant young historian, holder of a doctorate in history from Harvard and a former student at Oxford and Cambridge. Still in his thirties at the time, he was a full professor of history at Washington University and, five years earlier, had become chairman of the Department of History, a post he was to hold for thirty-eight distinguished years. He already had attracted international attention with his book *Pan-Germanism*, published in 1913, which had accurately forecast the events in Europe leading up to World War I. In his career he would write twelve books, many of them to be widely used as college textbooks. His special fields of professional interest were Tudor and Stuart England (the period in which Patience supposedly lived) and Modern European History. He later was to become a Fellow of the Royal Historical Society of England.

I remember Professor Usher well. His cool, lucid radio analyses of world events were broadcast nightly for many years in St. Louis and were heard by large audiences. During the darkest hours of World War II, when the U.S. sought clarification and interpretation from H. V. Kaltenborn and Raymond Gram Swing and Elmer Davis, those of us in St. Louis tuned in loyally each night to Professor Usher, for we considered him at least the equal of any New York or Washington radio pundit. And I remember 1950, when I was a student at Washington University, and Pro fessor Usher was closing out his career. He had achieved what might be termed an academician's double crown: He was both the most respected scholar and the most popular teacher at the university. On the day that he ended his forty-three-year teaching career at Washington University, his lecture hall was filled with old students from past years who joined with his last class to give him a prolonged standing ovation after the final words of the closing lecture were said.

Professor Usher and his wife had been invited to meet Patience Worth late in 1915, and they attended occasional sessions at the Curran home, although they never became regular visitors as did some of his faculty colleagues. Usher, a calm, unemotional, analytic scholar, was careful to make no public comment about the case. He wanted to delve into it more deeply, much more deeply, before taking any position concerning it.

In 1917, however, after reading *The Sorry Tale*, Roland G. Usher decided that the time had come to take an open stand. It is easy to imagine the trepidation this rising young historian felt as he ventured into the arena of controversy that surrounded the Currans and their defenders. Yet, obviously, he judged that the new book was important enough to warrant the personal risk that such a statement entailed to his reputation as a scholar.

The July 6, 1917, issue of the *Mirror* carried Professor Usher's review of *The Sorry Tale*. I believe it should be quoted here at some length, because it added a highly significant new opinion, one that could not be scoffed at by the most skeptical bystander:

"Two thoughts come first to mind about this book. First, the quality of the book itself, the product, apart from its origin or authorship; second, a very active regret that so fine a book will be spoiled for many people by the query sure to be raised about its authorship.

"Of the two let us dispose of the latter, and to me personally incomparably the less important, first. Undoubtedly, the announcement that a personality unknown, and claiming distinctly close relationship with the world beyond the veil, has written at length upon the era and life of Christ, will arouse interest, amazement, incredulity, scorn, according to the personality and previous training of the individual. What will seem to some a book almost on a par with the Gospels themselves will seem to others merely evidence of an attempt at literary impostership more extraordinary than that of Chatterton and more surprising than the fond delusion that Bacon wrote Shakespeare. Whoever the real author, and on this point I find myself more indifferent than most, I am convinced of Mrs. Curran's absolute innocence of any conscious attempt at authorship or deception.

"What I do feel to be distinctly more important than the possibility of communicating with the other world by a ouija board or by any other form of automatic writing is the book itself."

Usher explained the difficulty of cataloguing the book, as it is neither a novel or a history, in the strictest sense. Of the book's characters, he said: "Certain adjectives come to me . . . cameo-like, vivid, dramatic. All are weak to convey a sense of the startling definiteness with which a man is invested with presence and reality in a line or even a phrase. There is local color totally unlike that of the encyclopedia-crammed author of the usual novel of the Holy Land."

And here perhaps is the key paragraph of the entire long article: "I must however confess that the real interest of the book for me lies in the appearance of Jesus and the length at which the Gospel story is retold and elaborated. The sheer beauty of the chapter on the Sermon on the Mount; the spirituality of the passage descriptive of the Last Supper and the evening at Gethsemane; the moving narrative of the last days of Jesus, and the terrific climax of the Crucifixion I shall not soon forget. Everyone can read the last ten chapters in two hours and will be the better for it. The dramatic handling of these incidents, the reverent treatment of so lofty a theme as divinity upon earth, is noteworthy. *Unquestionably this is the greatest story penned of the life and times of Christ since the Gospels were finished.* One leaves it with a sense of understanding much previously dark and vague." (Italics added.)

As to the book's historical accuracy, Usher said the book seemed accurate to him, although he took pains to note that "Patience Worth's method is to hint rather than to enumerate, to allude in stately phrase rather than to employ the sort of specific statement which historians could check. None were demanded by the tale itself and the tone of the story would make them as much out of place as a joke in *Paradise Lost*."

He added that historians really don't know much about the events in Palestine at the time of Christ and "upon that little they are not well agreed." He concluded that ". . . this story seems to me historically well enough. There is little plain ordinary history in it, but the background is, for all I can see, accurate." He did raise a mild question about the use of the term "Jesus Christus" while Jesus was still alive, saying that he thought that the term didn't come into use until after the Crucifixion.

But, historical considerations aside, Usher proclaimed himself thoroughly impressed by the local color of the book: "One thing impressed me particularly. I have been told by travelers that the most characteristic thing about the Near East, as about the Orient, is the smells. From these one is never parted in the *Sorry Tale*; the reek of the camels, the acrid taste of the sands, the stink of the kennel are unforgettable because they are part of the story, not mere lumber lugged in by the struggling author, trying vainly to make real a scene which lacks all reality to him and padding his manuscript with enumerations of things he has read about."

And later: "These are not nineteenth century Americans masquerading as Jews and Romans, falling off their camels, and hobbling around on their bare feet as if walking upon the ten millions of swords' points of one of the Hindu hells. They seem to be, inside as well as outside, men and women of the years when Christ was on earth."[19]

So a brilliant historian proclaims himself utterly convinced by the reality of the book, by its amazing ability to immerse the reader in the sights, sounds, and smells of Palestine at the time of Christ.

And the question bores unceasingly into the mind: Where could Mrs. Curran possibly have secured the knowledge to write this book? Scholars and literary critics agreed that even a lifetime of reading all available knowledge of the Holy Land (reading that apparently never took place, but even if it had) still would not have given her the information to produce a book with such verisimilitude.

For that matter, if one prefers to take the spiritualist route in this case, where did Patience Worth get the knowledge? Even if she was an entirely separate entity from Pearl Curran, the spirit of a dead woman as she implied, she had lived in England and later in America. She never mentioned any personal experience with Palestine. Where did *she* get the knowledge necessary to write *The Sorry Tale?* The only effort to answer this question was a rather lame assertion by some exponents of reincarnation that either Mrs. Curran or Patience had lived a former existence in Palestine at the time of Christ and somehow had the ability to delve back into memories of that time.

The "problem of knowledge," as Casper Yost termed it, was always to be one of the most perplexing mysteries of the Patience Worth case. Earlier in 1917, in a national magazine article, Yost had pointed out again that Mrs. Curran never had read anything archaic, any books on English literature, and her education had not covered this field. And, in addition to her exhaustive knowledge of English life and customs, Patience Worth in her newest book "enters the Palestine of 2,000 years ago and reveals a knowledge of the minutia of its life that is simply amazing."

Because of this, Yost wrote in the article, "it is difficult to avoid the conviction that here, at least, is something outside of human personality . . . it seems indubitably to be something that has lived in the flesh and that yet lives when the flesh is gone."[20]

For months *The Sorry Tale* was a major topic of conversation in the literary world. The book and its author had their share of vehement detractors who refused to admit that the work had any literary value or that Patience was anything more than an offbeat joke. But they were more than balanced by the many prestigious writers and critics who insisted, with equal vehemence, that the book was indeed a superb piece of literature and that the whole case, with particular reference to the real identity of Patience Worth, was deserving of long, serious study.

Indicative of the interest was an article by critic and scholar H. W. Boynton in *The Bookman,* followed immediately by an analysis of the case by a psychoanalyst, Dr. Wilfred Lay.

Boynton had reacted favorably to Yost's book the previous year. Now, in his latest article, he pointed out as many others had that, until the advent of Patience Worth, all other alleged spirit communications "have been invariably negligible from the literary point of view. The greatest names have been identified with the most trivial or commonplace utterances." It was truly disheartening, Boynton said, to hear Shakespeare credited by occasional mediums as the author of "ghostly piffle." But, he went on, the important thing about Patience Worth "is that the work published under this name is worth assaying."

Boynton admitted to some irritation with Patience's language: ". . . it was such a tongue as no seventeenth-century Englishwoman, no man or woman of any century, could have written—a strange farrago of strained and clipped and grammarless utterance which just escaped being gibberish. The irritating thing about it was a kind of self-consciousness, a deliberate smartness, as of a spook posing. Yet there was gold; now and then one had the sense of a creative intelligence breaking through its self-imposed barrier, and expressing itself in terms of undeniable simplicity and beauty. This occurred oftenest in the verse, but in the prose, too, phrases of rare quality would emerge from a context bristling with wanton obstacle."

Also a bother to Boynton were "some of those pure illiteracies over which Mr. Yost seeks to cast a rosy glow by calling them 'verbal and syntactical peculiarities' and 'freedom from grammar.' Patience is helpless in the presence of the verb lie, and the archaic endings—eth and est—she almost habitually misuses, as well as the singular and plural second persons." (One can almost picture Patience verbally shrugging her shoulders at these objections and responding, "I be dame.")

Boynton also makes note of a few modern expressions in *The Sorry Tale*, but then he adds: "But—and this is the main thing—the style as a whole has much of nobility and force—a biblical style with abounding color added. There are tiny pictures full of beauty . . . or of astonishing realism . . . the Oriental detail of the narrative is amazingly lavish and vivid throughout, and its general accuracy I, who am ignorant, am not disposed to question."

The book, Boynton wrote, was built upon a striking conception which makes one of the thieves on the cross a son of the Emperor Tiberius by a Greek slave girl. He said the story, particularly in its early portions, is often weighed down and smothered by overly long sections of dialogue. But, with these technical comments out of the way, Boynton went on to his conclusion: "The chapter describing the crucifixion—a chapter of five thousand words which Mr. Yost says was dictated in a single evening—is a composition of appalling force and vividness, and an interpretation upon a high and sincere plane. I, for one, own myself converted by this story from a mood of languid curiosity about an odd 'psychic' phenomenon, to a state of lively interest in the future published work of the powerful writer who, whether in or out of the flesh, goes by the name and speaks with the voice of 'Patience Worth.' "

Boynton's newfound "lively interest" in the activities of Patience Worth hardly was shared by the psychoanalyst Wilfred Lay, whose comments on the case immediately followed Boynton's in the magazine. Dr. Lay made it clear from the start that he saw nothing too unusual in the case from a psychiatric standpoint.

He began: "To a psychoanalyst the books of 'Patience Worth' would appeal merely as the automatic activities of the Unconcious of the person who has found a ouija board to be the easiest method of bringing them into consciousness. The well-known manifestations of the Unconscious are quite analogous in every way to the mental activities of the transcriber of this remarkable book. The split-off personalities which, apart from the main conscious one, are found frequently to exist parallel with it, may well express themselves in literary or any other artistic form. A reader of the Bible and of early Christian history could easily have objectified in this manner the results of an imaginative dwelling on the sights, sounds, smells . . . and on the emotions aroused by the recurrence of thoughts concerning the happenings of those times."

The character of Hatte in *The Sorry Tale* and the Crucifixion scene were, according to Dr. Lay, manifestations of two common characteristics in human beings: "the mother imago" and "masochism."

"There is much of literary interest in *The Sorry Tale*," Dr. Lay went on, "but much more which is reiterated monotonousness, even apart from the impossible grammar and curious interchange of parts of speech and inconsistencies in usage...."

He conceded that some of the language in the book is "highly poetical" and "worthy of comparison at least with [an] Elizabethan dramatist." Dr. Lay then proposed a pretty sure way of solving the mystery: As Dr. Prince had urged the use of hypnosis, Dr. Lay proclaimed that psychoanalysis could very likely answer all the questions that the case had raised:

"Our wishes to behold the miraculous, which would be gratified if this book could be proved to be the communication of a disembodied spirit, are very natural wishes, springing from a desire to be ourselves omnipotent and to annihilate, still more than we have, the limitations of time and space. But I think that modern mental science, whose conservativeness has combated even the deductions of psychoanalysis concerning the working of the unconscious mind, can find ample explanation for both the appearance of this book and for the desire for the bit of omnipotence which its issuance demonstrates. We do not need to suppose that it is the utterance of the spirit of a lady who lived a couple of hundred years ago, if we can show that it is merely the utterance of the Unconscious of a lady living at the present time. Only a thorough psychoanalysis of the medium will be able to show this, and, without such analytic study of the person who held the ouija board, all scientific measures will not be taken, and therefore the spiritistic claims of the book will not be proved."

If it could be shown, he went on, that the language and other materials of the book were a part of Mrs. Curran's "unconscious mental life," then this would explain the whole affair. "Until this most modern of scientific instruments of precision, psychoanalysis, is tried on the communicator of the story, and has failed, it will be impossible to say . . . that the book is not the outward manifestation of the working of the contemporary lady's unconscious mental activities."[21]

One of the most entertaining side effects of the Patience Worth case, which had William Marion Reedy as one of its main victims, was the efflorescence of spirit writings, or "spook literature," as Reedy preferred to call it, as a result of the wide publicity given to Patience. Reedy frequently and loudly complained, both publicly in his *Mirror* and privately to his friends, about the flood of writings allegedly composed by spirits of the dead that now poured in upon him. This was about the only thing that caused him sometimes to regret that he ever had become involved with Patience Worth.

"St. Louis," Reedy wrote in the *Mirror,* "has no monopoly of the spook literature output. That is in progress everywhere. I've been swamped with spirit-communicated literature from all over the country since I gave publicity to my experiences with Patience

Worth. Most of it is poor stuff, not literature at all. A deal of it is sheer twaddle."

But, Reedy said, he could not resist discussing one such work: a drama sent to him by a Kansas poet which was called *Hamlet in Heaven* and which supposedly had come from Shakespeare, as a contribution to the celebration of his own tercentenary. This play, Reedy said, is perhaps better than other stuff purporting to come from Shakespeare, but "that is not saying much." This new play, Reedy judged, is "a curiosity worth the fifty cents" asked for it. "There are splashes of bastard Elizabethanese that almost deceive one into belief in their legitimacy and then there are awful descents to the banal and the absurd."[22]

A few weeks later Reedy printed a letter from the Kansas poet who had claimed to receive the play from Shakespeare's spirit. He didn't protest too strongly over Reedy's comments about the play, but took the editor to task for missing what he said was the central feature of his book. What we need, the poet proclaimed, is a spirit telephone: ". . . arguing on the belief of all religions in life beyond the great change, I urge the invention of machinery, employing some vibratory force, such as electricity, for instance, as the motive power for driving the machine, to the intent that communication may be put on a basis that cannot be questioned as to sincerity." If such a telephone is invented, announced the poet, "we would know absolutely about Heaven and Hell. We would have that realm mapped and know its history. . . . We would have our news and views of Heaven in the daily papers every morning."

Insisting that his idea was "real news," the poet demanded: "Why did you miss this big story in my book? I am astonished at your lack of perception. Peer in your *Mirror* and find out what manner of man you really are."[23]

But one of the most surprising developments in the Patience-inspired renaissance of spirit literature involved an old familiar name: Emily Grant Hutchings, the writer and friend of Mrs. Curran who sat with her when Patience first appeared. In recent years she had largely dropped out of the Currans' inner circle, although she and her husband still attended a session with Patience on occasion.

Sometime before the summer of 1916, Reedy related in the

Mirror, he was visited by Mrs. Hutchings, who occasionally contributed articles to his publication. She brought a story of ten thousand words, uncompleted, and asked him to read it, which he did. Reedy wrote: "I sat down and wrote her that if the story finished as it began it would be a 'go' like the works of Gene Stratton Porter and other highly popular novelists. I congratulated Mrs. Hutchings on her workwomanship. The story was of newspaper and political life in Missouri—a story smacking of the soil, of campaign oratory and even campaign whiskey and printer's ink."

A week later Mrs. Hutchings came to see Reedy again, accompanied by Mrs. Lola Hays, also an occasional writer and the daughter of a small-town Missouri newspaper editor. The manuscript, they told Reedy, had come to them via the ouija board and its author was, they insisted, Mark Twain himself. They pulled out a ouija board and forced Reedy, by now cursing the day that he had been born, to sit down and take notes. "The pointer began to work," he wrote later, "and Mrs. Hutchings got fearfully rattled. She could hardly keep her chair and her nervousness was distressing." The board spelled out a continuation of the story that Reedy had read.

The manuscript, which was called *Jap Herron*, finally came to 50,000 words and was completed. And it was accepted for publication by a leading New York publisher, Mitchell Kennerly.

Reedy was persuaded to write the introduction to the published work, but that he did so under great pressure was indicated by these comments in a letter to publisher Kennerly: "I hate the spiritist smear.... My heart is not in this project of my going into that book.... I don't want to be used to the extent of going in the book as a sort of sponsor. Not that I doubt the authenticity of the phenomenon or the integrity of the people producing it. I simply don't like spiritist obsessions. I'm sick of 'em. To treat 'em as news matter in the *Mirror* I don't object. But somehow when it comes to going into a book of such stuff I want to wash my hands.... The spiritists get on my nerves."[24]

Once again, however, when the book finally was published, Reedy was much kinder in his reaction than one would expect from a man of such acute literary perception and such a decidedly hostile attitude toward spiritualism. The book, he wrote, is "very

Mark Twainian, very Missourian," although decidedly un-Twainian in its sentimentality. It is a well-written story, he said, and unlike anything Mrs. Hutchings has ever done. Although not so remarkable as the Patience Worth works, Reedy concluded, *Jap Herron* is a story of quality far above the ordinary story of the day.[25]

About a year later Reedy did another story in the *Mirror* on *Jap Herron* and again spoke of it appreciatively, calling it second only to *The Sorry Tale* among spook-produced literature. It is a good story, he said, with rich humor, nice sentiment, and some deep pathos. "It is agreeably readable, whether done by Mark Twain's spook or by mere mortals."

Reedy didn't seem to mind the association of St. Louis with such books: "I wish the country knew the city more as the headquarters of spook literature than as being across the river from East St. Louis. Our spook authors should glorify us as Indianapolis has been glorified by its literature of the quinine belt."

Reedy also noted that *Jap Herron* did not bear Mark Twain's name on the cover, although it carried a reproduction of a drawing of the famed Missouri-born writer. The reason for this was that another publisher held the rights to all of Twain's work and had expressly forbidden the labeling of this purported creation with his name.[26]

The other publisher, Harper and Brothers, eventually went to court seeking to forbid the sale of *Jap Herron* on the grounds that its quality was an injury to Twain's reputation and memory. Reedy, by now enjoying the whole thing immensely, commented in the *Mirror*: ". . . suppose Mark Twain in spirit realm did write *Jap Herron*, does the Harper and Brothers copyright 'run' on his productions as a citizen of the Hollow Land? The trial of this case should bring the whole question of the truth of spiritism into court. Can the dead communicate with the living? That is an issue of fact in the case. If *Jap Herron* is not as good a piece of writing as Mark Twain did in the flesh, still a good writer may fall down in his work here, so why not hereafter? Will the court permit the alleged spirit of Mark Twain to testify over the ouija board and say that the rights in his pen name here which he signed away should not stand in the way of his sending us proof that the souls set free come back to the souls that stay? Does the law *outre tombe* care for such trifles as mundane trade-marks and copyrights? Can the live hand reach out into the dark and dominate the dead as the dead hand often reaches back and controls the living? Let us put the spooks on the witness stand and hear their tale under the strictest rules of evidence."[27]

The whole episode of *Jap Herron* had one more bizarre flourish before it subsided from the attention of Reedy and his readers. It won the enthusiastic praise of Dr. James H. Hyslop, who had so bitterly condemned Patience Worth and those who supported her.

The respected head of the American Society for Psychical Research, a man who declared himself unwilling to accept anything that couldn't be demonstrated scientifically, wrote in the *Journal* of his society that "*Jap Herron* is much better accredited than the volume on Patience Worth. It should be studied in the light of that fiasco." He charged also that friction had arisen between Mrs. Hutchings and the Currans over "her desire to have the material treated scientifically." Hyslop also claimed that Mrs. Hutchings had contacted another medium and that Patience Worth "reported there also with her usual style and mode of expression." (Which, if true, would seem to support the Currans' belief that Patience was a spirit and not a reflection of Mrs. Curran's subconscious, as Hyslop had contended.)

As to *Jap Herron*, Hyslop concluded that "there is abundant evidence that Mark Twain was behind the work connected with his name." And, still apparently feeling the need to strike at the Currans and their allies, he added, "The Patience Worth case might have been more useful in this way, but deception of the public will make more money than the truth."[28]

Hyslop always had insisted that scientific evidence was lacking in connection with Patience Worth. What scientific evidence he had that caused him to reach so different a conclusion with regard to *Jap Herron* he never publicly announced.

Reedy interviewed Hyslop, who, he said, "knows more about high-class spookery than anybody." Reedy pointed out that *Jap Herron* in itself showed no inherent evidence that Mark Twain had written it. Hyslop agreed. "But," he said, according to Reedy, "Mrs. Hutchings and Mrs. Hays have visited me here and submitted to all tests, through a psychic having no knowledge of them or of their 'control' and I have obtained indisputable evidence of the fact that *Jap Herron* is the work of the discarnate spirit of Samuel L. Clemens."

Reedy noted that Hyslop's continued blasts at Patience Worth, taken in conjunction with his acceptance of *Jap Herron*, indicated that "there is already a battle on between the two schools of spooks. But if *Jap Herron* has the *Journal of the American Society for Psychical Research* on his side, the wraith that visits the Currans has her own organ, *Patience Worth's Magazine*. The spook-book boom will probably not be hurt by the dispute that has begun as to the orthodoxy of the rival schools."[29]

7

The Top of the Hill

DURING 1917 and 1918 Patience Worth reached the high point of her fame. Two of her books (in addition to the one by Yost) were published about a year apart, and the appearance of each stirred up a new whirlwind of controversy and discussion concerning both the literary value of her work and the origin of the author. She and the Currans were the subject of numerous magazine and newspaper articles during this period. Imitators sprung up everywhere, as Billy Reedy had mournfully attested. Not only were novels and poems purportedly written by spirits blossoming all over the landscape like crab grass, but some individuals at various times would insist that they, too, were in contact with Patience Worth, the same caustic spinster from Dorsetshire who had brought worldwide attention to the Currans. The Patience Worth devotees in St. Louis regarded such claims as obviously spurious, citing the poor quality of the literary productions involved as sufficient evidence to disprove the allegations.

Patience herself was once asked to comment on such claims and replied: "Aye, they tear at the heart o' her [Mrs. Curran] through thy handmaid. List ye, my bairn [child], list ye. I say me that the thing that be thine, be thine; and what hath come unto

Earth from out thee of thy handmaid, may not be but through thee; aye and shall not be! Aye and he who shall for to set up wordin's for to set as thy handmaid shall weave his own noose."[1]

While the books and magazine articles were spreading the story and words of Patience to readers throughout the world, an even more intensive effort to keep Patience in the forefront of attention was being made in St. Louis. Casper Yost saw to it that poems by Patience appeared with regularity on the editorial page of the *Globe-Democrat* during 1916, 1917, and 1918. Billy Reedy continued to write about Patience frequently in his *Mirror*, although not on the weekly basis that had been his wont earlier. (Reedy's biographer, Max Putzel, states that Reedy became quite bored with the "spook literature" about this time. If this was so, it was not reflected in Reedy's occasional comments in the *Mirror*, and all indications were that he remained on friendly terms with the Currans until his death, attending sessions with Patience periodically and always bantering with her and querying her, as in the past.)

In July 1917, after almost a year of planning, the first edition of *Patience Worth's Magazine* came off the press. It was published by the "Patience Worth Publishing Company."

St. Louis newspapers reported a few months later that papers to incorporate the publishing company had been filed by the St. Louis Recorder of Deeds. The incorporators were Mr. and Mrs Curran and Casper Yost. The capital stock was $50,000, divided in 5,000 shares of $10 each. According to one newspaper story: "Property in the company consists of all the writings, except the books, of Patience Worth, the subconscious spirit dictator of literary productions, who communicates via the ouija board through Mrs. John H. Curran. . . . These works, amounting to more than 700,000 words, consist of 700 poems of varying length, up to 4,000 words each; about 500 epigrams and sayings, hundreds of prayers, parables and religious and philosophical discourses, and records of witty conversation with prominent St. Louis and other people, besides several short stories."[2]

The offices of the publishing company were given as an address on Cates Avenue in St. Louis's residential West End, the home address of the Currans at the time. Also mentioned was a business office in downtown St. Louis (presumably John Curran's place of work) where advertising for the magazine could be purchased.

The creation of the magazine and the accompanying solicitation of subscriptions and advertising for it would seem to lend some support to allegations that the principal parties in the case were trying to make money from it. Yet everyone involved steadfastly denied that such was the case. Yost wrote a few years later that no thought ever was given to making a profit from the magazine. The hope, he said, was simply that sale of advertising and subscriptions would earn enough to pay for the cost of producing the magazine. It was a fruitless hope. The magazine never paid its own way and was suspended after the publication of ten monthly issues. Yost also emphasized again that the Currans never had charged a cent for admission to the sessions with Patience, that they uncomplainingly had entertained the hundreds of persons, many of them not known to them personally, who had visited their home to meet Patience. In addition, Yost pointed out, the voluminous accretions to the Patience Worth records and the necessity for making additional copies of the records had required the Currans to hire a secretary and stenographer. All these expenses more than offset the proceeds paid to the Currans by the publisher of the Patience Worth books.

Yost's statement was supported by John Curran, who told a reporter in 1922 that he estimated the Patience Worth affair had cost him a personal financial loss of more than $4,000. "And in figuring the expense," he added, "we haven't counted the cost of entertaining some eight thousand persons at our home; our callers have come twice a week."[3]

From all indications the only parties who really profited financially from the Patience Worth case were the manufacturers of ouija boards, and the Currans and Yost held no stock in such companies.

My research uncovered only two of the ten issues of *Patience Worth's Magazine*. It was a handsome, professional-looking magazine of eighteen to twenty pages per issue. The clean, readable layout undoubtedly reflected Yost's many years of newspaper experience. The issues were devoted entirely to the Patience Worth case—to articles on some aspect of the case by the Currans or Yost, or by others with comments on it, and to long excerpts from the writings of Patience, with discussion of the contents. The magazine was unillustrated, except for some art work on the cover. It was priced at fifteen cents per copy, with a subscription cost of $1.50 per year.

Carried prominently in each issue were two major statements. The first, unsigned, set forth the reasons for the magazine:

"The sole purpose of this publication is to spread and to interpret the words of Patience Worth. It is not a medium of occultism nor of psychical research. It will not concern itself with kindred phenomena of any character. It is not related to nor associated with any cult or society, nor has it any theories to present other than those based upon the words and the personality of Patience Worth. It is, in short, Patience Worth's magazine, nothing more, nothing less.

"It should be clearly understood that Patience Worth is not a 'fortune-teller.' She does not 'read the future.' She does not find lost lovers, lost relatives or lost property. She does not give advice upon business. She does not pretend to be a physical healer. It is, therefore, utterly useless to ask her service in any such matters, and it is worse than useless to send money to this publication, or to anyone associated with her, for such purposes."[4]

The second major statement appearing in every issue was a large box headed WHAT PATIENCE WORTH TEACHES. Written most likely by Yost, who had meticulously analyzed the religious philosophy of Patience, it was, in essence, the core of her theology:

There is a God.

He is our Father, and His other name is Love.

He knows His children, their feelings, their weaknesses, their errors—and He understands.

He sympathizes with their pain and sorrow, and He whispers consolation if they would but hear.

He would tell them the trials of life are the building of the soul; that earth is but a starting place for eternity and its troubles and its difficulties are essential to the soul's foundation.

He would tell them that the building may not be finished here but goes on and on, until it is fully complete, and always His love streams o'er it.

He would tell them that He condemns not, but ever seeks to lift. He may grieve at their transgressions and anger at their perversity, but it is the grief and anger of love.

He would tell them that He destroys not His children, but preserves them for an immortality which must be won, but which all can win and shall win.

He would tell them that He is ever with them, that He never forsakes and never will forsake them, in this world or the next.

He would tell them that He would not be feared, but loved; for in the exercise of love—love for Him, love for His own, His children, is the soul built to its fullness.

He would tell them: Wait! Be patient! It shall be.[5]

The September 1917 issue of the magazine devoted considerable space to the publishing, for the first time, of Patience's earliest long work—*Red Wing*, a six-act play of about 20,000 words, dictated more than two years earlier. The introduction to the play noted that "the time seems to be medieval and the 'atmosphere' is English, but the land is an imaginary one. It is the only one of Patience Worth's productions that has no discernible spiritual significance."

A major department of each issue was "Evenings with Patience Worth," long excerpts from the official records of the sittings at the Curran home, with appropriate interpolations for clarification by Yost or the Currans. The September issue contained also a detailed report on a visit by Dr. John Wesley Hill, identified as a former minister and "now Chancellor of Lincoln Memorial University" in New York City, plus an article by Mrs. Curran on "The Purpose of Patience Wee," and a report by her husband on the procedures followed in keeping and maintaining the records of the sittings. There also was a detailed analysis by Yost of "The Language of Patience Worth."

There was a good deal of display advertising in the two copies of the magazine that I saw—for a dramatic school, a painting company, a concert pianist, a railroad, and for a Chicago patent attorney who had written a letter to the editor, printed in the same issue, which proclaimed *The Sorry Tale* to be "by far the greatest book I have ever read; beside it all other books sink into insignificance." There were a few classified ads and the inside back cover was given over to a large advertisement for the books of Patience Worth.

With the United States having entered World War I by then, the October issue of the magazine led off with an article on "Patience Worth and War," which recapitulated many of Patience's poems and statements on war.

The Currans and Yost obviously were not reluctant to air opinions about Patience that differed from their own. The October issue carried a lengthy discussion of an article that had appeared in the *Chicago Evening News* concerning the origin of Patience Worth. The editor of the newspaper's literary page apparently had commissioned someone experienced in psychical research, and whose honesty the newspaper vouched for, to offer his explanation of the case. The "expert" preferred to remain anonymous.

His explanation, as reprinted in *Patience Worth's Magazine*, was this: "Now, this is how I account for Patience Worth. The group that receives her communication does not consist of professed spiritualists, but of highly intellectual 'dabblers,' who fancy themselves immune from the conventional beliefs about departed spirits. Nevertheless, these scholarly people are, in the periods of the spirit manifestations, subject to precisely the same sort of group hypnotism that controls ordinary spiritualists. The difference is that here we have a group of intellectuals; people who have clear and, perhaps, correct conceptions of the historic period in which Patience professes to have lived and who, consciously or unconsciously, are more or less saturated with the romance of that time, its life and methods...."

The anonymous author goes on to suggest that a form of group hypnosis is the basic cause of the phenomenon and that, although the literary works are better than anything heretofore produced by spirit writers, they do not exceed the capabilities of the "intellectuals" who are part of the group and, in fact, usually do not rise to their level.

The response (unsigned) to this argument in Patience's magazine was that it was founded on insufficient information and lacked the elementary essentials of truth: "By far the greater portion of the Patience Worth matter has come when not one of them [the intellectuals] was present or in communication in any way.... Nor has any group of 'intellectuals' such a relation to Patience Worth as this writer suggests."

The communications come, the article pointed out, when the Currans are alone, when they have only visitors who could be considered non-intellectuals, or when they have visitors of acknowledged brilliance, "but the quality and character of the communications are the same. . . . With the single exception of Mrs. Curran, it makes not the slightest difference who is present when Patience Worth speaks."

Each issue of the magazine apparently featured the record of a visit to Patience by a well-known guest, and the individual spotlighted in the October issue was writer Fannie Hurst. The magazine also carried a letter from Miss Hurst granting permission for the record of her visit to be printed, and adding, "I am deeply interested in your new enterprise and await my first copy of the magazine with keen anticipation. *The Sorry Tale* I see is receiving the sort of reviews its high literary quality warrants."

Along with an article on "Spiritual Power of Patience Worth" by an admiring clergyman from Iowa City, the October magazine also contained a significant article by Mrs. Curran discussing the role played by the ouija board in the Patience Worth affair. It must have surprised some of those who had followed the case, particularly those who had rushed out to buy ouija boards in the hope of tuning in to a sort of cosmic radio broadcast, to find Mrs. Curran declaring that the only value of the board for her had been to serve as a "thought dispeller," enabling her "to put my own thoughts away for the moment. As soon as this happens . . . the dictation of Patience Worth begins. . . . It is I who moves the board, in response to the subconscious or conscious impulse. There is no mystery in the movement; the mystery, if any, is in the source of the impulse."

The ouija board, she said bluntly, "is just a piece of dead wood, nothing more."

The back page of the October issue was given over to a big ad for a special Christmas issue of the magazine, to be devoted entirely to the devotional and religious utterances of Patience.

It was a time of war and the circle around Patience Worth could hardly be untouched by it. Some of the husbands who, with their wives, had been regular visitors to the Curran home for meetings with Patience came to see her for final words before leaving for military service. Mothers whose sons were in combat in France asked Patience for words of hope and were always granted their wish. And, on some occasions, good friends of Patience who had loyally visited her through the years came to request a poem, a comment—anything that would ease their grief over the news that had just reached them. The records relate many touching episodes during those months in 1917 and 1918 when the ghostly writer was doing her best to console the bereaved parents and wives who sought her aid.

On September 30, 1917, after being visited by several grief-stricken friends, Patience dictated this plea:

> Peace, oh gentle sister, hast thou fled?
> White-winged, hast thou made away
> Unto some summit far
> With thy golden urn of plenty?
> Hast thy smile faded and thine eyes teared,
> Blinding thee unto the woe thou leavest,
> While thy sister, Mercy, claspeth to her bosom
> Earth's children, succoring hosts with love?
>
> Peace, oh gentle sister, why tarriest thou?
> Come! Come upon a new morning!
> Fan the fevered earth with thy soft wings.
> Pour o'er earth's wounds from thy urn
> Plenteousness and joy.
>
> Peace, oh gentle sister,
> Hearest thou not the calling?
> Knock thee at the hearts of men,
> Turning the key of love
> Within the lock of hate.
>
> Peace, peace, oh gentle sister,
> Make haste! For Mercy is weary,
> And the earth perisheth![6]

Patience frequently was called upon to comment on headline figures of the day: President Wilson, General Pershing, the Kaiser. She usually did so, but her comments were general and as allusive as always. They were not predictions of the future for these people, but only a generalized sort of reaction to them. But there was no ambivalence about Patience's attitude toward war. She hated it with a furious passion. During a period when most Americans had been whipped into a fever of righteousness about making the world safe for democracy, Patience offered these bitter lines:

Father, is *this* thy will? God! the din!
Blood, thick-crusted, still living, I saw it fall unto the dust;
Hunger, gnawing like a wolf, whose teeth do whet upon my vitals,
 crouching before me—
A hideous thing, whose hands show dripping, and whose tongue
 doth feed upon the new-sprung streams, licking life from liv-
 ing things!
Father, is this thy will?
Damn the discord garrulously belched forth from burning throats!
Hell is within the eyes that look across the wastes;
Hell crawls upon earth dragging its robe of fire,
Sprinkled of scarlet its hem, and the sound it makes upon its
 trailing way, is like the shriek of womankind in labor.[7]

The late months of 1917 and the early ones of 1918 continued to be frantically busy ones for all of those who surrounded Patience. Along with the regular flood of poems, conversation, epigrams and what-have-you that issued from the semi-weekly sessions, Patience continued regularly to give long segments of *Hope Trueblood,* her big new novel, and of *The Merry Tale,* the lighthearted medieval story that she had begun months before as a counterpoint to the seriousness of *The Sorry Tale.*

Meanwhile, Yost was working diligently on his book about the philosophy of Patience. He attended almost every session during those months and often would bring portions of his manuscript with him. He would read them aloud and ask Patience to comment on them, or perhaps to clarify a point that he could not quite pin down.

The depth of Yost's emotional immersion in the entire affair is still surprising, considering his long experience as a newspaperman exposed to all sorts of oddity. Yet he regarded Patience with a kind of rapture usually reserved for love-struck knights or lovesick adolescents. He would write this kind of poetry and bring it to Patience as a love offering:

> Sister mine:
>
> I see thee not, and yet I know
> That somewhere thou art close at hand,
> So close that were my eyes to ope
> To vision of that other sphere
> That lies within and yet without

> My own, I'd find thee standing face
> Unto my face, with shining eyes
> That shed a radiance of love,
> And yet do hold within their depths
> A twinkling gleam of merriment
> That doth foretell the break of smile.
> Ah, sister it is hard for me to say
> Which most delights me in yourself—
> The loving smile or yet the smiling love.
>
> Brother[8]

It is almost eerie to read how Yost looked on Patience as a person, as real to him as Mrs. Curran or her husband. And, because he saw her as a person, not a God, he sometimes teased her and sought to embarrass her:

YOST: I know what I'd like to give you. . . . I'd like to put my arms around you and kiss you!
PATIENCE: I said it were so!
YOST: I'm going to do it some time if I have to chase you all over heaven.
PATIENCE: Tarry, brother mine, tarry! I tell 'ee I shall for to down o' my bonnet's curtain [veil]! I wot a spinster be plegged e'en though she be thrice thy grandsire's, grandsire's, grandsire's age!
YOST: This is only brotherly love, Patience.
PATIENCE: Lor', I hae heard that too!
YOST: You shall get that present.
PATIENCE: Aye, and the simper shall be thine.[9]

On October 22, 1917, the final installment of *Hope Trueblood* was dictated. The novel, which would total 363 pages when published, had been given in a period of about seven months. The manuscript was sent off to Henry Holt in New York.

The social status enjoyed by Patience in St. Louis at this time was typified by a program given on the evening of November 9, 1917. It took place at the Victoria Theatre and was billed as "The Patience Worth Evening" given for the benefit of the St. Louis branch of the American Red Cross Society and sponsored by the "Friends of Patience Worth."

Those "friends" included among their numbers many of the top leaders of St. Louis society. Listed in the program as sponsors of the evening were, among others, the wives of E. Lansing Ray, publisher of the *Globe-Democrat*, former Governor and cabinet member David R. Francis, Professor Roland G. Usher, Professor Tyrrell Williams of the Washington University School of Law, and Isaac Hedges, business and civic leader. Another sponsor was Miss Avis Blewett, sister of the St. Louis superintendent of schools and a patron of the arts in her own right.

Reedy helped promote the Red Cross benefit with another story in the *Mirror* that came out the day of the program. Of Patience, he said: "The words of Patience Worth are real, if she be not. Her poems and stories have a substance of truth and loveliness. They have brought comfort and much joy to many people." Of the benefit program scheduled for that evening, he wrote: "Those persons who have been captivated by the charm and power of the Patience Worth writings and have undertaken the social sponsoring of the entertainment are not such as succumb to the cheap and tawdry appeals of mystagogy. They are those who know the true value of the works that have so strangely come through Mrs. Curran. 'Patience Worth,' unseen, unheard, but vividly present ever in the words writ by other hands, will receive at the Victoria this evening. The audience should be large. Those who attend will be partakers in an experience the like of which has never before been known."[10]

The printed program for the benefit declared that Patience wanted to do her bit for the Red Cross, "thus reflecting the purpose for which Patience Worth came back to Earth, to give balm to the wounds of mankind."

The first part of the evening was a musical program, part of which consisted of songs composed by E. R. Kroeger to words of Patience Worth. The second part included an address by Mrs. Curran on "The Secret of Patience Worth," followed by a dramatization of a scene from *The Sorry Tale* by students of the Morse School of Expression, a well-known St. Louis dramatic and elocution school.[11]

While the Currans and their friends read the proofs of *Hope Trueblood* and awaited its publication, new honors came to Patience, and each additional accolade tended to bolster even more the contention of those who believed in her that Patience and her writings were unique in human history.

The Joint Committee of Literary Arts of New York announced

its list of outstanding authors of 1918 and Patience Worth was included for *The Sorry Tale*. Chairman of the committee was the noted writer Hamlin Garland, who had long been interested in psychic phenomena, which doubtless accounts for the willingness of the body to take seriously the work of Patience Worth. An invitation to attend the reception for the honored authors was sent to Patience. William Lyon Phelps, Amy Lowell, and Rupert Hughes were among those on hand, but Patience—through Mrs. Curran—sent her regrets.

Another and perhaps even more significant tribute to Patience came with the publication of the 1918 edition of the *Anthology of Magazine Verse and Year Book of American Poetry*, edited by William Stanley Braithwaite. Braithwaite's annual volume was one of the most authoritative and respected of poetry anthologies and was considered one of the most reliable guides to the best American poetry of the time.

Braithwaite and Patience Worth had had an on-and-off relationship until 1918. The 1916 edition of the anthology had, without any comment about the author, included two of Patience's poems: "Lullaby" ("Dream, dream, thou flesh of me . . .") and "Food o' Moon's Beams" ("Athin the even's hour/When shadow purpleth . . ."), both reprinted from *Reedy's Mirror*. In addition, the 1916 edition carried an index of poems published in American magazines from October 1915 to September 1916. A limited number of these poems' titles were marked with an asterisk, indicating "poems of distinction," the selection being made, apparently, by Braithwaite. The index lists six Patience Worth poems, of which four are ranked as poems of distinction. By way of comparison, the same index lists five poems by William Carlos Williams, but none was accorded Braithwaite's asterisk of honor.[12]

The 1917 edition of Braithwaite reprinted no poems of Patience's and made no mention of her. In 1918, however, she hit the anthological equivalent of the jackpot. Braithwaite printed the complete text of five of her poems: "The Weeping Earth," "Tutored Not, Unlearned Am I," "The One Thing," "The Shadow Land," and "Sweet Hath Hung the Eve." Faring not quite so well in the same volume were such leading poets as William Rose Benet, with three poems reprinted, Amy Lowell, three, and Edgar Lee Masters, one.

Braithwaite's index of magazine verse for 1918 obviously was not geared for the assembly-line production of Patience, but the editor gamely went ahead and gave her her full due. While the same index listed the titles of ten poems by Amy Lowell and five by Edna St. Vincent Millay, it required almost three pages to list the titles of eighty-eight poems by Patience that appeared in magazines during the twelve-month period.

More important than the voluminous indexing of the Patience Worth poems was Braithwaite's judgment as to their quality. He used a somewhat more detailed rating system in this edition than in the earlier ones. Instead of simply indicating certain ones as poems of distinction as he had in the 1916 edition, Braithwaite in 1918 rated many of the poems from one to three stars, with the latter being the highest accolade. Poems considered to be of lesser merit were given no stars. Of the eighty-eight Patience Worth poems listed in the index, Braithwaite rated forty-nine as one-star quality, twenty-nine as two-star, and eight as three-star. Only two of the eighty-eight works were considered by Braithwaite to be lacking any distinction.

By way of comparison, of the ten Amy Lowell poems listed, Braithwaite rated two as one-star, five as two-star, and three as three-star. Of the five poems by Edna St. Vincent Millay, he judged one to be one-star, three to be two-star, and only one to be of three-star quality.[13]

So, although Patience's three-star batting average according to Braithwaite was not quite as high as the other two feminine poets of great reputation, her showing was, by almost any standard, a remarkable one.

Undoubtedly posing quite a dilemma for Braithwaite was a feature that had been added to his anthology since the first appearance of Patience's works in 1916: a section at the end of the volume giving brief biographical information on each poet whose works were included. It is easy to sympathize with the staid editor and critic as he wrestled with the problem of how to handle the biography of Patience Worth. (It should be emphasized that Braithwaite always attributed the poems to Patience, not to Mrs. Curran.)

He resolved it this way: The biography was listed under Patience Worth, in its proper place between George Edward Woodberry and Annette Wynne. The statement began: "In regard to this author, I can only quote what Mrs. Curran writes: 'Nothing is definitely known of Patience Worth's life except that she seems to have lived during the middle of the 17th century and was not an author. She was a spinster whose mother was a sempstress to certain neighborhood nobility. They seemed to have lived in Dorset, England, near the sea, but in her effort to hide herself and withdraw her personality in favor of her work, she has been so meager in her facts relating to her life and surroundings that what we know is almost nil.'"

Braithwaite then gave a brief biographical summary of Mrs. Curran, which she had supplied to him. Her statement noted that Patience by this time had written "1,500 poems, seven short stories, three complete novels, one in blank verse of 70,000 words, five other stories and a one act play in process of writing, in all about 1,500,000 words."[14]

After her moment of triumph in the 1918 edition, Patience largely dropped from Braithwaite's view. Whether he was the object of criticism for devoting so much space and attention to such a controversial writer, we do not know. But in his 1919 edition he reprinted none of Patience's poems and listed only one in the index. After 1919, Patience received mention only in the 1924 and 1928 volumes, when several of her poems were listed in the index of magazine verse for those years.

On March 18, 1918, the ever-productive Patience began the dictation of a new novel, another story of nineteenth-century England, which was to be called *Samuel Wheaton*.

During this period John Curran began to note what he considered to be changes in the facility with which Mrs. Curran passed on the words of Patience Worth and in her general demeanor during the sessions with Patience. In the record for March 20, 1918, he made the following report:

"During the later conversation this evening Mrs. Curran endeavored to explain her state of mind while the stories are coming. It seems that now there is practically no dividing line between her conscious self and the ability to listen to the dictation of Patience Worth. In other words at this time the fact that she is writing and calling letters does not interfere with her ability to see and hear everything around, see the expressions on the faces of the watchers and be conscious of numerous other things at the same time. A number of times lately spectators have noticed Mrs. Curran do practically all the following things simultaneously. With one hand on the board she would be pushing the pointer practically in a circle, calling the letters, say in a poem or story, watching with her inner vision the pictures of the story unfold and being conscious of the relation of characters to each other and their passing emotions as well as the details of the surrounding scene. At the same time she would rub her nose which evidently itched a little or pull her ear for the same cause and turn her head half around at a whimper of the sleeping babe in the next room. At the same time she declares she can catch a meaning glance of any of her audience within the circle of her vision and be thinking of what they are evidently thinking of with approval or wonder or disapproval. There is only one thing that seems to disturb all these conditions and that is some sharp noise as an impact. At times she seems totally oblivious of a whole sentence which she might have been calling as though some one else than herself was telling the story yet there is something which guides her not to go on until the full meaning of what is written has come to her. Often times the characters are speaking different from the words that she dictates off the board.

"I am setting these things down here as they may help to mark the milestone in the development of her ability to produce. I am thoroughly convinced that the conditions set forth above are not the same as they were when she first began receiving the messages on the board from Patience Worth and I am also convinced that they are not the same as they were six months ago."[15]

If Mrs. Curran's approach to the sessions had changed, there was no marked change in Patience's caustic personality. And her dearly beloved Pearl Curran remained one of her pet targets. She particularly resented any effort by Mrs. Curran to take credit for the writings. On one occasion, when Mrs. Curran made reference to the poems *she* was writing, Patience snapped, "What meanest thou, wee whit dame, that thou shouldst set thee up and o'er thy dame at the bakin' o' wee loaves?"[16]

On another occasion Mrs. Curran rendered a word as "soup." Patience impatiently interrupted: "Lor', the follied one [Mrs. Curran] putteth o' her puttin's athin my brewin's! Nay, she deemeth a thinnish brew be a soup! Lor', it be brothed."[17] While dictating a portion of *Hope Trueblood*, Mrs. Curran spelled out the phrase "and my eyes fell upon the floor." To which Patience objected, "How be it that ye cast eyes upon the floor, ye dullard? Say ye 'glance'!"

In May 1918 Henry Holt and Company published *Hope Trueblood*, the second of Patience Worth's books (excluding Yost's volume) to go on the market. The novel ran to 363 printed pages, about 90,000 words. The book jacket referred to it as "A Mid-Victorian Novel by a Pre-Victorian Writer." The author was listed as Patience Worth, with Casper S. Yost credited as editor.

According to the jacket: *"Hope Trueblood* differs materially from the previous productions of Patience Worth. In this she abandons her archaic dialect and constructs her story in standard English of the present day, free from grammatical irregularities. Modern in its language, the story is relatively modern in its time, which is about the middle of the nineteenth century. . . . It is a simple tale of life in an English village, the autobiography of Hope Trueblood, born in that village without the knowledge of a father and suffering the tortures which that stain applies to a sensitive soul in a narrow community."[18]

We previously gave the opening passage of the book, which so startled the Currans when it was dictated due to its radical departure from the earlier speech patterns of Patience. Here are a few more short excerpts from *Hope Trueblood* to illustrate the style of the book and some of its dialogue:

Page 90:
"Naw," Rudy answered, spitting upon his sore and smearing more earth. "Naw, I didn't."
"Where, then?" I begged.
He pointed to the tall tree that stood over the grave of Willie Pimm Passwater. I flew at him. There was a dreadful mixture and the bowls and pottery were spilled. I came out of the fray with two birds that were acting strangely. Rudy held the others and they hung their necks very long and one of them did not move. I cried aloud:
"Look you, Rudy Strong, they are all mussed."
"They're dead. That's what," Rudy shot at me. "That's what!

You see, girls always make musses."
Pages 220–1:
I shall never know what possessed me then, and even now, as I write, I seem another self. It seemed to me that my feet bore me, but were not mine; that my lips spoke but were not mine. I could not stop.

Dawson shivered. I started up, flung the chair from me so that it overturned the sup that lay upon the little table, ran to the door, tore open the latch and with my whole strength burst the door open. I all but fell, righted myself, then plunged down the pathway. I can feel the Sabbath's cool and stillness upon me, yet it seemed to me that the village shrieked and that the air stifled me. The hour now was not early. I knew it by the empty houses. I fled down the miry way. My garments were soon wet with the muck. I stumbled and slipped on, my locks flying wildly and my garments torn and displaced.

The book concludes this way. The conversation is between Rudy Strong, now an old man, and one Brighton, who had just arrived in the village:

"Strong? Mr. Strong, I believe."
"Yes."
"Brighton, sir. I have come to take the vicarage. You no doubt remember my sire?"
"I have heard, sir, of layman Brighton."
"I cannot understand. My sire took the vicarage at the time the vicar, I believe Vicar Gifford, went to London for the Willoughby's. It seems to disturb you, sir."
"Yes, yes. But a moment. You seek me?"
"Yes. You are Rudolph Strong. I should be glad if you would come with me to the chapel. There are certain things which I will have to put within your hands as an elder. 'Tis but a little way down. Would you be so kind as to walk with me? ... The chapel yard is sorely in need of a gateway. ... And the chapel—wait, I shall open the doorway. There, enter, Mr. Strong, and I shall join you. ... The altar—see, the flooring is quite rotted and even this volume—wait. ... Strange, isn't it? Look, my eyes fell upon this: 'Suffer little children to come unto me.' And, let me see—it seems a bit of record; two scraps—of no account, sir, I judge."
"Wait! Wait! Let me see them. Read."
"It is torn raggedly. 'diah Willoughby."
"Yes! Yes!"

"And here is a scrap; 'Sarah Trueblood' quite plain. Yet more scraps: 'Stephen'—are you ill, man?"
"No, but answer; was Brighton a layman?"
"Why, no. He and Vicar Gifford were made of the cloth at one time."
"What!"
"Wait sir. You are overcome. What does it mean?"
"Nothing, nothing, nothing."
And through the chapel windows showed the mounded chapel yard, and the larkspurs nodded, and a white butterfly fluttered up, up, up.

And so the book ended. Although these fragments are meaningless insofar as the plot of the story goes, they illustrate how sharply different the novel was from the previous Patience Worth productions. The language is old-fashioned, but it is readable and understandable, in contrast to Patience's usual tongue, which poses a verbal bramblebush for most readers to struggle through.

(Actually, Patience's everyday speech tended, as time passed, to become more readily understandable to her listeners and readers. She periodically was asked by investigators to account for this noticeable change toward more comprehensible language. Her reply usually was to the effect that, if she had spoken in simple, easily understood phrases from the outset, her hearers quickly would have assumed that Mrs. Curran was the source of the words. She deliberately had muddied the waters, she implied, to discourage false conclusions that she and Mrs. Curran were the same being.)

Once again the wait began for the reaction of literary critics and the reading public to the newest work. The reviews for *Hope Trueblood* were more mixed than those for *The Sorry Tale*, but once again leaned strongly to the favorable side. I can point to the 1918 edition of the *Book Review Digest*, a reference library favorite which has for many years served the valuable function of excerpting reviews of new books in a fashion to show a good representation of the book's reception. The *Digest* listed seven reviews of *Hope Trueblood* and the ratings, again using the *Digest*'s code of plusses and minuses, were four favorable and three mixed but tending to be favorable. In other words, the book was not a smash hit, but it had received generally favorable reviews—the kind that most hopeful novelists would accept quite gladly.

The *Book Review Digest* included excerpts from five reviews. Once again some of the kindest words came from the august *New York Times*: "The dramatic situations in it are many and striking, and each one is approached along a road that, after it is traveled, can be seen to lead inevitably to that situation, although it makes no advertisement beforehand of its direction. And the plot is contrived with such skill, deftness and ingenuity as many a novelist in the flesh might well envy. There is much appreciation of mundane beauty in the book, and it is permeated with spiritual fineness and beauty, with a conception of God as an expression of universal love that has been a characteristic of nearly all of Patience Worth's writing."

Boston Transcript: "It is the kind of book that encourages tarrying, each paragraph full of simple detail in which lies the real strength of the novel."

Review of Reviews: "The touch of a literary artist is evident in this book."

Less complimentary, but not hostile, were the other two excerpts.

ALA Booklist: "The story itself is not without interest but would ordinarily find few readers. Rather doleful."

Dial: "Viewed as literature and by not too rigid a standard, this novel—like former works from the same 'pen'—is not without interest and not without merit. Like the others it is a rather spontaneously mechanical, a fluently uninspired performance. Considered in terms of the manner of its composition, as a labored kind of automatic writing, it is a formidable effort."[19]

Other favorable reviews, presumably gathered by Mrs. Curran and Yost, were reported in the book written several years later by Walter Franklin Prince.

New York Tribune: "Whether in the body or the spirit, the author of *Hope Trueblood* is singularly gifted with imagination, invention and power of expression. The psychological analysis, and invention of the occult, the dramatic power displayed in the narrative are extraordinary, and stamp it as a work approximating absolute genius."

New York Times (additional comments not cited above): "No

teller of tales who has studied his craft could read this story without the keenest admiration for the finished technique with which Patience Worth handles this story. Notwithstanding the serious quality and the many pitifulnesses and tragedies of the story it tells, the book has much humor of a quaint, demure type, a kind of humor that stands out as a characteristic of all her work and her personality. . . ."

New York Sun: "Pages could be filled easily and we think entertainingly with report of quaint curiosities of speech in the text. There is much of the fine old English, the English that people of culture affect to disdain. There are paragraphs of power and paragraphs of mystery."

Chicago Mail: "You will wonder at the sheer beauty of the story's thought and diction. You will be convinced that here is a tale from the pen of a master word builder."

Los Angeles Times: "One cannot escape the realization that here is a masterpiece. Can it be that this is some Bronte from Spirit land who has found a tiny aperture through the bleak wall of death to which she has pressed her lips?"[20]

One of the most intriguing facets of the publication of *Hope Trueblood* was its issuance in England by a London publisher. For reasons we don't know, perhaps as a test to seek unbiased reaction, there was no indication given in England as to the unusual manner in which the book had been written. The author was given as Patience Worth and no further information was provided about her. (Although by this time the Patience Worth case had aroused great interest among psychic circles in England, her name apparently had remained quite unknown to book reviewers and readers generally.)

Since the book was about life in a Victorian village in England, it would seem logical that from England would come any challenges as to the authenticity of the book—its physical setting, language, attitudes, customs, etc. The Currans and Yost waited anxiously for the response from the British.

The reviews of the book in England turned out to be quite extreme—either ecstatic in praise or bitterly scornful of the work. Yet, according to Yost, who wrote later about the reaction in England, there were no challenges, with one minor exception, to the authenticity of the book. Yost wrote: "Throughout England the story was generally accepted as the work of a new English writer. The reviews reflected no suspicion of an alien origin, though many of them called attention to verbal peculiarities . . . but, with one exception, no doubt that the writer was an English woman was anywhere expressed."[21] That one exception was a trivial one: A reviewer mentioned in passing that he assumed the writer of *Hope Trueblood* was American.

Yost also pointed out that when his own book on Patience Worth had been reviewed in England, the critics had agreed that Patience showed an amazing knowledge of English life. The *London Times*, according to Yost, had said: "She reveals a familiarity with nature as it is found in England, and with the manners of English life of the older time." And the *Liverpool Post* had commented, "Selections in this volume appear to show an uncanny knowledge of English social life in the 17th century and before."[22]

Here are excerpts from some English reviews of *Hope Trueblood* as quoted by Prince. As mentioned, the reviews in England tended to be extremely favorable or extremely critical, and what follows does not purport to be a representative sample but only some of the favorable reports which were provided to Prince by Mrs. Curran and Yost:

Athenaeum (London): "This is a novel of decided promise. Written by a new author the story is noteworthy in more than ordinary measure. Definite and clear cut in characterization, good dialogue, quaint and arresting turns of expression, and deep but restrained feeling. . . ."

The Bookseller (London): "Undoubtedly a book out of the common, powerful and realistic."

Lady's Pictorial (London): "Will stand as a landmark of fiction by a new writer, who will take a prominent place among great writers."

Ladies Field (London): "A new writer of such unlimited promise as Patience Worth is an event in a world of literature. The pathos and poignancy of what might almost be said to be on a level with those of our greatest writers."

Independent (Sheffield, England): "Patience Worth must command a wide field of readers by the sheer excellence of *Hope Trueblood*, which contains sufficient high-grade characters, splendidly fashioned, to stock half a dozen novels."[23]

Some time after the book made its initial appearance in England, the true story of Patience Worth was made public. The book soon exhausted its first printing (in England) of 10,000 copies, and a second printing was ordered. The Currans and Yost, however, apparently did not realize much money from the comparative success of the book in England, for the record at one point made reference to "the laughably small return for the English rights to *Hope Trueblood*."[24]

One of the most striking features of the Patience Worth case during these years was the willingness of certain well-qualified scholars to enter the controversy and risk the scorn of their colleagues, if not their censure, by publicly and enthusiastically endorsing the literary efforts of Patience. Some of the professors, like Usher, were historians, some were philosophers, but there also were a goodly number of specialists in the academic field most closely related to the data of the case: the scholars of English Literature.

Among the most outspoken of these, in 1918, was W. T. Allison, professor of English Literature at the University of Manitoba in Canada. In the fall of 1918 he traveled to St. Louis to make a personal investigation of the Patience Worth phenomenon. Allison interviewed the Currans and Yost, carefully studied the written record of the five years of sessions with Patience, reread the published books and also attended a few of the sittings at the Curran home, where he joined Mrs. Curran at the ouija board.

In an article written later for a Winnipeg newspaper, Professor Allison concluded from his inquiry that the Patience Worth case "must be regarded as the outstanding literary phenomenon of our age, and I cannot help thinking of all time."

Like many of the other academics who had looked into the affair, Professor Allison strongly emphasized that he held no brief for spiritualism: "I have always regarded so-called spiritualism with suspicion, not to say derision. . . . [Mediums] indulge in hocus-pocus tricks, carry on in rooms where the lights are dim, charge admission to their seances, and tickle the ears of credulous people with trivial messages from the supposed spirits whom they pretend to bring back from the beyond.

"But," he continued, "the Patience Worth phenomenon is

different from all others of which I have heard or read. I have read all the books she has so far dictated, hundreds of her poems, practically all the communications, conversational and formal, which she has made through . . . Mrs. Curran, and I have not found one objectionable sentence, one sentence which I could have wished might have remained unwritten."

Of *The Sorry Tale*, Professor Allison wrote, "No book outside the Book of Books gives such an intimate picture of the early life of Jesus, and no book has ever thrown such a clear light on the manner of life of Jews and Romans in the Palestine of the day of our Lord."

The article summarized the history of Patience Worth's coming and her personality and religious philosophy. Describing one of the sessions he had attended, Allison said, "I have been amazed at the rapidity of Mrs. Curran's utterances. Her husband . . . takes down the matter to dictation while his wife spells out her letters so quickly that the words merge into each other and the letters rattle out like bullets from a machine gun." Despite the speed of the dictation, the scholar said, when the words of the novel then in progress were read over, "each paragraph . . . made not only sense, but beautiful English; such poetry also as was perfect in meter and rich in imagery."

On one evening, he noted, fifteen poems were written in one hour and a quarter, an average of five minutes for each one. "All were poured out with a speed that Tennyson or Browning could never have hoped to equal, and some of the fifteen lyrics are so good that either of those great poets might be proud to have written them."

Of *Hope Trueblood*, Professor Allison commented: "It is one of the most gripping stories of English peasant life, one of the most powerful character novels I have ever read."[25]

Rather surprisingly, there were not many hostile articles by scholars or other writers to counteract the praise being lavished on Patience by admiring observers such as Allison and his predecessors. Oh, there were some very unfavorable reviews of the books and of course there were the attacks by Professor Hyslop, but these were more than balanced by the statements of wonder and appreciation appearing in many newspapers and magazines.

In August of 1918, however, the rather benign, sympathetic, interested atmosphere in which Patience had been existing was rudely punctured. A single magazine article did it, but it was an article which turned one of the most powerful of all weapons on Patience—a scathing feminine wit—and delivered a broadside with it.

The article, titled "Dead Authors," appeared in the *Atlantic Monthly* for August. It was written by Agnes Repplier, a biographer, essayist, anthologist, and critic who contributed frequently to the major intellectual magazines of the day. Protesting against "the recent and determined intrusion of spirits into authorship," Miss Repplier wondered "why should disembodied spirits force an entrance into our congested literary world, and compete with the living scribblers who ask their little day?"

Isn't it strange, she asked, that the dead who seek to communicate with the living should use the alphabet as a connecting link? "Dying is a positive thing . . . but letters are artificial and complicated. They belong to fettered humanity, which is perpetually devising ways and means."

She turned the flame of her ridicule on some of the devices of spiritualism: "table-rapping (which combines every possible disadvantage as a means of communication with every absurdity that can offend our taste)" and the use of furniture such as the table employed by Sir Oliver Lodge, a noted British spiritualist. "The frolicsome moods of the Lodge table must have been disconcerting, even to such a receptive and sympathetic circle. It performed little tricks, like lying down, or holding two feet in the air, apparently for its own simple diversion. One day, in emulation of Aesop's affectionate ass, it 'seemed to wish to get into Lady Lodge's lap, and made caressing movements to and fro, as if it could not get close enough to her.'"

Having fragmented the spiritualist furniture, Miss Repplier moved on to consider Patience Worth. Describing her as "that most prolific of spirit writers," Miss Repplier wrote that "a sympathizing disciple once ventured to ask her if there were no less laborious method by which she could compose her stories. To which Patience, who uses a language called by her editors 'archaic,' and who likes to 'dock the smaller parts-o'-speech,' replied formidably,—

" 'The hand o' her do I to put be the hand o' her, and 'tis ascribe that setteth the one awhither by eyes-fulls she taketh in.'

"The disciple's mind being thus set at rest, he inquired how Patience discovered this avenue of approach and was told,—

"'I did to see at crannies for to put; aye, and 'twer the her o' her who tireth past the her o' her, and slippeth to a naught o' putting; and 'twere the me o' me at seek, aye, and find. Aye, and 'twer so.'

"The casual and inexpert reader is not always sure what Patience means to say; but to the initiated her cryptic and monosyllabic speech offers no difficulties."

Miss Repplier continued, with fine scorn: "All fields of literature are open to Patience Worth, and she disports herself by turns in prose and verse, fiction and philosophy. Other spirits have their specialties . . . but Patience writes six-act dramas which, we are assured, could, 'with a little alteration,' be produced upon the stage, short comedies 'rich in humor,' country tales, mystical tales, parables, aphorisms, volumes of verse, and historical novels. In three years and a half she dictated . . . 900,000 words. It is my belief that she represents a spirit syndicate, and lends her name to a large coterie of literary wraiths. The most discouraging feature of her performance is the possibility of its indefinite extension. She is what Mr. Yost calls 'a continuing phenomenon.' Being dead already, she cannot die, and the natural and kindly limit which is set to mortal endeavor does not exist for her. 'The larger literature is to come,' says Mr. Yost ominously; and we fear he speaks the truth."

Bringing a few other so-called spirit writers into her view, Miss Repplier declared that their didacticism is their most striking characteristic. "Free from any shadow of diffidence, they proffer a deal of counsel, but it is mostly of the kind which our next-door neighbor has at our command."

She cited some of the absurdities which had been published purporting to be spirit communications such as the "repulsive" spiritualistic seance, reported by a magazine, in which victims of the *Lusitania* sinking supposedly had recounted the horrors of their drowning. Miss Repplier commented, "And this shocking travesty of death is supposed to bring comfort to the living. The grossness of the process fails to offend; the puerility of the result fails to discourage. 'There is a set of heads,' wrote Sir Thomas Browne, 'that can credit the relations of Mariners, yet question the Testimonies of St. Paul.' We seem to have changed very little in the course of three hundred years.

"There is nothing calamitous in death," Miss Repplier declared, ". . . and we accept it reverently. But to escape from time, only to enter upon a futile and platitudinous eternity, upon the manufacture of sham products, and the authorship of unreadable books—which of us has courage to front such direful possibilities!

"It is strange," she went on, "that the spirits who are driven by the stress of these terrible years to communicate with a desolate world should be untouched by the source of our desolation. . . . Patience Worth, with the ruthless self-concentration of the author, is too busy dictating novels and plays to waste a thought upon our assaulted civilization. She is a trifle impatient of earthly authorship (potter hates potter and poet hates poet) and she bids us know that truth is not to be found in 'books of wordy filling'; but she adds without compunction 900,000 more words to our overflowing measure, and leaves untouched the problems we desperately face."

As to Mrs. Hutchings' pride and joy, *Jap Herron*, Miss Repplier branded it "a sin and a shame to plunge him [Mark Twain] now into the murky fogs of spiritualistic revelations. . . . If anything could disturb Mark Twain's spirit, and bring it stormily back to earth, it would be the linking of his name to the volume called *Jap Herron*."

But having turned her withering barrage on other spirit communications, Miss Repplier was not finished with Patience Worth: "To be reintroduced to earth as the author of books as silly as they are dull is hard luck for the scholar and the wit. Patience Worth is fortunate in so far that she has no earlier reputation at stake. In fact, we are assured that three of her stories are told in 'a dialect which, taken as a whole, was probably never spoken and certainly never written. Each seems to be a composite of dialect words and idioms of different periods and different localities.' It is Mr. Yost's opinion, however, that her long historical novel, *The Sorry Tale*, is composed 'in a literary tongue somewhat resembling the language of the King James version of the Bible in form and style, but with the unmistakable verbal peculiarities of Patience Worth.' 'What bringeth thee a search?' and 'Who hath the trod of the antelope?' are doubtless verbal peculiarities; but for any resemblance to the noble and vigorous lucidity of the England Bible we may search in vain through the six hundred and forty closely printed pages of this confused, wandering, sensuous, and wholly unreadable narrative, which purports to tell the life-history of the penitent thief."

She goes on to quote a paragraph which she said was "snatched at random from the text" and then cries out: "six hundred and forty pages of this kind of writing defy a patient world. And we are threatened with the 'larger literature to come'!"

Admitting that Patience's poems are somewhat more intelligible, Miss Repplier quoted some of Yost's praise for them and his comment that "In these poems there is both beauty and depth—and something else." To this, Miss Repplier replied, "Whatever this 'something else' may be, it is certainly not rhyme or rhythm. The verses brook no bondage, but run loosely on with the perilous ease of enfranchisement."

The long, rather angrily sarcastic article closed with these paragraphs: "Patience Worth as a 'psychic mystery' has no significance for the reading public. With her ouija-board intimacies, and her 'feminine tastes'; with the baby of 'patrician mould' whom she persuaded Mrs. Curran to adopt . . . we have no concern. It is only her incursions into the field of authorship which make her liable to criticism. It is only the literary ambitions—and disqualifications—of the spirit-world which disturb our serenity.

"Ghosts there have always been since men began to die. They have played their part in disquieting the world since the world awoke to trouble. Vengeful, prophetic, fantastic, and invariably *de trop*, they have come down to us through the centuries, discredited but feared. Now our old apprehensions, our old creeps and shivers, are exchanged for new and reasonable misgivings. Spirits soothing as syrup, didactic as dominies, prolific and platitudinous, are dictating books for the world's betterment; and never a word which can add to our store of knowledge, or stand the 'dry north light of intellect.'

"We are told that once, when Patience Worth was spelling out the endless pages of *The Sorry Tale*, she came to a sudden stop, then wrote, 'This be nuff,' and knocked off for the night.

"A blessed phrase, and of a certainty, her finest inspiration. Would that all dead authors would adopt it as their motto; and with ouija boards and table-legs, and automatic pencils, write as their farewell message to the world those three short, comely words, 'This be nuff.' "[26]

It was just one article in one magazine by one articulate woman who, though respected in the world of letters, wielded no particular influence. Yet, more than any other single thing, the article by Agnes Repplier marked the beginning of the fadeout for the international fame of and interest in Patience Worth. The article in itself was not particularly damning. It did not, in any way, expose or explain the mystery of Patience Worth. It did not prove, or even allege, any fraud or other culpable actions on the part of the Currans, Yost, or anyone else. In normal circumstances it could have been—like the bitterly critical article by Hyslop some two years earlier—merely shrugged off by the followers of Patience.

Patience herself reacted to the Repplier article as she had to all other criticism, with an attitude of resignation and unconcern. In fact, she rebuked those sitting around the ouija board for spending so much time in discussing Miss Repplier and criticizing her: "He who bloweth with his pipe of wisdom, beauteous bubbles of wit, knoweth not that a barb of keen wit should prick them. . . . It be a sadden thing that men create o' their fancies babes that they fondle and make wax strong. Aye and they be things not fitting their sires, for they be weasoned and crypt, aye and not fitting that they stand the days' dealing. I say me then that the men that begot them stand forth and show them proud, ne'er seeing that they wither and shrink.

"He who begetteth o' his fancy destructive imps, shall watch the havoc and that havoc shall be the undoing of the sire. With nimble words fools begarland folly in a mask of fool's wisdom. This thing goeth then forth so clothed, unto the day, and there be men who look upon the folly cloth as wisdom, but he who is wise watcheth the shoddy cloth to fall, for he knoweth no fool weaveth taut and wisely.

"There be nay trick in what I hae set. Man measureth, aye and hath taken within his hands thy handmaid's cloth and hath looked upon it and spake: 'This is a goodly weave.' Yet ye mouthe o'er a wench's gabbin'!"[27]

The Repplier article, however, could not be so blithely discounted as Patience seemed to ask. The simple fact was that the Patience Worth novels had not found a large audience. Unlike the first book, by Yost, which had sold well because it revealed and discussed a most puzzling case, the two novels of Patience were difficult to read and were a long way from meeting the needs of the mass reading public for pleasure reading. It was a difficult task to get through them and, despite the kind words of literary men and despite the tantalizing possibility that the books had been written by a ghost, the public just was not buying them.

The Repplier article, therefore, coming when it did and bringing into the open the ridicule which many intellectuals long had been tempted to pour on the spirit-writing fad, helped persuade Henry Holt and some other publishers who had been issuing such books that perhaps it was about time to call a halt.

The first concrete indication of this in St. Louis was the rejection by Holt of Yost's book on the religion and philosophy of Patience, on which he had been working for months. A few months later, Yost compiled a small volume of Patience's poems of courage and consolation which had been written for those visitors who had relatives in the war and especially for those who had lost loved ones. It was hoped that the book, if published, would serve as a help to thousands of persons across the country in similar circumstances. However, the record for November 20, 1918, noted: "As we had expected, the book of poems came back from the publishers with various excuses. . . ."

Into 1919, despite the increasing coolness of publishers to the works of Patience Worth, she lost no favor with the leading intellectual and social lights of St. Louis. The records of sessions in those months continued to list the presence of many of the most prominent citizens of St. Louis and many faculty members from Washington University and other institutions. And the rebuffs from publishers seemed to have no effect on Patience. She had as many as four separate books in the works during this period and would dictate varying segments of each. Sometimes, just for kicks, she would astound her guests by rapidly writing sections of each book in sequence, alternating the fragments so fast that it was almost impossible to keep up with her. Other times, she would dictate a line of one book, then a line of another, then throw in a line or two of an unrelated poem, then back to the first book. All were given at such a speed, according to witnesses, that even if someone had the ability to write the lines beforehand and then memorize them, it would have been nearly impossible to deliver them in such fashion without stumbling.

Her zest for give and take with visitors never faltered, nor did her willingness to provide spur-of-the-moment poems or dissertations on almost any subject specified. On one such occasion a guest called for a poem on "prairies." Without hesitation, Patience gave these vivid lines:

> *That arch, that vasty blue,*
> *Flecked of the fleece, where, like*
> *Whited doves driven upon the wind*
> *The clouds stream southward;*
> *That spread of gold, that flaming*
> *Flower-strewn plain, swept of winds*
> *That woo too fiercely, beating down*
> *In anguish upon the spreading ways;*
> *And the far, far line, marking*
> *The skies' bowl; and the circling*
> *Of the great black-spread wings*
> *Of the vulture; and the heat*
> *Of oppression at noontide, descending*
> *Like the burning kiss of passion*
> *Withering its beloved.*
>
> *Then the cool of the night,*
> *When the vasty arch becometh*
> *A silver dome, filled of glist'ning*
> *Gems, and the unwinding, across*
> *Its curve, of the night's shroud,*
> *The winding sheet which is created*
> *Of myriad pulsing stars. Mark*
> *The silence. Deathy, save for*
> *The hushing of the wind and the*
> *Companionship of the guardian moon*
> *Which hangs afar as if retreated*
> *Upon her vigil.*[28]

On another occasion Professor Cory of Washington University, who had been investigating the case, indicated that he was going to contact certain scientists to ask their opinion. Mrs. Curran expressed the fear that attempts would be made to "argue Patience Worth out of existence." To which Patience quickly responded, in one of her best-known verses:

> *I am molten silver,*
> *Running. Let man catch me*
> *Within his cup. Let him proceed*
> *Upon his labour, smithing upon me.*
> *Let him with cunning smite*
> *My substance. Let him at his dream,*
> *Lending my stuff unto its creation.*
> *It shall be no less me!*[29]

During 1919 two new figures entered the lives of the Currans, both of whom were destined to play important roles during the remaining years of the case. From Los Angeles came Mrs. Alexander Smith, a widow who had heard of Patience, then had carefully read her writings, and had become a confirmed and devoted believer. After corresponding with the Currans for some time, she was invited to visit them in St. Louis and, during the summer of 1919, lived with them for three months. She became a favorite of Patience, who wrote many poems for "Dotsie," as Mrs. Smith was called, and a close friend of Mrs. Curran. She was to remain an intimate and loyal companion until Mrs. Curran's death.

The other newcomer was Herman Behr, a wealthy New York businessman, a native of Germany, who also had become deeply interested in Patience and her work. He had begun the translation of a number of the poems into German with the hope of having them published in his native country. In 1919 he and his wife also came to St. Louis to meet the Currans and to get a firsthand taste of the personality of Patience Worth. The record notes that Behr offered to pay for the publication of Yost's book on the philosophy of Patience, but the newspaper editor apparently declined with thanks.

During that summer of 1919 Patience wrote another short poem which became one of her most famous and beloved. As she had when she began *The Sorry Tale*, she indicated that this poem was exceedingly important to her and that she would put into it all the skill that she possessed. The episode began when Mrs. Smith passed on a request from her niece in California that Patience write a child's prayer because, said the niece, no such adequate prayer already existed.

Patience agreed to provide such a prayer, but obviously was fearful that she could not do the task justice: "How for to put within a babe's lips, whom He loveth so, words for to tell unto Him the love He hath bought from them! Woe is he who putteth but love within a babe's utterance. Fear hath nay part. Yea, for to bring the great God down unto the whisperin' lips aye and disturb not the comin' sleep with awe."

Patience then did something she had only rarely done before—she prayed for help in creating the prayer: "Let my throat sing a song that shall fall as a dove's coo. Oh, make my throat dulcet, aye and my words as the touch of sleep. Give me the tongue, aye and the power of simplicity."

Then, after a long period of silence, she said, "Aye, I hae the singin'." Then there was another long pause and she said, "I may not sing 'O Lord'; for what babe knoweth the words' lilt?"

John Curran's record goes on to describe what happened next:

"'Father,' went on Patience and we thought she had commenced it. But she stopped and said: 'It meaneth not a nearness.' Then later: ' 'Tis like unto making the first babe's swaddling cloth.' Letters and words were slipping by in streams as though Patience was selecting from all the literature of time. Then Mrs. Curran saw a little child on the shore of a vast sea. Then this passed and the prayer came. The first time 'Dear Father' was interjected. Then the first line read: 'I am Thy little child, dear Father, I shall play.' Then after much feeling of unsatisfactoriness and some changes we arrived at the final copy:

CHILD'S PRAYER

I, Thy child forever, play
About Thy knees this close of day.
Within Thy arms I now shall creep
And learn Thy wisdom while I sleep.
Amen.[30]

In his exhaustive analysis of the Patience Worth case (about which we shall have more to say later) Walter Franklin Prince devoted considerable time and effort to a careful study of that brief prayer and to a comparison of it with many other children's prayers, both popular folk prayers that had come down from antiquity ("Now I Lay Me Down to Sleep," for example) and also prayers composed by leading poets. From this study, Prince decided: "I conclude that of all prayers for children which I have discovered, this seems incomparably the best, that it is entitled to be called a masterpiece, and that under all the circumstances of its composition, it constitutes a distinct and remarkable phenomenon in the case of Patience Worth."[31]

Prince, it should be noted, was in no sense a professional literary scholar or critic, but he was a well-educated man, a student of poetry and the classics and, in any case, a man not given to making sweeping statements. His opinion, while it might not carry much weight today with *The New York Review of Books* or the Modern Language Association, hardly can be shrugged off as meaningless, either.

In the fall of 1919 another event occurred which was to have considerable significance in terms of the diverse explanations being offered for the mystery of Patience Worth. From the very beginning, one of the cornerstones for the argument of those who hailed the uniqueness of the case was the fact that Mrs. Curran never had shown any writing ability nor had she expressed the slightest interest in creative literary activity. Her insistence that she never had wanted to write and her professed inability to do so seemed to underscore the possibility that Mrs. Curran might well be a totally separate entity from Patience, as the spiritualists insisted she indeed was.

During the few years after Patience's first appearance, however, it became obvious that Mrs. Curran either was developing with amazing rapidity into a person of some literary ability or that she had possessed the ability all along, and either had kept it hidden or hadn't realized it herself. Hints that she had some facility with the written word had been given in some of her published letters (such as the one to Henry Holt, quoted from earlier) and some of the speeches she gave concerning Patience Worth.

Obviously, if it could be shown that Mrs. Curran possessed

substantial literary or even journalistic ability in contrast to the general understanding that she had none, this would add considerable weight to arguments that Patience simply was a subliminal personality of Mrs. Curran, reflecting and refining the literary ability which the young St. Louis housewife always had possessed on her own.

It seems obvious that, since the Currans professed a belief that Patience was in fact the spirit of a dead woman and since most of the attention that had come to them was based on speculation over that premise, it would have been convenient for them to suppress any indications that Mrs. Curran was able to write on her own with some skill. To their credit, however, they made no effort to hide such indications and, in fact, were quite open about making them known. This seems to bear out again the feeling of almost everyone closely connected with the case that Mr. and Mrs. Curran were completely open and truthful about the facts and themselves sincerely wanted to get to the truth.

In the spring of 1918 the record had noted that Mr. and Mrs. Curran had been collaborating on short stories and had sold six of them to the Publicity Bureau of the Liberty Bond Committee. Mr. Curran frankly stated in the record that patriotism was involved, but that financial gain was the primary motive in writing the tales. He noted that the stories "were considered so good that we were figuring on writing up a series of dialect stories about the Ozark people, something of which Mrs. Curran has dreamed for many years."[32] That last phrase also seems to contradict the claims that Mrs. Curran never had entertained any literary ambitions until the appearance of Patience.

Then, on September 1, 1919, the record noted that Mrs. Curran had just completed her first major short story. It is made quite clear that Mrs. Curran, not Patience, was the author, yet the record added: "There was no doubt that Patience had helped. The story reeks of her, yet it was all Mrs. Curran's personal material."

Patience was asked to comment on the story and replied, "The tastin' be the tellin'. 'Tis but a babe's mixin', but nay sae sorry a loaf!"[33] Later, referring to a second story on which Mrs. Curran had begun work, Patience said, "I say 'tis well that the wench be she. There be within mine words a thing she may not deny and within hers a thing I may not deny. There be two streams runnin' forth from one fountainhead, I say, the throat with two songs. And earth shall be confused before the task of knowin' what be upon them, and in the confusion they shall be drawn within the net, for they shall look upon the flesh of me for the flesh of her and see it not. Yet shall she take in the ears of them that list unto her for the words of me."[34]

Mrs. Curran's maiden literary effort met with instant success—just about the greatest success a short-story writer could have in 1919: The story was submitted to and accepted by the *Saturday Evening Post*. If there ever had been doubt that Mrs. Curran possessed the ability to write, this should have dispelled it. She had hit the jackpot on her first try. And, it must be emphasized, her sale to the famous magazine was made, so far as is known, without capitalizing on the Patience Worth publicity. Mrs. Curran did not mention her connection with Patience when submitting the story and the magazine editors, in their correspondence with Mrs. Curran and in the publication of her story, did not mention it, leading to the assumption that Mrs. Curran's name hadn't rung a bell with the *Post* editors. She expressed guilt later over not having informed them of her involvement with Patience when the story was submitted.

The short story, for which Mrs. Curran was paid $350, was published in the November 22, 1919, issue of the magazine. It ran to several thousand words, one of the longer stories in that issue, and covered almost seven pages. The story was titled "Rosa Alvaro, Entrante" and the author's byline was Pearl Lenore Curran.

The style and language of the story were completely different from anything attributed to Patience Worth. And yet the subject matter of the tale and some of the dialogue inescapably link it to Patience and to Pearl Curran's role in the case of Patience Worth. The story seems to offer a wealth of psychological clues and yet none of the many people who carefully studied the case gave any serious consideration to the story. They seemingly regarded it as insignificant because it had little literary merit and because it differed so strikingly from the works of Patience Worth.

Pearl Curran's story was of a lonely salesgirl in a Chicago department store. She has no family and lives with another salesgirl in a boarding house. She is bored with her job and is growing increasingly depressed.

To give an indication of the style, here is the way it began:

> To Mayme Ladd the morning had dragged through mechanically, the hours mere incidents of commerce—incidents which had necessitated the insertion of her nervous hands into various qualities of hosiery innumerable times; incidents which claimed her disinterested attention, threatening to sap her remaining strength after a sweltering night at Mrs. Winthrop's home boarding and rooming establishment.
>
> Gwen Applebaum watched her narrowly and quizzically as she Frenched a stray strand of pale hair which had extracted itself from one of the hornlike protuberances at either ear, and chewed ruminatingly a bit of paper, at the same time irritating an elderly patron of Goldman & Co. to exasperation by her air of condescension assumed in answering an inquiry for cotton lisles at thirty-five cents the pair; murmuring as she resumed her chewing and Frenching after the patron's departure: "Don't they know they was a war?"

The quality of the prose never rose appreciably above that rather unpromising start. The dialogue was full of what apparently was the popular slang of the day: It's grub at 'leven-fifteen and back at it. . . . Ain't you the morgue, though? . . . Cut that stuff, Mayme, and tuck this under your dome. . . . Us for a feed. Cheer up, kid, and don't boob the act—and more and more of the same.

The salesgirl, Mayme, finds a card that someone had left behind advertising a fortuneteller. Trying to stir up a little excitement in her drab life, she visits a fortuneteller, a drunken old woman who is an obvious fraud. The old woman tells her that she has a spirit-guide, a young Spanish woman named Rosa Alvaro.

From then on, the story begins intriguingly to parallel real life. Mayme finds herself slipping in and out of a second personality—that of Rosa Alvaro. Her friend persuades an eminent psychologist to treat the girl. He is convinced that it is a case of personality dissociation. The girl eventually confesses to her friend that she deliberately assumed the new personality in order to change the miserable pattern of her existence. Attracted by her new personality, the manager of her department at the store asks her to marry him and she immediately accepts. The psychologist, after several therapy sessions with her, pronounces her completely cured. The story, however, ends on a note of mystery as Mayme and her new husband leave on a honeymoon cruise (and brace yourself for one of the worst dialects in memory, the dialect used to indicate the personality of Rosa):

> A strong arm encircled her and the voice of Mr. Peacock whispered: "Senorita, Senorita."
> "Yeaz, Senor."
> "Tomorrow has come!"
> "Yeaz. Look, Senor, look yondair!" One hand made a sweeping gesture toward the fast disappearing shore. "Yondair is yesterday, Senor. Look, Rosa would nevair forget yesterday. See, tomorrow is yondair in the wide open way, Senor. We go tomorrow. Ah, Senor, shall Rosa go weeth yesterday or stay with tomorrow? Speak, Senor, speak!"
> "Rosa, Rosa, stay forever! Forever, amor mio!"
> "Siempre jamas," came the soft answer, and Rosa's little head fell confidingly upon Mr. Peacock's shoulder.

This story, which never rose above the level of bad soap opera, nonetheless was important, I think, for the insight it seems to offer into the entire Patience Worth affair. The psychologist in the story, for example, was a serious, rather bumbling fellow who never gained a really clear understanding of what Mayme was up to or why she was doing it. His fiancée, a rather hard, cynical society girl (with whom he apparently freely discussed his patients), insisted from the very start that the entire Rosa Alvaro personality was a fake, that the girl was "putting on."

Even more significant, it seems to me, were several speeches of Mayme in the story, in which she tried to explain to her friend why she had devised the secondary personality. For example: "I told you I was afraid of her! Oh, Gwen, I love her! She's everything I want to be. I can't be nothin'. What's the use of me? Nobody ever sees me. I tell you, you shan't stop her! She has a right! Didn't I find her? It don't make no difference. I can slave on, but they shan't touch her, do you hear? It ain't me. It's what used to be me before the world buried it. . . ."

Or this passage: "Well, I just didn't want to be me. I was sick of myself. I wanted to feel, feel like a woman that somebody cared about; not like a alley cat. And that's what done it. I just made Rosa out of a shawl and a bunch of rag flowers, but there was somethin' else in her. It was my fight for life! Every rusty hope in me broke loose. I forgot myself in Rosa and commenced kiddin' the world back! And the world liked it, hon; honest it did."

Perhaps, in that single, rather unimportant magazine story, Pearl Curran revealed much more of herself and of the real secret of Patience Worth than she ever intended or even realized.

8

"A Nut for Psychologists"

ALTHOUGH, BY 1919, publishers and editors were no longer too interested in the Patience Worth case or in her writings, Mrs. Curran and her unseen literary companion still were the objects of great curiosity, interest, and affection on the part of many people throughout the country.

In November of that year the Currans accepted an invitation from Herman Behr and his wife to visit them in New York. They spent more than two weeks in Manhattan and almost every evening a session with Patience was held before large, enthusiastic groups of onlookers. Many of the meetings took place in the Behr apartment, others in private clubs. A number of celebrities attended the sessions, according to the record, including actresses Blanche Yurka and Ethel Barrymore, writer Hamlin Garland, and poet Edgar Lee Masters. Crowds as large as 150 persons, including a number of newspaper reporters, were in attendance at some of the evenings.

According to a newspaper report, Masters, whose *Spoon River Anthology* had thrust him into the front rank of American poets, was invited by Mrs. Curran to join her at the ouija board. After he sat down, Mrs. Curran asked Masters what he was thinking.

"I'm not thinking," Masters replied.
"Dullard," immediately commented Patience.

Mrs. Curran then suggested that Masters join her in writing a poem to their mutual friend and admirer, William Marion Reedy. Masters agreed and this brief tribute to Reedy resulted:

He who speaks with a barbed tongue,
Direct as an arrow,
He whose eyes are deep as midnight, and as covering,
He whose heart is the tabernacle, yea the sanctuary.

As Masters had approached the ouija board after observing Patience dictate poems for some time, Mrs. Curran had asked him to tell the guests if anyone, in his opinion, could write poetry in the way that the Patience Worth matter was produced. Masters answered, "There is only one answer to that—it simply can't be done."[1]

After his own turn at the board, a reporter asked Masters to comment. The poet replied, "I am not prepared to give an opinion as to whether her stuff comes from Patience Worth or not. There is no doubt, however, that she is producing remarkable literature. How she does it, I cannot say."[2]

During that same evening session Mrs. Curran told the guests that a prominent neurologist, Dr. Victor Haberman, had that day offered to devote a month to the study of Mrs. Curran. She flatly rejected the offer and denounced scientists "who cannot understand me."

She angrily told the guests: "I have just got an offer from Dr. Haberman to subject myself to a scientific investigation—vivisection, I would call it. I have received thousands of offers from doctors, psychologists, and the like, and I want to say here that I have turned them down and will continue to turn them down. All these people think I am abnormal. It is they who are abnormal in that they cannot see that I am receiving this beautiful literature from Patience. Scientists cannot understand me. That is why they are trying to call me names. But I don't care. I have the goods: one and a half million words of literature."[3]

Many of the guests at the New York meetings were clergymen of note and they continued, as had their colleagues for the past six years, to pepper Patience with questions concerning her present existence and the so-called spirit world. There was this conversation, for example, with a Dr. Huckle:

> DOCTOR: In Mr. Yost's book . . . he intimates that she might not have had a previous existence, but was solely a spirit personality.
> PATIENCE: Aye, this wert when the youngins were young. (This was interpreted to mean when those making the record of her remarks were still inexperienced.)
> DOCTOR: May we expect sometime from Patience Worth a novel of eternity with scenes and characters of the immortal life as vivid as *The Sorry Tale* is for the land of the Savior, as true to that place as the England of *Hope Trueblood*?
> PATIENCE: Ah, Sirrah, this be His kingdom. Would thy handmaid mar it with her touching?
> DOCTOR: Has Patience met the Savior in the other life? Has she heard His words there? Can she tell of His sayings there?
> PATIENCE: There be nay stranger which enters the gateway, and this gateway is but the phantom of man's tongue. And all must pass the Shepherd. But the things that God hath locked thy lips to make thee know, and sealed thine eyes that they see—ah, what folly that ye ask to prate of them!
> DOCTOR: Shall we all one day see the face of God?
> PATIENCE: There be no thing that is denied. Ah, that ye babes might know that He be but a Sire neither aloof nor withdrawn. Nay, His face be as thy sun before thee.
> DOCTOR: The message of Patience Worth, as I understand it, is the simplicity and sublimity of love. It is just the vital and essential message of Jesus unencumbered by doctrine, dogma or ceremony. It is primitive Christianity. Is this correct?
> PATIENCE: Yea, I'd show him a Shepherd, nay a king.
> DOCTOR: Many of us have found great interest in the communications of W.T. Stead in the letter of Julia, of Sir Oliver Lodge in Raymond, in Basil King and others. Can Patience Worth assure us that all that is true in these comes to us in the same way from the immortal world?
> PATIENCE: This be not the pratin' o' thy handmaid. I say me naught of my brothers. The thing that I utter is truth. Take the stuff of the weavin' of these and smite it. If its metal ringeth true, then is it truth. Or if it crumbles into naught by the quirt of thy wit, then 'tis folly.[4]

The greatest single triumph of the trip to New York came on the evening of November 14. Among those present was none other than Professor James H. Hyslop, head of the American Society for Psychical Research and the man who had bitterly attacked the Currans and Yost in the past with such words as "a fool adventure . . . a fraud and delusion . . . lying literary productions." By his very willingness to attend a session with Patience Worth, Hyslop seemed to be openly admitting that he may have been wrong about her. If this were a blatant fraud and lie, as he had charged, would he have been willing to participate in it?

It was a dramatic moment when Hyslop was introduced to Mrs. Curran, who invited him to sit at the ouija board. She asked him if he still believed she was a fake and, according to the record, he denied having ever made such a claim. The record placidly noted, "We took the denial as a retraction, shook hands and called it off as far as we were concerned."

Patience always had refused to get excited about Hyslop's past comments and now she reminded Mrs. Curran of this, saying, "I sayed me, follied one, ye wert a donkey." Then she gave these lines to Hyslop, a poem given the title "Is Thy Quest Honest?":

> *Through that vast vale, black, pitlike,*
> *Wouldst thou hold a taper? Wouldst thou*
> *Lend thy hand to them who seek?*
> *Is that yearning born of Truth?*
> *Eating thy heart in hungry anticipation*
> *That thou shouldst leave a beacon*
> *On the sands? Oh, dost thou behold the regal*
> *Barque of day floating upon the sea of Eternity*
> *And no beacon, no light, no chart?*
>
> *In benediction do I bow before thee!*[5]

Hyslop obviously was not displeased by his reception. On November 21, the day of the final Patience Worth session in New York, the famous psychic investigator telephoned and asked permission to attend once again.

That night, Hyslop got into a bit of a wrangle with Patience herself. Patience had reeled off fragments of *The Merry Tale* and *Samuel Wheaton*, two of the novels then in progress. Hyslop insisted to all present that he could easily explain the situation: There were two spirits writing the stories. Patience objected to any attempt to divide her work up in that way and said, "I tell ye

I be seein' the pigs in mine ain pigsty. Aye and I be shellin' the grain for the feedin' wi' mine ain hands, and the sow who hath bringed them forth wert me!"

According to the record, Hyslop continued to insist that a number of spirits were taking part in the writing of the literature. Patience came back again: "Aye, but I say me, why need I a one to chew the feed which I take? When thou dost eat thou dost chew and swallow the stuff thyself. Nay, nay, this be one path that be not trod by hosts."[6]

During the more than six years since Patience had first identified herself, it had been made clear that the ouija board itself played a rather incidental role in the whole affair. Mrs. Curran had freely admitted that she used the board only as a means of concentrating on thoughts and that the words of Patience Worth came from her head, not from the board. Suggestions were made periodically that she might some day discard the board entirely, but she and her husband expressed apprehension over trying to do so, fearing that somehow, once the established pattern was disrupted, there might be danger of a complete break in the communications.

Late in 1919 someone raised the question again and Patience remarked, "The grister [the ouija board] be wearyin' the follied 'un [Mrs. Curran]." She then was asked if the board could be set aside and answered, "Crawl afore thou runnest. This shall be a perfect thing."

Then, as an experiment, but still using the board, Mrs. Curran for the first time dictated an entire poem word by word, without spelling out single letters as she always had done in the past.[7]

From that day on, Mrs. Curran generally dictated the poems word by word. Her speed didn't falter under the new system and her husband once timed her delivery at 110 words per minute. On occasion Mrs. Curran would begin receiving dictation from Patience when she was not sitting at the board. Once she was in the midst of typing a letter to Mrs. Behr when, she said, she heard Patience "softly, insistently dictating" and she wrote down a poem.

On February 12, 1920, the ouija board was discarded for good. It had been decided to risk experimenting without the board. With Yost joining Mrs. Curran, the pointer was removed from the board itself and placed upon a smooth chair between them. The pointer began to circle on the surface of the chair and then, after a moment, Mrs. Curran began to recite the words of a poem, just as if the pointer were, as always, gliding on the board's surface. The next step was to discard the pointer and simply rest their hands on the chair. Mrs. Curran continued to pronounce words, but said she felt somewhat confused and lost. Patience seemed to be trying to reassure her and dictated a poem which was titled "Be Not Confused."

Finally, Mrs. Curran, wishing that she had something to hold in her hands, was given a scarf pin by Yost. Holding this, she continued to offer the words of Patience Worth, just as always. The scarf pin, too, was soon set aside.

From this day forth there were no physical objects serving as any type of intermediary in the case of Patience Worth. Pearl Curran simply saw the pictures and the words in her head and called them out, as coming from the hand of Patience Worth.

Every once in a while the Currans would attempt other experiments as they continued to probe the boundaries of their knowledge about the phenomenon that had so dominated their lives for the past years. On one such occasion Mrs. Curran expressed confidence that she could write with her own hand something entirely separate from the work of Patience Worth, while simultaneously dictating a poem from Patience. It was decided to try the experiment.

Mrs. Curran sat down and, without pausing, wrote a letter to Dotsie Smith in California. As she wrote, she also dictated a three-stanza poem from Patience called "Will o' the Wisp." To indicate the clashing styles of the two projects, here is the first stanza of the poem followed by the letter to Mrs. Smith which was being written simultaneously:

> *Oh you marshlight, flashing*
> *Across the marshes, beckoning!*
> *Is thy light that I see*
> *A beacon to tomorrow? Give me*
> *A sign, oh, you banshee!*
> *Give me a sign! Make*
> *Tomorrow's question marked against*

The sky fitfully, as thy flash.
Oh you marshlight, flashing, then
Shall I be more accustomed
To the questioning that I live.

DEAR DOTSIE: I am writing you while I write a poem. It is a new trick. Do you like it? See here, honey, my hands are full! I don't like it, honey. It's like baking bread and stirring soup! I am sick of the job. I wish you were here and that we could go over this together. This is a mess of a letter, honey bug. I'm nuts! This is some chase! Slinging slang and purring poetry! Jack is doing his best in this Marathon. This is fine business and I'm up against it. 'Finis' honey, and I call it going some!
PEARL[8]

The letter was thoroughly banal and the poem was far from the best of Patience's work. Yet psychologists regarded this experiment with considerable interest. In virtually every other reported case of split or dissociated personality, the separate personalities had alternated in taking command of the body. Here, if Patience was a separate personality of Mrs. Curran, apparently was an instance of alternative personalities able to function concurrently.

During those early months of 1920 there were frequent references in the record to the increasing discouragement of Yost, the Currans, and all the other members of Patience's inner circle over their continued inability to arrange for the publication of new books. Yost had revised his *The Task*, the analysis of Patience's religion and philosophy, but still was unable to get it accepted by Henry Holt. Patience had completed a new work, a poetic drama called *The Pot Upon the Wheel*, but it, too, could not find a publisher. Yost and the Currans began to discuss the possibility of publishing the drama on their own, with financing being provided through private subscriptions.

Although all those in the inner circle were bitter and unhappy over the complete loss of interest on the part of publishers, they never could get Patience to offer any expression of regret. On one occasion, in May 1920, after a particularly mournful meeting at which the wisdom of publishers, editors, and the general reading public had been challenged, Patience gave this consoling poem:

SATISFIED

Beloved, I would confess.
I would make me humble
And contrite, but behold, I may not
For I am exalted!
I have cried out "love me!"
And have been loved. I have
Cried me "trust me" and have received trust.
I have commanded "list" and behold,
They have bended unto me!
I have commanded "take thou this"
And it hath been taken up.

Behold, I have spent a song
And buyed a kingdom. How then
May I be contrite in this full knowledge?

During those difficult months there was still much interest in Patience Worth in St. Louis. Mrs. Curran received a steady flow of invitations to speak before clubs and schools about Patience and to demonstrate her communication with the ghostly writer. In April of 1920 she addressed a large audience at Harris Teachers College and made these comments:

"Seven years association with this—shall I say phenomenon?—I hate the word. It is cluttering to so simple a thing as the beautiful gift that is mine—has transformed me from a sort of ordinary garden variety of woman with no aspiration save to gain some selfish recognition for a mediocre voice, keep in style and please my husband, sucking in all the good things of the day like a hungry baby until I was comfortable, then forgetting it—to a different being. Poetry or deep reading of any sort bored me to distraction, though once in a long while I admit there was a feeble stirring of something which might have been called a soul. Think of being such a person and after a miracle engraced you, waking to it and having a wonder book laid before you which turned its pages day by day, year by year, illuming the pit that was once you. This is what happened to me. If Patience Worth is a part of me, I auto-educated myself. You will admit this is a rare feat!"

Mrs. Curran admitted in the talk that there were many different explanations offered for Patience, but she left no doubt with her audience that she firmly believed Patience was the spirit of a woman of the seventeenth century: "I have heard the sounds. I have received truly spiritual evidence in the spirituality of her words. I hear her voice. I almost see the twinkle of her eye when she jests. I know she *is*."[9]

In the spring of 1920 there appeared in print the most detailed personal statement ever made publicly by Pearl Curran concerning her own reaction to the entire affair, its influence on her life, and her opinions as to the origin of Patience Worth. Her article, called "A Nut for Psychologists," appeared in the March–April issue of Henry Holt's magazine which had changed its name, formerly *The Unpopular Review*, to *The Unpartizan Review*. Although Holt was unwilling to publish any more Patience Worth books or Yost's second volume about her, he obviously still was interested in the case or considered it to be good copy. He devoted more than fifteen pages of his magazine to Pearl Curran's article.

Mrs. Curran began by describing, in somewhat bitter terms, the effect of the Patience Worth case on herself:

"Let any man announce himself a psychic if he would feel the firm ground of his respectability slip from beneath his feet. He may have attained through rigorous living an enviable reputation, but if he once admits himself an instrument differing in any manner from the masses, he will find himself a suspected character. Science with side glances will talk secretly of dire and devious matters, connecting with his name such doubtful associates as dis-associations, obsessions, secret deviltries of all manner and kind. They humor the subject and listen tolerantly to his effort to prove himself sane, while they cast wise eyes and smile.

"He will find that the mere act of honestly trying to give the world the truth, has opened the door of his soul to ridicule and abuse. It is my honest belief that the humiliation the world has offered to the psychic has kept many splendid examples of God's mysteries hidden and that there are many true and wonderful phenomena that are not disclosed or announced, for this reason only.

"Because one produces a superusual phenomenon, is he to be immediately classified as a monstrosity, and mentally and physically placed upon the dissecting table? Is there no gentle means by which we may . . . get the full result from him? . . ."

Her feelings about scientific investigators, however, had moderated a bit: "In my own case, at my first encounter with science I developed a sensitiveness which caused, on both sides, a deep distrust, and it has only been through frequent meeting with broad men of that cloth that I have at last become enough interested in their attitude to try to present whatever I may have that may interest them."

A long conversation with Professor Hyslop, she said, had convinced her that serious psychic investigators "were pursuing their investigations in the manner I have suggested, with the confidence of the subject retained. This has stimulated me with the desire to aid them with all my power."

Because the psychic immediately comes under suspicion, Mrs. Curran wrote, his word is worth less than the results of his work and science seeks to disprove the case without really looking at it. She is presenting facts about her own case "with no desire to offer proof or to try to convince anyone of anything whatever, but merely to jot down some of the incidents which might be interesting to the interested." She recognizes that her own opinions are worth nothing to a scientist, but offers them for him to do as he pleases.

Mrs. Curran went on to describe her health as normal: "I sleep normally, have no queer obsession or wakefulness, or urge to write. . . ." Then she added, with bland understatement, "Patience Worth never obsesses me, and I feel as normally about her as I do about any other friend who has gone into the great beyond.

"Whatever may be the association which I describe as the presence of Patience Worth, it is one of the most beautiful that it can be the privilege of a human being to experience. Through this contact I have been educated to a deeper spiritual understanding and appreciation than I might have acquired in any study I can conceive of. Six years ago I could not have understood the literature of Patience Worth, had it been shown to me. And I doubt if it would have attracted me sufficiently to give me the desire to study it."

Mrs. Curran proceeded then to describe the visions that accompanied many of the writings: "I am like a child with a magic picture book. Once I look upon it, all I have to do is watch its pages open before me, and revel in their beauty and variety and novelty.

"Probably this is the most persistent phase of the phenomena, this series of panoramic and symbolic pictures which never fail to show with each expression of Patience where there is any possibility of giving an ocular illustration of an expression.

"When the poems come, there also appear before my eyes images of each successive symbol, as the words are given me. If the stars are mentioned, I see them in the sky. If heights or deeps or wide spaces are mentioned, I get positively frightening sweeps of space. So it is with the smaller things of Nature, the fields, the flowers and trees, with the field animals, whether they are mentioned in the poem or not.

"When the stories come, the scenes become panoramic, with the characters moving and acting their parts, even speaking in converse. The picture is not confined to the point narrated, but takes in everything else within the circle of vision at the time. For instance, if two people are seen talking on the street, I see not only them, but the neighboring part of the street, with the buildings, stones, dogs, people and all, just as they would be in a real scene. (Or are these scenes actual reproductions?) If the people talk a foreign language, as in *The Sorry Tale*, I hear the talk, but over and above is the voice of Patience, either interpreting or giving me the part she wishes to use as story."

The article went on to describe in greater detail some of the visions she had seen, including one with a particularly mystical quality in which a vast play of colors, especially an "indescribable white purity, purer than dew, whiter than young lilies, not dazzling, but soothing like a smile" culminated in the appearance of "a river of forms, all in white . . . their eyes lighted with a wondrous light, and each glance fixed upon their leader who walked before them with outstretched arms, Jesus of Nazareth." The vision preceded a poem which was given the name "The White River."

On occasion she had received in an instant the entire detail of a long story. Mrs. Curran quoted from her husband's record for June 22, 1917. Mrs. Curran had been walking with her mother to a grocery:

"All at once, without any preliminary warning, as in a single flash, she was overwhelmed with the entire framework of the story which she felt had been on the way. In the twinkling of an eye, like the bursting of an inner veil or the sudden drawing of a great curtain, she found herself immediately in possession of practically the entire mechanism of a wonderful story, the plot, the characters, that subtle spirit essence of the central idea, the purpose, and with it came a great exaltation. Even the name of the story came, which was 'The Madrigal.'

"It took Mrs. Curran two hours to tell me what she had received in a flash...."

The article then gave a summary of the plot of the story. The manner in which it came to her in a flash, wrote Mrs. Curran, "still remains upon me as the most startling and wonderful thing that Patience Worth has brought me."

Another aspect of the case, brought out in the magazine article, which had not been generally known, was Mrs. Curran's claim that she had often seen herself in the visions: "I have seen myself, small as one of the characters, standing as an onlooker, or walking among the people in the play." She described the tiny figure of herself boldly taking part in the play, perhaps taking up a piece of fruit and tasting it or smelling a flower in a garden. "And the experience was immediately my property, as though it had been an actual experience: but it was as real to me as any personal experience, becoming physically mine, recorded by my sight, taste and smell as other experiences."

In this way, she said, she had become familiar with many exotic flowers which she had never actually seen, but recognized when she saw them in pictures. In this way, also, "I find that I possess an uncanny familiarity with things I have never known—with the kind of jugs and lamps used in far countries in the long ago, and the various methods of cooking, or certain odd and strange customs or dress or jewelry. I know many manners and customs of early England, or old Jerusalem, and of Spain and France."

Mrs. Curran pointed out also that Patience had given evidence countless times of knowing the "inner life" of those who attend the sessions with her. ". . . every time we write, if there are newcomers, Patience shows that she knows them and what they are doing, what their sorrows are, if any, what are their dispositions; in fact she has shown that in a pinch there is nothing about them which is kept from her if she desires to know it." Patience, Mrs. Curran claimed, would refer to things in the lives of people that no one else knew and "she often tells people things about themselves in such a way that I cannot understand what is meant, yet the person interested does. . . . This happened scores of times in New York on my recent visit."

The article also explained, as we have described previously, Mrs. Curran's ability to be aware of mundane things happening about her in the room while she is taking dictation from Patience.

Also described was Patience's propensity for literary stunts: "Things she does which no mortal man may do, according to our wise writers, form a large share of the wonderful evidences of superusual power." She cited the unusual language of *Telka* as analyzed by Casper Yost and these other stunts:

"Patience is writing on four novels at once, part of each at a time. She has written a line of one in its dialect, then a line of another in a different dialect, then back to the first for a line, switching from one to the other at top speed and without a break; at times she has assembled two persons in each story, engaged them in conversation, and made the characters of one seem to reply and even argue with the characters in the other. When the stories are stript [sic] apart, it is found that they read right along in the proper continuity of text.

"She has also written a line of a poem, a line of story, and then alternated them for some time to the completion of the poem. When stript, it is invariably found that each is whole and unhurt."

She went on to describe the composition by Patience of the 120-letter inscription for the Missouri State Capitol. Mrs. Curran implied that this was an exceptional achievement because Patience had, on order, given a statement that was exactly the required length and she "gave this as fast as it could be written in longhand." Actually, Mrs. Curran was not being completely honest in making this claim (or else her memory had failed her), for, as we have described, Patience was given the required length of the inscription on a day prior to the one when she actually gave the words for it.

Mrs. Curran described her own efforts at writing without the aid of Patience. The work has been most interesting, she said, "to watch the functioning of my own mind and feel the difference between the conscious effort of the ordinary manner of writing, as against the unconscious manner in which the Patience Worth material comes to me. My own writing fatigues me, while the other [Patience Worth's] exhilarates me. That's a queer mess of a statement, but quite true."

Having mastered the use of the typewriter to facilitate her own writing, she found that it offered "a perfectly good means of communication, unhampered with conscious effort" to talk with Patience. She had already written one of Patience's poems on the typewriter, as it was received: "Every other condition was the same, her presence, the pictures of the symbols, the pressure on my head,[10] and everything except that I was at the typewriter." The article had been written prior to her decision to abandon the ouija board and she concluded the long statement by reporting that she expected eventually to discard the board: "I hate to do this, for think of the check there will be upon the sale of Ouija boards!"[11]

On July 28, 1920, news came that was a bitter personal blow to Patience, the Currans, Yost, and all the others in the inner circle: William Marion Reedy had died of a heart attack in San Francisco. Patience's beloved "Fatawide" would no more write the long, flowing articles about her in his *Mirror*, would no longer be there to defend her skillfully in print against the onslaughts of her critics. Though he never had believed in the "spiritist" theory of Patience Worth and he deeply regretted at times that he had become involved with "spook literature" to the degree that he had, Reedy never lost his strong admiration for the literary achievements of Patience Worth and his personal belief in the integrity of those involved in the case. Patience had lost one of her most formidable allies. The day after Reedy's death, Patience dictated this tribute to him:

> He who fared forth
> Upon that expectant voyage
> Watching the far horizon
> With the same joy, the same faith,
> The same untrammelled security
> Which marked each day,
> Behold no thing within the new glory

> Of a newer day one whit
> The fairer than that he hath
> Presented unto this.[12]

The record for the summer of 1920 cites two more incidents that deserve mention. Yost periodically would seek to test Patience with new questions in a continuing effort to determine just how much knowledge she possessed and from where she obtained such knowledge. On one such occasion he asked if the word "Selborne" meant anything to Patience. Neither Mr. or Mrs. Curran remembered ever hearing the word. Patience immediately gave to Mrs. Curran an impression of crossing the ocean and then a vision of the English countryside, complete with several characters from the area. Mrs. Curran described the scene and the costumes of the people. After the vision, Patience commented, "Oh think ye 'pon it. How a lark arising from the field may sing, sing heavenward, with dust upon its wings."

Yost was very impressed with the response. Selborne, he told them, was an English village. Gilbert White had just written a new book called *The Natural History of Selborne*. Yost had heard of the book, but hadn't yet read it. He was even more impressed the next day as he read the book. Remembering Patience's remark to Mrs. Curran, he came across a passage in the book in which reference was made to "the lark dusting its wings."[13]

Another experiment was tried a few days later. Yost asked Patience if the word "Plotinus" meant anything to her. She responded by showing Mrs. Curran a long, detailed scene, apparently from ancient Rome. A man appeared in the scene, apparently a writer, and Patience gave some information about him. The record noted: "When it was all over, Mr. Yost said that Patience again had demonstrated that she was confined to no time or place in her knowledge of things, for this was a complete picture of Plotinus, the writer, whose complete works had just been translated into English. . . . The encyclopaedia describes Plotinus in a way that fits Patience's picture of him. . . ."[14]

The material in the Currans' encyclopedia obviously was readily available to Mrs. Curran, but it seems apparent from the record that Yost had given no one any advance knowledge of the question that he would put to Patience concerning Plotinus.

In October 1920 another sharp criticism or, more accurately, a downgrading of the Patience Worth affair appeared in a national publication—Henry Holt's *The Unpartizan Review*. It was a reply by a writer named Mary Austin to Mrs. Curran's article in the same magazine a few months before. The basic point of Miss Austin's piece was that the Patience Worth case contained nothing really extraordinary or without precedent:

"All or nearly all utterances of the kind that man has cared to preserve for reasons wholly apart from their value as fact, whether made vocally or in written words, seem to the speaker to have come from some source outside itself. The poet or philosopher or prophet has felt himself a medium through which the valued communication is made. . . .

"Also," the article continued, "it has been characteristic of all ages and cultures that these unpremeditated and often uninvited messages, on arriving at the doors of consciousness, present themselves as Beings."

Mrs. Curran's description of her "mental flashes of white radiant light" was said by Miss Austin to be a very frequent occurrence. She compared it to the vision seen by Paul on the road to Damascus. "I recall discussing this with a neurologist who suggested that the effect of light might actually be the register on the brain centers of an excessive discharge of phosphorus accompanying acute cerebration."

The frequent accompaniment of Patience Worth ideas by symbols in the mind of Mrs. Curran was also nothing to excite anyone, according to Miss Austin. "This is one of the oldest methods by which truth not yet rationalized is presented to the conscious mind. . . . Indeed the whole theory of dream interpretation . . . depends for its validity on this universality of the disposition of the human mind to state its profoundest surmises and conclusions in symbolic form."

The visions seen by Mrs. Curran, the article declared, are seen by certain types of people with "this faculty for visualization . . . [and] few people realize . . . that this faculty . . . is common to all artists." And so, wrote Miss Austin, "here are four of the concurrent manifestations of supposedly spiritistic automatic writing, shown to be quite the ordinary accompaniment of creative work in general, and without the least suggestion of spirit intervention."

As to Mrs. Curran's claim that she had acquired—through Patience Worth—information which could not come to her in any normal way, Miss Austin countered that psychoanalysis had demonstrated that much material may be in a person's subliminal self which had arrived there by perfectly normal means that since had been forgotten. ". . . without competent analysis, to which I understand Mrs. Curran has declined to submit, no statement of previous unacquaintance with facts, however sincerely made, can be accepted at its face value.

"There is nothing" in Patience Worth's mode of composition, according to Miss Austin, "which cannot be duplicated in the experience of the literary writer." Mrs. Curran's claim that Patience appeared to know the inner lives of the people who call upon her was rather glibly disposed of by Miss Austin, who related her own experience at a spiritualistic session and charged the experience to coincidence and the giving of unconscious hints and clues by the visitors.

But the supreme crime committed by Mrs. Curran in her article, apparently, was to speak in glowing terms of Patience's writing. Miss Austin declared: "For here she renders the one touch which convincingly relegates her automatic writing to the lower strata of productivity. She naively speaks of it as 'all literature,' and uses the words 'great' and 'wonderful' without hesitation. No artist could go on with his work who did not think it tremendously worth while, as he is doing it. But no artist goes far who cannot afterward subject it to the strict censorship of the canons of criticism.

"The work of Patience Worth, though superior to most automatic writing, is by no means 'all literature' by the prevailing standards. Mrs. Curran is reported as having great natural gifts as a story teller, and her paper gives evidence of the possession in her own right of much more than ordinary writing power. One wishes, one ventures to prophesy, that her gift will become robust enough to throw off the obsession of Patience Worth and continue in her proper character to make genuine contributions to the elucidation of the Unconscious."[15]

Miss Austin's rejection of the Patience Worth case as anything out of the ordinary did not assume the same damaging proportions as had the article by Agnes Repplier several years earlier. It simply added some lubrication to the downward path on which the literary career of Patience Worth already was embarked. Ironically, though, the criticism of Mary Austin did bring Patience back briefly as the subject of discussion in many literary and intellectual salons. Less and less attention had been paid to her. Now, for a few moments, she was in the limelight again.

In 1921 Patience's poetic drama *The Pot Upon the Wheel* was issued privately by the Currans and Yost under the imprint of The Dorset Press. Although sales figures of the book are no longer available, all indications are that few copies were sold.

It was a most difficult year for the Currans in more than one way. In addition to the rapidly declining public interest in Patience Worth, John Curran—who had been working very hard in organizing a new business, a shale company—became ill and was in and out of the hospital for months. During his hospital stays Patience frequently sent him tender messages of concern, such as this one: "Beloved, I am come unto thee not anew. Lo, have I offered thee balm o' my very soul, as thy pillow, and even though flesh crieth out, remember thou, best beloved, I am come and ne'er shall depart."[16]

In the summer of 1921 Casper Yost realized an ambition that had been swelling in him ever since he first became acquainted with Patience Worth. With his wife he prepared to leave for England and a visit to Dorsetshire, supposedly the home of Patience before she left England. On July 4, just before the Yosts left St. Louis, Mrs. Curran saw a detailed picture of a hill overlooking a seacost, ruins showing part of a monastery, then for a moment a view of the original building, views of the countryside, then a small village. Mrs. Curran was given the impression that this was where Patience had lived. There was a church, a couple of manor houses, a few smaller cottages, and a blacksmith's shop.

Patience commented, "The hand of time be a banisher of men's baubles. Aye, but I say me, when thou hast stood 'pon this spot and lain hand 'pon the stuns, thee'lt have stood 'pon the spot thy damie hast stood upon and gazed seaward. . . ." Then Mrs. Curran saw a scene at a boat landing with a huge three-masted schooner docked there. She saw Patience traveling toward the ship on a horse, accompanied by other riders. They board the ship. Mrs. Curran then gave a detailed description of the interior of the vessel.

Then, Mrs. Curran reported, she saw Patience: "Patience pushed back her hood and fully disclosed her face. She was much younger than Mrs. Curran had thought, being probably about thirty years. Her hair was dark red, mahogany; her eyes brown and large and deep, her mouth firm and set as though repressing strong feelings. Her hair had been disarranged by her cap and was in big, glossy soft waves." Mrs. Curran, the record went on, "felt the motion of the ship as it put to sea, but Patience sat lonely and silent, a part of the twilight inside the ship—a grey, tired, lonely figure, leaving her land—to what? It was late afternoon."

The scene continued with various scenes of the voyage and then Mrs. Curran saw the vessel landing on a wooded coast.

Later in the same session she reported seeing a monk meet Yost and lead him. She saw the back of a bald monk working on a window for a church or cathedral. She gave a detailed description of the drawing and its inscription, the words in French, the lettering in Old English: Ange . . . Felice . . . Enfant . . . Aime Amour.[17]

In August a letter from Yost, posted in Weymouth, England, was received by the Currans. Its contents were dutifully included in the Patience Worth record:

"This morning we engaged a car and went to Abbottsbury. There are the ruins of the old monastery Patience told us about. There are old walls, ivy-grown and a massive building which looks like a chapel. It is said to have been used by the monks as a stable. Whether that is true or not, the whole ground about is used as a stable now. Far up on the hill above is St. Catherine's chapel, a small building of massive stone. The village of Abbottsbury is exceedingly picturesque. All its houses are very old, built solidly of stone and with thatched roof. The few streets are narrow and crooked and the few inhabitants look as ancient as the town. We touched the stones and then we sped down the road to Portisham, the village of Patience. It fits exactly in her description and her direction.

"About three miles inland from the monastery on a road that runs inland and branches. It is still a wee village perhaps 300 inhabitants. It is beautifully situated and its houses look as old as Patience's days. The little church was there, no doubt, in Patience's day—a stone building with a square Norman tower overgrown with ivy. . . . Found no existing signs of colored windows.

Churchyard is filled with gravestones, many of them so old that no inscription can be seen. Deciphered one in the side of the chapel dated 1670. The chapel looked as if it might have been the one Hope Trueblood entered upon a certain occasion. Maybe one of those graves holds the black box. It is a beautiful place and, by the way, it is the birthplace of Thomas Hardy, the novelist. . . . I am quite sure I've been in Patience's own country, stood where she stood, touched the same stones, and as I write I can look out as I raise my eyes from the paper and see the sea where she has looked. . . . No one but you can understand what this day has been to me."[18]

After his return from the trip, Yost is reported to have said that he found the area generally true to Patience's descriptions and there were many specific buildings and locations that accurately conformed to her reports, but he apparently did not feel he had discovered any really striking evidence to convince skeptics that he actually had visited places once walked by the spirit who had spoken to him through Mrs. Curran.

During the last months of 1921 John Curran's health continued to fail and he was hospitalized much of the time. Mrs. Curran was almost constantly depressed over her husband's ill health and repeated setbacks. Patience sought to console her and give her courage. On a bleak day in November, as Mrs. Curran wept, Patience gave her these poems:

BABE AND SIRE

I am a babe and He the Sire.
At His feet I sit; Lo, my wisdoms,
My deepest words are but the lisping
Prate of a babe, beside His.
Lo, my labors, my greatest labors
Are as a babe who plays with pebbles beside His.
And my sorrows, my wailing sorrows
Are as a wilful babe who wails for self.
I am a babe and He the sire.

LEST I FORGET

Lest I forget to hope,
I must recall a clustering vine

> Begarlanded which hangs o'er a swinging nest.
> I must recall the shuttling wings,
> The ceaseless, ceaseless voyages,
> The o'er-spilled joy, the faint complaining,
> And a certain morning when the wonder
> Hath become apparent.

> ## MY STAFF OF FAITH
>
> Should I lay down the staff of faith,
> Then doth my voyage become heavy-footed,
> My path bestoned, the hillocks mountain high
> And the mountains defeat.
> Cleave I unto the staff of faith,
> My path is sunnied o'er. There are no stones,
> The hillocks are lendful in their curves,
> And the mountains bring exaltation to my soul.
> I long for that instant, when I
> May crest them with my victory.[19]

In December Mr. Curran was stricken again and lost the use of one hand. Responding to Mrs. Curran's grief and fear, Patience for the first time indicated that it might be better if she withheld her words for a while:

> Mine ain, my wee 'un, my willin' harp,
> Lo, are the winds upon thee.
> If thy strings whir to their very depth,
> Then shall thy song be sweeter.
> Yet in thine agony I fain would withhold my hand.
> I fain would leave thee weep thy heart free.
> For youth can forget tomorrow and smile at today.
>
> I shall make my prayers illume the altar of thy day.
> I shall pray that I become the flame within the
> Sense of thy soul. I shall pray that the hand
> Of God will hold thee upon its palm, in secret
> And confidence. I would say be strong, be tender.
> These two are the requisites of being Godlike.[20]

During the next few months, with Mr. Curran home again and slowly regaining his strength, the sessions with Patience continued once or twice a week. Among the guests in February, the record noted, was Roger Baldwin, the famed civil-liberties leader. Later that month the three-million-word mark was passed by Patience as she continued to work on the several novels in progress, as well as turn out her usual fund of poems, discussions, and conversations.

On March 13 Patience gave one of her most succinct statements on immortality. She had been asked whether we meet our loved ones again after death, and she responded: "This be a cunning earth, a wise set play in which we meet and learn farewell. There be nay truth in this farewell. It be the one thing man must unlearn. Flesh be finite and may not conceive the infinite. This be a simple thing. He who is, is uttered forever. I say me, today is neither a pledge or a troth. It be a certainty. And the shuttling of light and shade means naught. The day is without light and darkness. Likewise the soul of man."[21]

On June 1, 1922, after an illness of more than fourteen months, John Curran died. His death was front-page news in St. Louis newspapers, partly for his prominence as a businessman but more for his involvement with Patience Worth. He was buried in Mound City, Illinois, the village where his wife had been born. Patience dedicated this poem to him and it was read at his funeral:

THE TRIUMPH OF DEATH

These are the things I have laid down:
Sorrow, doubt and confusion.

These are the things I have taken up:
Labor, love and understanding.

He who hath laid down his armor,
When the sword hath finished his victory,
Letteth his soul forth as a young eagle
In the early morn, with the sun upon its wings,
And the rose kiss of morn upon its crest,
Unfettered of the day,
Freed for the heights.

The death of John Curran marked a major change in the lengthy record of the Patience Worth case. The meticulous businessman who had kept the record since 1915 had carefully, painstakingly filled it with complete details of each session with the mysterious writer—not only the words she had uttered but information about the guests attending the session, discussions among the guests and the Currans—a variety of details which, in their fullness, provided a comprehensive history of the case.

From here on, others would take over the record-keeping, well-meaning friends and followers. But they would not have the concern of John Curran that the record of Patience Worth should be kept with such thoroughness that it would be useful to posterity. As a result, during the remaining years of Pearl Curran's life, the Patience Worth record is episodic, fragmentary, with long gaps of time unaccounted for. Little substantive information is given, except for the words of Patience herself. The context of those words —which John Curran carefully had supplied—is henceforth left mostly to the imagination of the reader.

For Pearl Curran the death of her husband, a shocking blow in itself, came at an especially difficult time for her: At the age of thirty-nine, she was pregnant with her first child. During the weeks after her husband's passing, Mrs. Curran continued to hold the regular meetings with Patience, despite her grief and depression. She looked forward gratefully to the words of consolation and hope given to her at the sessions. There were few outsiders involved; most of the sessions involved only Mrs. Curran, her mother, and faithful friend Casper Yost.

Patience was constantly reassuring: "Confide in me, beloved, for I shall make myself deep of sympathy; I shall make myself tender of mercy; I shall make myself strong of understanding. My love shall be as a cloak, as a staff and as shoon. These will I lend unto thee. Make thee confident."[22]

In December 1922, six months after her husband's death, Pearl Curran gave birth to a baby girl, which she named Eileen. There was scant communication with Patience during those weeks; Pearl had been ill for several weeks prior to the baby's birth. Afterward, however, the sessions with Patience resumed as before and she wrote poems to Eileen, referring to her as the "little bud of hope."

Mrs. Curran faced a difficult future. She had a family of four to support now: herself, her mother, the new little daughter, and

Patience Wee, the "daughter" of Patience Worth, now six years old. As her husband had once told a reporter, the activities of the past few years had left the family poorer than before, rather than enriched as many people supposed. The financial situation was bleak.

One devoted friend came immediately to the rescue. Herman Behr, the wealthy New York admirer of Patience, fondly referred to by the Curran family as "Papa Behr," sent money to Mrs. Curran and announced that he would continue to do so as long as she needed it. I was told that Behr provided Mrs. Curran with an income of $400 a month for a number of years.

In March 1923, just a few months after the birth of her child, Mrs. Curran left for Chicago to give a series of public lectures on Patience Worth and to communicate with her unseen companion for the edification of all who wished to look on.

There is evidence that Mrs. Curran undertook this trip in order to make some money. Heretofore one of the strongest arguments against charges that fraud somehow was involved in the case had been that the Currans never had profited nor attempted to profit from Patience Worth. The decision of Pearl Curran to accept money for her services as Patience's communicator would seem to raise more doubt as to her motives throughout the case. And yet—could she be blamed? She had a family to support, little money of her own, and presumably a reluctance to go on accepting charity from admirers of Patience, no matter how well intentioned.

Mrs. Curran remained in the Chicago area for several weeks, speaking at a number of private homes and also at clubs such as the University Club in Evanston. Her usual format involved a discussion of the history and background of the Patience Worth case, followed by opening of the meeting to talks with Patience on pretty much any subject requested. At one such meeting, Patience wrote poems requested on such subjects as Friendship, Brothers of Wood and Field or God's Littlest Creatures, Love, Hate, Sunset on the Rockies, a poem to the hostess of the evening, Patriotism, poems to Denmark, Sweden, Greece (each of which was represented on that evening by their respective consuls), France, Chicago, the Goddess of Liberty, and Drama.

How Patience felt about such writing to order is not indicated in the rather fragmentary record of the trip, but she doubtless was aware that such tailor-made poetizing was not too remote from the activities of bards and balladiers of old.

A few months later came another hard blow for Mrs. Curran: Her mother, Mrs. Mary Pollard, also died. It was she who had sat alongside the ouija board on that hot summer night in 1913, carefully noting down all that was said, the first pages of what was to be a twenty-nine-volume Patience Worth Record. It was she who had been the loved butt of Patience's acid jests, who had provided a kind of matronly comic relief at those first puzzling confrontations with the mysterious writer. Now she was gone, along with John Curran, and Pearl was more alone than ever.

The sessions with Patience still continued regularly at Mrs. Curran's home. At one of them, in September 1923, little Patience Wee asked for the first time to speak directly with Patience. Her message is worth citing, not simply as the happy greeting of a child but as further indication of the seriousness with which Mrs. Curran regarded Patience. It seems to me inconceivable that, if Mrs. Curran had not considered Patience, with utter earnestness, as a being entirely separate from herself, her little daughter hardly would have been inspired to speak in these terms. A cynical or even a questioning attitude toward Patience in the home would undoubtedly have filtered through to the little girl, for children are acutely perceptive about such things. It is hard to doubt the sincerity of Mrs. Curran toward Patience when one reads these words of her daughter:

"My angel Patience, I love you very much; you've never known how much. Also I love dear Jesus, for He was our Saviour. He was honest and true. He was the one that helped us. He was the one that loved us. He, who loved us, He is our Lord. Dear Patience, I love you and sometimes I have wanted to speak to you, but I was outdoors. You are just like a wee whit angel. Dear Patience, I love you millions. I am going to mind my mother. I have thought of God and wanted to speak to Him too because he sent Patience. Everything that dear Jesus thought of nice to do, He has done. He sent my mamma and papa and Aunt Dotsie and Father Behr and Dame [Mrs. Pollard] to me."

Patience responded to the child's greeting, "See ye upon it, the love hath thrived and become manifest and pours like a golden fluid unto my thirsted lips."[23]

During those months the literary works of Patience Worth continued to sink deeper into obscurity. The novelty had long since faded, leaving only the words themselves. And, despite the encomiums of many thoughtful critics, the mass reading public remained apathetic. The poems and novels were too difficult to fathom, the themes were weighty and demanding. It was so much easier to just pick up the latest romance or mystery novel.

Herman Behr paid for the publication of a collection of Patience's poems in 1923. He edited the volume, which he titled *Light from Beyond*, and wrote an introduction in which he left no doubt that he considered Patience, without fear of contradiction, to be a spirit voice. The book was published with the imprint of the Patience Worth Publishing Company of Brooklyn, New York. The volume apparently had a very small sale.

There was another reason for the disappearance of the Patience Worth literature from general attention during the early 1920s. It seems quite apparent that many critics and anthologists turned away from Patience simply because they feared becoming involved with a writer of such questionable, controversial origin. The case somehow seemed to bear a taint—of what? fraud? sensationalism? lunacy?—and self-respecting critics and anthologists steered away from it, disdainfully lifting their skirts like a crusty old Victorian lady crossing a mud puddle.

Walter Franklin Prince, in his book on the case, pointed out that he knew of several literary authorities who, during this period, lauded the work of Patience in private but would not do so publicly. Prince wrote: "I heard one man, a professor of literature of high standing in a university, talk for perhaps fifteen minutes in terms of high eulogy of what Patience Worth has produced, yet when I asked him to reduce to writing a part of what he had said so enthusiastically to a local audience, he looked at me doubtfully nor did he answer the letter echoing the request. Several other literary experts who I know admire these same productions did not answer my letters, even though I offered, if necessary, to conceal their names. . . . Here is ground for my belief that if nothing had ever been said about Patience Worth and the ouija board, the literature would have produced a much profounder effect even than it has done. If this is so, it will take its rightful rank some day. . . ."[24]

It is very difficult to believe that critical tastes would have shifted so much in just five years that the work of Patience Worth —once lauded in the highest terms by reviewers for the *New York Times* and many other major publications—suddenly would be utterly inconsequential from a critical standpoint. It seems obvious to me that the occultist cast of the affair led most critics, once the novelty aspect of the case had faded, to turn up their noses and say, "This is no concern of mine."

In the course of my research I checked more than twenty anthologies of American poetry published during the 1920s. The poetry of Patience Worth, rated so highly by Braithwaite just a few years before, regarded by William Marion Reedy, a major American critic, as "literature of no mean order . . . wonderful for content and for form," was not even accorded a mention in any of these volumes.

Even in her home region, Patience was ignored. The *Missouri Historical Review*, journal of the state historical society, in 1924 carried a lengthy two-part article on "Missouri Verse and Verse Writers." There was no mention of Patience Worth in the text of the article or in the appended bibliography.

9

"Patience has shown me the end of the road..."

THE NEXT THREE YEARS were lonely, rather despairing ones for Pearl Curran. No longer a celebrity, largely ignored by the public (although she often still received and accepted bids to speak about and communicate with Patience before various clubs and organizations), periodically in ill health, she was often depressed and morose. Sometimes she found herself regretting that she ever had allowed herself to tell the world about Patience Worth and open herself to the barbs and insults of strangers. But, she told friends, she held steadfast to the belief that her involvement with Patience was the greatest blessing of her life.

Her old friend from California, Dotsie Smith, came to spend several months with her in 1923. At the conclusion of her visit it was agreed that Patience Wee would go with Mrs. Smith and live in California for a year in order to lighten the physical load on Mrs. Curran. Patience was asked about this plan and approved, saying, "I hae said that the harp wert breaked. I said this and if it wert breaked asunder, then must I cease to sing."

In October the final installment of the latest Patience Worth novel, *Samuel Wheaton*, was dictated. It was dedicated to "Dame and Laddie"—to Mrs. Pollard and John Curran. There seemed to be no prospect of interesting a publisher in putting out the book.

During the next few years Mrs. Curran's closest friends were two sisters, Williamina and Grace Parrish. Daughters of a wealthy St. Louis laundry owner, they were patrons of the arts. Williamina assumed the primary responsibility for typing and maintaining the Patience Worth Record during this period. Sessions with Patience continued regularly in Mrs. Curran's home, and large groups often were in attendance, including many of the social leaders of St. Louis, prominent jurists, clergymen, and university professors.

Mrs. Curran sometimes would go to another person's home and put on a Patience Worth session. She would receive a fee, generally $100, for such meetings. *The Censor*, a gossipy publication that covered the activities of St. Louis society, carried this item in November 1925:

> Mrs. Curran has long since passed the probationary stage with her followers and has been accepted. Hence, to put in issue the source of her power today or its validity would be unthinkable. When she presents a program, therefore, suffice it that "the oracle hath spoken." She gets the "proceeds" and her select audience a novel entertainment—something to while away an idle afternoon or evening. Fair enough! Mrs. William N. Bemis placed her pretty home at the disposal of Mrs. Curran Wednesday for such a divertissement, and approximately 100 matrons were duly electrified, if not flabbergast.[1]

The gossip sheet's reference to Patience as an "oracle" was hardly justified and, of course, Patience never claimed such status for herself. She consistently refused to make predictions of the future, despite repeated requests. Often, however, she was asked to comment on major events or personalities in the news of the day and such comments tended to become oracular in nature. That Patience was no better at gazing into the future than any of her hearers is indicated by this comment, given in 1924, on the League of Nations:

A brat in swaddlin' clothes,
And yet it hath wailed—
And lustily;
And shall crawl and walk,

And declare itself
Before Man.²

Even though Patience had little success in forecasting the course of the world and its leaders, there were claims from time to time that she had demonstrated knowledge of things that, by normal standards of cognition, she had no way of knowing. They were claims made by her friends and admirers—hardly disinterested people—yet they lend an eerie air of mystery to the chronicle of the literary wraith.

Mrs. Hazel Leete, a long-time friend of Mr. and Mrs. Yost, who attended some of the Patience Worth sessions, told me of one such incident that she had witnessed. One of the guests at the sitting was a Judge Corliss. The judge, with no prior warning, gave Patience the word "Sockman" and asked her what it meant. No one else in the room ever had heard the word before, presumably including Mrs. Curran. Yet she was immediately given a vision by Patience of a man walking behind a plow with blood running down his hands. Patience went on to write a poem about the workman.

Judge Corliss, according to Mrs. Leete, was astounded. The word was so terribly obscure that he was certain no one, even the ubiquitous Patience Worth, would know it. He explained that in feudal days a tiller of soil was called a sockman. Such men often worked so hard in pushing a plow, he said, that it was not uncommon for their hands to become raw and bloody.

I found a note in the record by Williamina Parrish about another occasion when a friend of Mrs. Curran in the East, a Mr. Hoskier, had mailed a letter to her with a sealed envelope folded inside. He asked her not to open it until she had received Patience's comment on it. (Obviously there is no proof that Mrs. Curran didn't open the envelope, but let's take it on faith that she didn't.) Mrs. Curran put the sealed envelope on the table beside her and Patience gave the following lines:

> Life is the garment of eternity
> Which be the vestment of God Himself.
> Each man be the keeper of a golden thread
> Spun from the radiant Heart of God.
> This he plies at will,
> Making or marring the Perfect Pattern.

Yea, Man is a bobbin,
Slipping the woof of Hope
'Twixt the warp of Faith
Upon the loom of Love.
Despite his rebellions, he *must* lend him
Unto the weaving,
And that which is not perfect
He shall re-weave.
This is the Mercy of this Just God
Whose labors are perfect.
Man, in his fulfillment of this Perfection,
Having inherited the power of creation,
Createth Himself unto perfection.
This is the law of the Perfect.
Man is the bobbin at weaving the vestment of God
Who in His love requireth Perfection
Wherein is reflected His own Countenance,
And Man's kinship in full is declared.

Mrs. Curran then opened the sealed envelope from Mr. Hoskier and read the contents:

SOCRATES: And what is it with which we weave?
HERMOGENES: A shuttle.
SOCRATES: Is it not then assuredly the discriminating and interpenetrating implement of our Being, as a shuttle of the web?
HERMOGENES: Surely.[3]

Another strange incident involving Patience also was recorded by Williamina Parrish, but in this instance she was personally affected. Her father, Dinks Parrish, had died some months earlier. Her mother, Aggie Cooper Parrish, was fondly known as Miss Aggie or Little Miss Ag. Williamina Parrish made this statement:

"On the night of January 9 . . . Mrs. Curran had a vivid dream in which our Father came to her and asked her where was our Mother. Mrs. Curran said it seemed to be in our house, and little Miss Ag, hearing Dinks's voice, came running down the stairs, and Dinks opened his arms and folded her in, both of them laughing happily.

"We asked Patience: 'Did you give this dream to Mrs. Curran?'

"Patience: 'Ah me, nay! I say me this . . . 'twere he, thy Sirrah, who knocked for entrance.'

"We asked: 'Did you help him, Patience?'

"Patience: 'Inasmuch as I had found the path and had spaked with ye.'

"Mrs. Curran said, 'This is not plain enough, Patience. Did Dinks send the message through you?'

"Patience: 'Look ye . . . hae ye not seen the word and the fulfillment of the word? I fetched me not, nor showed me unto ye . . . yet he, thy Sirrah, in his radiance, came him for his Beloved.'"

Two weeks after this incident, Miss Parrish stated, her mother died suddenly.[4]

During 1925 and 1926 Mrs. Curran continued to make frequent appearances before St. Louis clubs. The record indicates such sessions with the St. Louis Women's Club, Miriam Lodge, the Junior League of St. Louis, the St. Louis Writers' Guild, and others. She also made periodic trips to New York and Chicago, where sessions were held in the homes of her followers and at clubs such as the Colony Club, Town Hall Club, and Writers' Club in Manhattan.

The sessions continued to attract prominent people and their wives. At one of the New York meetings in 1925, for example, were Mrs. Ethelbert Nevin, widow of the composer, Mrs. Walter Damrosch, wife of the conductor, and Mrs. Hamlin Garland, wife of the noted writer.

On one of the trips to New York Mrs. Curran met with John W. Ticknor, described by the record as "a psychic, clairvoyant and clairaudient. Sir Arthur Conan Doyle says that he is the greatest in the world." Patience quickly made it clear that she liked Ticknor. With that, Mrs. Curran suggested a new experiment: Perhaps Patience would dictate lines of a new poem to both of them alternately. Ticknor was perfectly willing to try and within a moment or two said he felt something coming through. The experiment ran into problems, however, for every time Ticknor attempted to supply a line, Mrs. Curran interrupted and corrected him, the interjections presumably being supplied by Patience.

Another try was made, and these lines resulted:

 TICKNOR: And black-mouthed waves beat high
 MRS. CURRAN: With bruised lips crying—chaos,
  T: Toward a stern rock-bound shore,

>   C: Mute of utterance, but flinging back
>   Chaos and the hiss of despair.
>   T: Woods, black brewed against the stormy skies,
>   C: And wild winged gulls beating 'gainst the wind.
>   T: The giant branches beat free, free, free,
>   C: Unloosed in agony.
>   T: And beating hard against the wind, a shuddering bark
>   C: Clings for an instant—and is gone.
>   T: Life, sorry and despair, but an atom of existence,
>   C: Flung as a phantomry before thee and the trick be done.

Ticknor was very enthusiastic over being included by Patience in the composition of the poem and pronounced this quite a wonderful feat.

> PATIENCE: Nor to good man, if his mouth be full o' words.
> TICKNOR: Well, it was surely full of words that time.
> PATIENCE: More words than thought, mayhap.[5]

That Mrs. Curran continued to be lonely and often depressed during those years was evidenced in the record by the frequent poems of encouragement and consolation given to her by Patience. Whatever the mood of her communicator, however, Patience was her own self: witty, confident, ever didactic. For example, these random comments:

Of Mrs. Curran: "Mine ain harp. A woeful one at times, tuned o' self a whit, but withal mine harp."[6]

On the difference between knowledge and wisdom: "Kennin' wisdom or kennin' learnin'? Man kens much that is not wisdom. Wisdom and understandin' be the same. Learnin' and understandin' be sweet wine and bitters . . . they will not mingle. Understanding is the conception of mercy. Wisdom is fundamental. The law of Wisdom be writ by the hand of God on the holy script of the soul. It be a simple word . . . Love. Mercy and understanding in union bring forth Wisdom . . . but humility be the key to the treasure-house."[7]

On Congress: "They be asses who set up their brayin' declarin' it be the voice of the people."[8]

On herself:

>   A phantom? We'el enough,
>   Prove thee, *thyself* to me;

> I say, behold, here I be
> Buskins, kirtle, cap and pettiskirts,
> And *much tongue!*
> We'el what hast *thou* to prove *thee?*[9]

On the question: Should women express themselves or should they stay home and work for the race? (These lines should be relished by our present group of militant feminists):

> When labor is done (the wench-taskies),
> What be it that a thirsted soul sup;
> That it sing; that it expand;
> That it give forth?
>
> The tide hath gone
> (And I may say, with thank)
> It hath gone when a wench be bound in a kirtle,
> Ribbed and shoon by law.
>
> Behold! Womankind shall lead,
> Yea, with a sweet intuition
> Shall pierce, shall expand,
> Shall hold a taper unto deeper vasts
> Than men may e'er stumble upon.
> For womankind goeth through the valley of death
> In darkness, with no taper for to lighten,
> Leading man to the brink of day;
> And *he*, finding the day made perfect
> *Through the agony of womankind,*
> Struts![10]

In February 1926 a new and important figure came into the Patience Worth case. Mrs. Curran never had quite been able to forget the rough treatment she had received a decade earlier from the nation's most renowned psychic investigator, Professor Hyslop. Since that time she and the various psychic and spiritualist groups had kept a respectful distance from each other. Now, however, she received a request from another such organization for her cooperation. Walter Franklin Prince, research officer of the Boston Society for Psychical Research and a nationally known and respected leader in the field, wrote that he wanted to make a full, careful, and detailed investigation of the entire Patience Worth case. He intended to spend several weeks in St.

Louis, where he wanted to study minutely the written record dating back to 1913, to interview Mrs. Curran about her entire life, and to talk with many of her friends. The purpose: to endeavor, once and for all, conclusively to answer the question that had been asked all over the world during the past eleven years—who was Patience Worth? Would Mrs. Curran cooperate?

Mrs. Curran years before had made clear her disinterest in studies of herself, her exasperation with those who wanted to "dissect" her. Yet she had always wanted, as much as anyone else and probably more, to find the answer to the mystery of Patience. She invited Dr. Prince to come to St. Louis and offered him her full cooperation. (A summary of his findings will be included in the next chapter.)

The Patience Worth Record includes a report of the first meeting between Patience and Dr. Prince, but unfortunately the account is slightly deficient: It lists thirty-five answers by Patience to questions put to her by Prince, but fails to quote the questions. One wishes fervently that the session would have been recorded by the careful, thorough John Curran.

The record is more complete, however, for the second session with Prince on February 15, 1926. Dr. Prince greeted Patience and asked her if she was ready to begin.

PATIENCE: I have brushed the hearth, polished the pewter and sanded and sit me kerchiefed and ready.
DR. PRINCE: Imagine that I am a resolutely sceptical psychologist. Give me the hardest raps and sharpest retorts you can—the harder the better. Now we begin. I cannot believe in you, since mind is but a function of the brain. Your brain died long ago—if you ever existed.
PATIENCE: Weel, better a resurrected dead than a dead living, eh?
DR. PRINCE: Nothing exists but what has substance. There is only matter or the properties of matter.
PATIENCE: Show *me* the fruit of thy word. I may not lay hand upon it! E'en so am I.
DR. PRINCE: If you once lived, you are now nothing. How can nothing remember?
PATIENCE: Thee art less than naught and thy memory is retained. I am as much as thee and the trick even so is mine.
DR. PRINCE: You are a continuing subconscious dream of Mrs. Curran.

PATIENCE: And what be thee, Sirrah? Nay, egad—thee art a sorry dream—over too much curd.
DR. PRINCE: Mrs. Curran probably pondered over some old stories when she was young. You are a dream founded upon them. She, perhaps, has forgotten the stories.
PATIENCE: And the lass fellowed an ass. Hast thou then become an asses man and is thy wisdom gleaned from the bray? Or hast thou fellowed with a king and become heady?
DR. PRINCE: Part of the odd words you use, she unconsciously remembers, others she has invented.
PATIENCE: Well, it be a trick—can thee do it?

The remainder of the record of this session with Dr. Prince is incomplete. Again the recorder—presumably Williamina Parrish—failed to note many of Prince's questions, although the answers of Patience are faithfully recorded, useless as they are in this fashion. Here, however, are some coherent fragments of the remainder of this meeting:

PATIENCE: Well, sirrah, many's the man has crowed and not o'er his ain labor.
DR. PRINCE: But I am not sure of this. She may have studied old words and customs purposely, to invest you.
PATIENCE: Weel then, what be the created thing? I BE. Canst thou deny me? Disseminate of word there be a thing apart which is me. No net of words containeth the zest and salt of personality save that it be uttered through the bein' of that personality. Sirrah, thy tongue be quick and thy wits nimble, yet thou art less thee than I be me. Record thy word and many's the man who spake the same—record mine and bid another for to do the same—I be cunningly contrived —a witch, verily.
DR. PRINCE: Perhaps you are the composite of all the knowledge of the persons who have sat with her. Each left a portion of himself, as it were, to add to the heap.
PATIENCE: The skimmin' o' the pot, eh?
DR. PRINCE: You are the result of her suppressed desires to become a great writer.
PATIENCE: Weel, you ken not the Folly then. Could she saddle me as a nag to job her to the mart, she might—but ne'er would she jog with me.
DR. PRINCE: Why do you not write of the history of your time?
PATIENCE: With pots and brush-broom, flax and bake and brew and the law and the clod wench, aside; you ask me this?

DR. PRINCE: Mrs. Curran is a hysteric. Of course, she does not know this—hysterics seldom do.
PATIENCE: Weel enough, if I be sic a thing a-settin' athin her—why be it not another fetch a fruitful ill?
DR. PRINCE: If I were allowed to hypnotize her I could find the solution of what they call the mystery—either the things she has forgotten would come out or she would confess her imposture.
PATIENCE: Mayhap, and yet I say me, shouldst thee sift the sand thee'st find few pebbles.
DR. PRINCE: You are witty, but wit is not logic.
PATIENCE: Nay, but wit unseats logic.
DR. PRINCE: You are clever in evading.
PATIENCE: Nay—na' wit is real wit save it has logic. Wit that has ridicule may part the skirt of a king and show him naked.
DR. PRINCE: I am too gallant, even to a fancied woman, to employ your methods.
PATIENCE: And I, sirrah, to a dullard return the same compliment. List ye, sirrah, no less fancy art thou. Flesh is a cheap garment. What shalt thou leave of thyself? Even thy labor is of shadowed stuff. Return and announce thee! I say thou art no less fancy than I.
DR. PRINCE: It has been a bore to live here—why should I want to live again?
PATIENCE: Thee art ne'er a good gamester.
DR. PRINCE: Couldn't I get out of living after my body dies, if I should prefer this?
PATIENCE: Sirrah, somewhere in chaos is God—go seek Him.
DR. PRINCE: Were you not bored not to have anyone to talk to for more than two hundred years?
PATIENCE: This be nae true.
DR. PRINCE: It seems to me from what spirits, so called, say—that the other world is far less interesting than this.
PATIENCE: Aye, and fra' what men, so called, call wisdom, I would call death chaos more amusing.
DR. PRINCE: May I question you about your romances? I suppose you had many?
PATIENCE: Weel, I say again—I be a wench.
DR. PRINCE: If you can so fight a sham battle, what would happen if I got you really angry?
PATIENCE: Weel, bein' a wench and ha'in a likin' to a lout, I'd lay my tongue light.
DR. PRINCE: May I submit an odd subject [for a poem by Patience]? "The Toad and the Fly."

Patience, as usual without any hesitation, gave these lines:

> Wattled, blink-eyed,
> Rested 'pon a lily pad of ease—
> Sunnin' neath a golden sun—
> Baskin' neath a frost white moon.
> Lollin' easeful, gazin' at the stars,
> He sits—hungered.
> An instant's whirr—
> A dartling fly seeketh and is gone.
> How like to wisdom!

DR. PRINCE: I heard Dr. Sullivan speak, on a great occasion, after two other men of world-wide fame had spoken . . . and his words were far more impressive than theirs, though he was quiet in body and calm in speech. Can you give a poem on such a subject, suggesting the secret of his power?

PATIENCE: Aye, sirrah—humility—certainty—faith and understanding:

> In Nazareth, a Shepherd bruised His foot
> Upon a stone,
> Layed the hand of labor 'pon a staff,
> Sweat beneath the sun,
> Hungered—knew life and living.
>
> In Nazareth a Shepherd spake,
> And His words were intermingled
> With the patter of sheep
> And the cry of the ewe.
> He knew living.
>
> In Nazareth a Shepherd spake,
> No mighty word,
> A word of understand,
> Tuned of Hope,
> Bathed of Memory;
> And the foundation of today
> Is that word.

Dr. Prince said good night to Patience and she responded with these words:

> Tomorrow comes
> A new, new tomorrow;

> Think on it, my beloveds—
> And then another morrow,
> And morrows and morrows yet to come.
> This instant we commune,
> No coming morrow, but shall hold
> This record, this holy instant.
> Am I a shadow—
> I, who love thee, with a love like thine?
> I, who speak as thou speaketh?
> Share as thou sharest?
> Then blessed be the coming morrow
> For then a twain of shadows we shall be.

DR. PRINCE: I am glad to meet you now, if not in the sixteenth century.
PATIENCE: Weel, sirrah, I say—I be a wench.[11]

During the next weeks Prince continued to attend many of the regular sessions with Patience in addition to carrying out his announced tasks of interviewing many persons who had been present at the sessions through the years, or had been connected with the Currans in some other way. He also traveled to the little mining town in the foothills of the Ozarks where Mrs. Curran had gone to school and talked with some of her old classmates about her and about such significant issues as the amount and type of reading she had done as a youngster.

At the meetings with Patience, Prince asked her many detailed questions about her books and her philosophy. Always he addressed her with respect and courtesy and always as a separate individual in her own right.

From one of those sessions a few weeks later the record gives a revealing account of the working of Mrs. Curran's mind just before receiving the words of a poem from Patience:

> DR. PRINCE: Now, I will ask Patience for a short composition—poems on two very diverse subjects. The first will be on the subject of that picture out in the hall. [It was a portrait of Nino Ronchi, an Italian artist and friend of Mrs. Curran's, which had been painted by Williamina Parrish.]
> MRS. CURRAN (after a short pause): I don't like what I see. It isn't pretty. It is a pretty *picture*, however. It is a bowl or cup; it might be jade only it is clear. In it is a wine that is yellow, but the yellow

wine has green edges—as the edge of the cup seeps into the wine. Now then, I seem sick myself. And I am listless—terribly listless and I seem to stretch out—long—just stretch out and hold something in my hand; I hold this cup—it is quite wide out and deep. The proportion is far too wide for a wine glass. [She draws a picture to illustrate.] The stem is so slender I can hardly feel it in my fingers and instead of it being a stem of glass, it is a very thorny little branch—full of thorns. It pricks my fingers. It seems to be growing and this bowl is attached to it. It seems to have a living quality. It is a living thing because there is an essence in it which gets into the wine. The bowl part is very shallow. And I have this in my hands. I am not getting words yet and I am so tired, so listless; just as though I were doped—only it isn't dope—a sort of lethargy. Now I lick my lips and they are dry—like corn husks. They almost rattle when I put them together and I open my mouth and go to speak. I am not me—I am this thing; and when I speak there comes from my mouth a green smoke that matches this cup exactly. The same color, but it is like a smoke and I want to get rid of it—just spit it out; it almost stifles me and I am sick all over and I want to speak, but the speech is an effort. [She pauses.] Now wait; something funny has happened. How can I tell you this? My eyes dropped out—like a doll's eyes—just fell out and instead of having eyes, I just have pictures there where the eyes were—weird things, and they don't match—these pictures don't match.

DR. PRINCE: When you get this last part, the glass has disappeared?

MRS. CURRAN: No, the glass is still in my hand and I am still in this position—just hang—draped on a chair, listless. And these eyes have dropped out—I think it is a sense of seeing wrong. The whole thing seems to be wrong and I see nothing else but that. I never was so tired—that terrible tired. I just feel *worse* than *wearied*.

DR. PRINCE: You don't only see these things, you experience the sensations also, do you not?

MRS. CURRAN: I not only get visual things, but the actual sensation. The thing I feel in this is as though I had moved up to a wall and couldn't get past—just as though it were no use trying.

She paused again, for a few seconds, and then gave the following poem, for which the visions she had seen apparently had been a preamble:

> *Here is my cup—*
> *Frail, white-lipped—and I*

> O, I would sup,
> But the dream is old.
> I know dreams;
> I have fed upon them,
> And there is no substance in the feeding.
> I would sup.
> There is wine but when I have supped—
> There is nothing but more dreams;
> Phantasies, phantoms, writhing mysteries,
> Bits of chaos which I cannot mould.
> I am oppressed with dreaming,
> Weary of fancy;
> I am hungered for reality;
> I am famished as a she-wolf
> With a brood to suckle;
> For I would feed—aye,
> I would feed the brats of fancy—
> And there is nothing but dream—
> Mocking dream.
> God, what a sup!
> Green as jade;
> Poisonous as the venom of an asp.
> Great God, give me REALITY.[12]

As part of his investigation Prince wrote an article titled "The Riddle of Patience Worth," which appeared in the July 1926 issue of *Scientific American*. In it he requested that anyone with any knowledge that might have a bearing on the case, anyone who perhaps would know of some childhood influences on Pearl Curran that might have provided her with the language and knowledge of the Patience Worth writings, contact him and provide him with such information. He was to announce later that no such information ever was brought forth.

In the article Prince described the history of the case and said of it: "Psychologically or psychically, the case is the most amazing one of its kind in history." He related some of the unusual requests he had made of Patience during his stay in St. Louis and how she had passed all the tests with ease: "A poem of 25 lines was demanded, the lines beginning with the letters of the alphabet, except X, in due order. It was instantly dictated. I asked for a conversation between a lout and a maid at a country fair, to be couched in archaic prose, and a poem in modern English on 'The Folly of Atheism'—first a passage of one and then a passage of the other, thus alternating to the end. This seemed to me an impossible mental feat. But it was done so rapidly as to tax the recorder—four passages of humorous prose abounding in archaic locutions, alternating with four parts of a poem in modern English of lofty and spiritual tenor; and when assembled each factor made a perfectly articulated little piece of literature."

Some months later Walter Franklin Prince's voluminous report of his exhaustive investigation and analysis was published, under the imprint of his Boston Society for Psychical Research, as *The Case of Patience Worth*. Publication of the book served to bring Mrs. Curran and Patience Worth briefly back into the foreground as a topic of conversation and argument. But, except in psychic circles, the book did not reach a wide reading audience and did not have the impact of Yost's original volume on the case more than ten years earlier.

There was a perceptible reaction to the book among the higher echelons of psychic researchers in England. Leaders of the pioneering Society for Psychical Research had long been aware of the Patience Worth case and were keenly interested in it. But their interest had never, until this time, taken the concrete form of discussion in their prestigious, widely circulated publication, the *Proceedings* of the S.P.R.

In the November 1927 issue of the *Proceedings*, however, there was a review of Prince's work by F. C. S. Schiller, a distinguished professor of psychology and philosophy at Oxford University and a leading figure in psychical research in Britain. The review summarized the background of the Patience Worth case and quoted some of the claims that had been made about the language used by Patience. Apparently accepting the analysis by Yost of the language in Patience's early novel *Telka*, Schiller wrote that "When we are told [about the language in *Telka*], we realize that we are face to face with what may fairly be called a philological miracle."

His study of Prince's book, Schiller went on, led him to three possible hypotheses for the case, each of them presenting certain obstacles of its own: 1) spirit possession; 2) Patience was a creature of Mrs. Curran's subconscious mind; 3) the case involved a revelation of the Absolute, some form of "cosmic reservoir" which has pooled the literary efforts of the ages.

After briefly discussing each of the alternatives Schiller wrote: "What, then, shall we do? I suppose that at present it is still *safer* to credit 'Patience Worth' to the unconscious and to class her, officially, as Mrs. Curran's 'secondary self.' But it is impossible to be comfortable about this theory, and it should certainly not be held fanatically."

Schiller announced himself as quite willing to subscribe to the conclusions that had been painstakingly reached by Prince (see next chapter) and then finished his review of the book by saying: "The general impression of the case on my mind is to deepen the conviction that orthodox psychology and orthodox philosophy are both very far from having plumbed the depths of the soul, and that it is unreasonable to require an open-minded man to endorse their prejudices."[13]

Except for the book by Prince, which contained liberal samples of Patience's writings, her words were having little more success in getting through to large numbers of people during the late 1920s.

Herman Behr paid for the publication of *Telka* in 1928, again with the imprint of the Patience Worth Publishing Company of Brooklyn, New York. He also had arranged for publication of *Telka* and *Light from Beyond* in Germany, after translating the works into German. And there is some evidence that a few other works were privately printed. I came across a small printed volume titled *Patience Worth—An Easter Greeting* which was composed of short poems written in early 1925. The front inside cover of the book contained a list of the Patience Worth books, but the only imprint read: "Brentano's New York City." Whether Behr paid for the printing of the book and arranged for it to be sold at the famous New York bookstore or whether Brentano's sponsored the publication of the volume is not clear.

An occasional religious or spiritualist magazine also carried a poem or two by Patience, and some of her works appeared from time to time in the publication of the American Society for Psychical Research. But, in general, the words of Patience Worth were being heard now only by the small groups of those who still devotedly followed her. The mass audience had been pretty well forgotten. In New York and Los Angeles there were followers who met periodically to read aloud the writings of Patience and to discuss their meaning. Dotsie Smith, Mrs. Curran's old friend, was the guiding spirit of the Los Angeles group.

Patience met "in person" with her admirers every once in a while. The record indicates trips by Mrs. Curran to Lake Forest, Illinois, and Orange, New Jersey, for sessions in the homes of friends. In October 1928 she was invited by the minister of St. Mark's-in-the-Bouwerie Church in New York City to spend an evening with his parishioners in commemoration of All Saints Day. Mrs. Curran was introduced to the congregation by Walter Franklin Prince.

About this time Mrs. Curran apparently had received an offer to go on tour for a full year, lecturing about Patience and communicating with her. She was undecided about accepting, but the question was answered for her by Patience, who commented:

> Behold, they would mask me, beloved,
> Take a pence for a song I would fling free.
> Couldst thou fling a pence at a nightingale?[14]

Though rejecting the request for a lecture tour, she did continue to go out of town periodically to speak. One of her appearances, in 1929, was in Detroit's well-known Town Hall Series at the Cass Theater.

Late in 1926 Mrs. Curran remarried. Her new husband was Dr. Henry H. Rogers, a retired physician considerably older than Mrs. Curran. As a matter of fact, he and his first wife had known her family when she was a teen-ager. Dr. Rogers' health was poor and the marriage was to last only a few years before it ended in divorce. Dr. Rogers apparently took little or no part in the Patience Worth activities (although he had been one of those interviewed by Prince during his investigation) because his name is rarely found in the case record as being present at the sessions during the time of his marriage to Mrs. Curran. (After the marriage, the record for a time referred to her as "Mrs. Curran Rogers" and then shifts over to "Mrs. Rogers" but, for the sake of simplicity, I shall continue to refer to her throughout as Mrs. Curran.)

In St. Louis one of the organizations most enthusiastic about

Patience Worth was, not surprisingly, the local chapter of the Theosophical Society, which sponsored on a number of occasions "An Evening with Patience Worth." A St. Louis newspaper gave a detailed account of one such evening in 1929 under the headline: "PATIENCE WORTH," GHOSTLY POETESS, EXTEMPORIZES. Here are excerpts from the newspaper report:

"Without a ouija board, Mrs. Pearl L. Rogers, sponsor and interceptor of the prolific and ghostly 'Patience Worth,' lectured and rattled off compositions in free verse last night before members of the Theosophical Society. . . .

"A tall woman, blue-eyed, and with greying hair, Mrs. Rogers chatted pleasantly with her audience, told funny stories, talked about 'Patience' as a distinct personality, and toward the end of the evening asked her hearers to suggest subjects for poems that 'Patience' might compose immediately.

"The audience called for a poem on Life After Death. On Success. On Heaven. On Duty. On the Soul. Mrs. Rogers, her subject given her, strode slowly from one side of the platform to the other. Back of her, at a table, sat her secretary, pen in hand.

" 'Heaven,' she repeated. 'Heaven.'

"In her hand was a green lace handkerchief which she placed intermittently to her forehead, to her lips.

"When the audience called for a poem on prohibition, Mrs. Rogers enthusiastically clapped her hands and burst into a roar of laughter.

" 'I must tell you Patience's joke about prohibition,' she said, striving to repress chuckles. 'Someone asked her for a poem on spirits and she said—"Distilled or deceased?" Don't you love that? I like her when she's saucy. You heard what she said when we started out?'

"Mrs. Rogers again laughed. The invisible Patience, as the evening began, had first made fun of her interpreter by saying—'Look, behold her 'n a white crown. Beflauntin' a brazen wench's pettiskirt.'

"Calling attention to her grey hair and her shimmering white robe, Mrs. Rogers laughed, commenting on Patience's sauciness.

" 'Success. Success,' Mrs. Rogers intoned.

"She closed her eyes and swayed from one foot to the other.

"'Back of this word is a fat self and a lean soul,' she whispered.
"'Patience wasn't at her best tonight,' Mrs. Rogers said in conclusion. 'Let's see. Twenty-seven poems tonight. Three thousand words. Not so bad, but Patience really wasn't at her best.'"[15]

One of Patience's most pleasant characteristics was her sheer unpredictability. She was willing, for example, to comment confidently and authoritatively on the most abstruse subjects, yet at other times would bluntly declare her ignorance. For almost anyone living in the United States during the first third of the twentieth century, a commonly accepted synonym for the utterly mysterious, almost the unknowable, was Einstein's Theory of Relativity. To understand, even in a general way, what was meant by Relativity, millions of Americans readily acknowledged that one would have to be a veritable "Einstein." Yet, one evening, Patience was asked to speak on "Relativity" and proceeded, without a moment's hesitation, to give this rather swaggering discourse:

"What be the mystery in this thing? It be but the law of harmony, which wert the first law. Yea, it be the law of kindred like unto kindred like. Man hath forgotten, in his tumultuous day and his discord and his confusions, the simplest law, which is that of harmony. Look ye 'pon it—this honey of God which holdeth one atom unto another and keepeth the universes spinning each in its own orbit, and outstrippeth man's imagination—this magic which hath planted in each man, that which is kindred with God, which maketh man to itch at conquest, to fret at the fetters of flesh—aye, and maketh his spirit to leap free of its fetters, for it is unfettered, limited only by man's own limitations, his egotry—which undoeth his humility—this thing a man hath called a mouthing word, aye, and hath forgot that God writ that simple law in the first urge of the first atom, and left the magic of His being as the honey which hangeth all things together. Who hath made such an word? He hath climbed a mountain when he might have found it beneath a sand's grain."[16]

Yet, on another occasion, when Patience was asked to discuss "Interstellar Worlds," she commented simply: "Gad! What a mouthin' for a wee wench. I ken not o' it. Yet I ken when a wench should say she kenneth not!"[17]

During 1929 Mrs. Curran and her friends compiled a group of

poems which Patience had written on various aspects of a garden, in which she related the flowers, birds, and insects to her philosophy of life. They discussed possibilities of getting the small collection of poems published, including asking the ever-generous Father Behr to sponsor the publication. Mrs. Curran was reluctant to ask any further favors of Behr, yet she knew that there was little chance that a commercial publisher would accept the poems, which the publishers would regard as having virtually no market value.

Discouraged at her continued inability to transmit Patience's works to the audience she felt they merited, Mrs. Curran one day put this question to Patience: "Is it your wish, Patience, that I continue to pour out your words as fast as I can, with no thought of their ultimate goal?"

And Patience made this rather poignant response:

"Beloved, I have delivered my trust and my faith, what more can I do? He casteth a cheap pence who BEGGETH for to sell his ware, and no sic an ware as a script may be marted save through hunger and that hunger be fed by the words therein. Wisdom which be befogged of creed and man's mouthing and his imagination may wound well, but it becometh ash beside the simplicity of real wisdom. Man may not create with words the plan of heaven nor the way of the spirit, nor the justice of life or living. Nay, the law IS and is simplicity. Man rooted in flesh and once he hath cast his flesh, his spirit be free, untrammelled of flesh forever. Man's rebirth is of spirit not of flesh. What I have writ from the first unto the last script, holdeth simple logic. And I say me, the price which I have paid for this communion with day, man may not comprehend. The grain is thine, entrusted unto them that love me that it be sown. Today IS—tomorrow may never be—for THEE. At thy labor, then, that THY task is well done."[18]

In the summer of 1930 Pearl Curran finally heeded the longtime pleas of her old friend Dotsie Smith and, with her family, left St. Louis for good and moved to California. Mrs. Smith had for some years been serving as Patience's emissary in the Los Angeles area, organizing reading and discussion groups and giving talks on Patience and her message. She promised Mrs. Curran a warm and sympathetic reception from her admirers. For several months after their arrival Mrs. Curran and her family lived with Mrs. Smith, then took up residence in Santa Monica.

Soon after her move Mrs. Curran began a busy schedule of personal appearances in the Los Angeles area. Many of the sessions were held at Mrs. Smith's retreat in the mountains near the city, which she had named "Patience Worth's Sanctuary." Several of the meetings, the record shows, took place at the home of Mr. and Mrs. Douglas Fairbanks.

Patience was kept busy at the sessions, as always, by requests for her comments on major topics of the day. At one such meeting, for example:

On Hoover: "His calm disturbs. His justice seemeth slow. His surety is a perfect thing, and his task shall be well wrought."

On Mahatma Gandhi: "Lit of an holy fire, a bearer of simplicity to a complicated day. Gad, what can the answer be?"

On Universal Peace: "A fine wish, but a wry hope."

On Time: "A jest, man would for to measure it. Egad, this is insolence. Time is naught but being."

On Predestination: "Nae sic 'n thing, beloved, nae sic 'n thing. That God who in His cunning cast Creation from His finger tips, as pebbles cast, writ no CERTAIN law. Man scribes his AIN SCRIPT."

On Evolution: "Man wert and is; if he becometh more, it be the measure of his intake."[19]

In the fall of 1930 Mrs. Curran went on a brief lecture tour into Washington, Oregon, and Idaho. The record indicates that she was well received at every stop and got a good deal of coverage in the local newspapers where she spoke.

At the Los Angeles sessions celebrities from various fields were often in attendance. Within one two-week period the record indicated the presence of Mrs. Jack Holt (wife of the popular movie star), writer Upton Sinclair, and Mr. and Mrs. Douglas Fairbanks.

One of the unusual things about Patience, given the circumstances of her appearance and the guise in which she appeared, was her continual disdain for most of those claiming clairvoyance or the ability to prophesy. At one of the Los Angeles sessions a guest who had taken up astrology asked Patience, "What of the influence on life of moon and stars?"

Patience tersely replied, "As a wench I hae heared they be monstrous fine for trystin' but for the governin' of man's lot they be large for man's swallow."[20]

There was one project on which Mrs. Curran was engaged after her arrival in Los Angeles which bears mention only because it represents such a discordant interjection in the voluminous song of Patience Worth. It is strangely, unexplainably incongruous.

The record indicates that Mrs. Curran was working on a book of short poems to be called "Light Wines and Cocktails." The record, compiled during this period by Mrs. Smith and other friends, is not completely clear but implies that the poems were by Patience because they are included in the Patience Worth Record and are noted as "given to Mrs. Curran Rogers." Yet they are so awful, so indescribably banal and trivial, that they are a total departure from the other work of Patience. Herewith a few mercifully brief samples of "Light Wines and Cocktails":

AFRAID

Love came to live with me,
I gave him bed. . . .
He took the rest
And thankless fled.
I be-wept no tear,
I wanted him to go,
I was afraid of love. . . .
I loved him so.

EVEN

I sold my soul and body for a song,
It wasn't new or old, it wasn't long.
I lost the price, I didn't give a dang
Love was a snake, I pulled its fang.

WHATHAP

They told me God was in the sky,
I believed it then—I know not why.
And now they say that love is hell. . . .
And I'm in love again—Oh Well!

NAUGHTY

If I should write the naughty things
I really, truly think. . . .
I'd have to burn the paper,
Or print it in red ink.[21]

Aside from the fact that these little concoctions are in rhyme and Patience almost never wrote rhyming lines, they are so witless, so devoid of any merit that we probably are justified in assuming that the compilers of the record got confused, or were misled by Mrs. Curran, and that these non-intoxicating wines and cocktails were entirely the product of the housewife from Missouri's Lead Belt, unaided or influenced by her more celebrated collaborator. Not surprisingly, they never were published.

On December 22, 1931, Mrs. Curran was married in Los Angeles for the third time—to Robert Wyman, to whom she had been engaged when she was nineteen, back in Missouri.

Mrs. Curran and her two daughters and Wyman and his teenage daughter from a prior marriage took up residence in Culver City, an area of Los Angeles. She kept busy with her Patience Worth activities, making a series of talks on the Wisdom and Philosophy of Patience Worth and appearing before a meeting of the prestigious American Society of Psychical Research, the same organization created and led in the years prior to 1920 by her old antagonist, Professor Hyslop.

She also had begun receiving a new long work by Patience Worth. It was a play about Shakespeare, which had been given the title "An Elizabethan Mask (three days in the life of William Shakespeare)." Mrs. Curran was assisted in the copying and editing of the work by Max Behr, son of her old patron, who also lived in the Los Angeles area.

In addition to the ever-present questions about world affairs and personalities in the news, the other consistent feature of the continuing sessions with Patience were the queries put to her about death and the hereafter. Put end to end, her responses likely could be codified into an Eschatology of Patience Worth. In the almost two decades of her existence, Patience never had varied her central doctrine: The law of God is a simple one and its key word is "Love." And, at death, man casts off the fetters of his body and lives on in spirit. There is no such thing as reincarnation; man, "once uttered," is forever.

At a session in 1933, Patience once again summarized her views for a guest, a Dr. Belmont:

> DR. BELMONT: Will I meet and recognize you when I go where you are?

PATIENCE: What be I save my word unto thee: And do I present unto thee through word my flesh? Nay, but the salt o' what I be. That thou hast come upon me a-here be not by chance, but that I hae sought thee. Thereby ye shall for to know that lo'e I ye so, thereby hae I sought and followed thee. A-here I shall do likewise when thou comest as a traveler unto my way. Aye, sire, wi' a glad voice I shall call me "Aday," and thou shalt for to know—for word be but the out-symbol o' an in-urge. Here the urge taketh the place o' the tongue.
DR. BELMONT: What becomes of the objective mind which we leave behind at death?
PATIENCE: Thy objectivity be the garment o' the flesh reality; but thy in-man kenneth little or careth little at the freeing. To be freed be for to be waked. Ye tarry not at the wakin', sire. Nay, ye waken and become eloquent o' the here. Thy doubts become clear, for doubt be a trick o' flesh and falleth with it.
DR. BELMONT: But what is the immediate experience at death?
PATIENCE: A bit weary wi' the fetters, a yawn, a blink and the wakin'.[22]

In March 1934 word came from New York that Herman Behr, Patience's devoted friend and admirer, had died. He had spent much time and money in publishing two Patience Worth volumes in this country and also translating them into German and publishing them in Europe as well. Patience offered messages of tribute to him and affirmed that he had joined her in the "here."

A few weeks later, on April 15, Patience Wee—the girl always considered by Patience Worth to be her own child and whose adoption by the Currans in 1916 at Patience's request created national news—was married. She was not quite eighteen years old. After the ceremony, Pearl Curran asked Patience for her blessing and was given these words: "Look you beloved mine, the task be done and thou hast come unto the estate of womanhood. 'Tis thine the task now for to shed thy love in selfless ministration unto thy day. Thy mither hath fulfilled her promise for to nurture thee and thy flesh mither hath dealt unstintin'. That which thou art shall now come to be—it hath no part with mitherin', for the mitherin' be o'er—now cometh the tide when thou shalt meet the twain who have served thee in lovin' as woman unto woman.

"Thou hast received richly and wi' nayself from her unto whom I have trusted thee. Serve thou in such fashion the day that shall be thine. I shall hover thee and look to see the fulfillment of the woman thou art. The answer thou shalt scribe in the service thou deliverest. Thou hast love—it is thine—and he whom thou hast chosen taketh on the task. 'Pon thee love be showered. The day is thine, oh my bairn. I have fulfilled the hope o' my heart and the promise I gave—not alone—for I have borrowed o' love for the labor.

"When thou leavest the seclusion o' the roof 'neath which thou hast nested, I shall follow as a shadow thy day, but the task o' lovin' now be thine. Born o' love, ta'en in love, nurtured o' love—he who takest thee unto him needs to take thee in love or his day shall fall short. Remember, love be thy talisman—I be satisfied dost thou jealously guard it.

"May God smile upon thee and keep thee close. May ye keep me in thy heart."

The blessing was signed "Thy Mither."

During 1935 and 1936 the written record of Patience Worth is fragmentary and lapsing. There are gaps of as much as six months in the chronological recording of her writings. Whether the writings were abandoned to a certain extent by Mrs. Curran or whether the friends to which she had entrusted the keeping of the record were less than diligent, we cannot determine. It is obvious, though, that the group of Patience Worth loyalists, led by Mrs. Smith, who had continued for several years to meet once or twice a week with Mrs. Curran for talks with Patience, was no longer so active. The record noted that a meeting on April 12, 1936, served as a reunion, since it was the group's first gathering in almost two years.

Meanwhile, Mrs. Curran was continuing her work with Max Behr on the Shakespeare play and occasionally still appeared before clubs and other organizations in the Los Angeles area.

In March 1937 Patience gave one of her last recorded statements on immortality:

LIFE AFTER DEATH

Life finite be the prologue unto life eternal. Who sayeth "life after death" hath jested, for behold ye he acclaims his doubt. The compliment o' the Creator be the pith o' Himself given eternally unto man—Once he hath uttered him, then He hath separated an atom o' His being from Himself and that atom contains the eternal everness o' Him. The jest be that man confronted wi' the endlessness and infiniteness o' His labor could e'en utter the question. Man's day being finite and his pith infinite, the war between man's flesh and his spiritual pith createth doubt, for the flesh sayeth "NAY" while the spirit yearns and hath not the power to endow infinite conception upon the finite vessel o' flesh. This be right and mete, for earth be but the rooting place where the spirit taketh form through flesh, the whathap choice o' man at his begatting limiteth or endoweth the flesh nohap—once uttered, man be ever uttered and the prologue which be his day 'pon earth announceth his entrance upon his everlasting BEING. The soul BE man, is—but his BEING is eternal.[23]

On Thanksgiving Day, November 25, 1937, came the final communication from Patience Worth. Max Behr, happy over the progress being made on the Shakespeare play, asked Patience for a Thanksgiving prayer. Patience's response to such requests usually was concise, though satisfying the need of the person making the request. This time, though, her response was unusually long. The prayer, as recorded by Behr, covers two pages of single-spaced material.

It began: "Before Thee, oh God of the universes, with humbled heart and proud mien, I give thanks. For I have beheld Thy countenance in its sublimity and its grandeur. I have communed with Thee through the ordered symphony of Thy faultless revelation of Thyself through man's finite limitations and may now reveal unto my brothers the beauty and perfection of Thy constant brotherhood with him."

Later came this passage: "If, then, oh God of all things, I may say unto Thee, 'Behold Thy servant!,' how proud, then, be my labour. For I have been at Thy task, a Kingly task! And if my hand be the instrument which Thou, in Thy creatorship, have used to draw the sable curtains of doubt and point unto the glory-vistas beyond, then am I mute with wonder and bow me in simple acknowledgement of the greatest grace delivered unto any man."

The prayer concluded with the following words. They are wholly appropriate as the conclusion to a Thanksgiving prayer, yet they also bear a strange, ineffable, wonderful sense of glory, of completion. It seems somehow compellingly *right*, almost mystically fitting, that, after more than twenty-four years, these should be the last words uttered by Patience Worth:

"My heart overflows. I am exalted. I am Thy child, and Thou hast *graced me*. Take thou my labour, oh gracious God, as but Thy grace reflected, and know Thy son glories in that reflection. Accept, then, the Alleluia my soul proclaims before the WONDER."[24]

There came at this time the final, and perhaps most significant, assertion by her followers that Patience was able, when the situation warranted, to reveal things otherwise unknowable. Such claims, as we have mentioned, were not prominent in the record of the case, but they were there: the birth of Patience Wee, the death of Mrs. Parrish, for example, and others.

Mrs. Curran had not been in ill health. However, according to Mrs. Smith, around the middle of November 1937 Mrs. Curran said to her: "Oh, Dotsie, Patience has just shown me the end of the road and you will have to carry on as best you can."[25]

On Thanksgiving Day Mrs. Curran caught cold. Pneumonia developed and she was taken to a Los Angeles hospital where she died on December 3, 1937.

At the funeral service the small group of relatives, friends, and followers gathered to pay their final respects to the woman who for almost a quarter of a century had been the faithful voice, the "harp," of Patience Worth. Max Behr read several of the Patience Worth poems and reminded the mourners of Patience's comment: "What a paltry pence is death to buy eternity; what a light price to pay for an everlasting abiding place."

He repeated Patience's statement made at the time of his father's death: "This be a day to exult, for the Here be far richer and the Knight hath rid home wearing the colors, his shield battered, his trappings worn, but his spear bright."

And this poem also was read:

> *Bairn o' my heart, art lonely?*
> *Weary and wonder-eyed at the day?*
>
> *Bairn o' my heart, art lonely?*
> *Soul-worn and tired o' play?*

> *What though the morning seems fearful;*
> *What though the twilight be grey?*
>
> *Bairn o' my heart, art weary?*
> *Lay doon thy head upon me.*
>
> *I would sing o' the sea, o' the morning,*
> *O' the lark, o' the sun, o' the lea.*
> *I would sing such a fanciful singing,*
> *Bairn o' my heart, for thee.*
>
> *Bairn o' my heart, art weary?*
> *And tears bedimmin' thine e'e,*
>
> *Bairn o' my heart, art weary?*
> *Then lay doon thy head upon me.*[26]

The official record of Patience Worth, which was begun in 1913, was closed on December 6, 1937, after 4,375 pages, with these final words, spoken at Mrs. Curran's grave: "And thus it is that we take leave of her, knowing well that her head is resting upon the bosom of Patience, whose words are as arms that would cradle the world."

With the death of Pearl Curran there came one last small flurry of publicity before the story of Patience Worth sank back into the fog of passing time. The St. Louis and Los Angeles newspapers of course carried news of the death, along with brief reminiscences of the case. The report from Los Angeles prompted the *New York Herald-Tribune* to run a nostalgic editorial a couple of days later in which Patience was credited, perhaps unduly, with starting a national ouija-board fad.

About two months after Mrs. Curran's death a national newspaper Sunday supplement ran a long feature article about the case, illustrated with photos of Mrs. Curran and even one of Patience Wee as a child, dressed in the old-fashioned bonnet and dress which a friend had made for her in accordance with the request of Patience.

The death of Mrs. Curran prompted extensive discussion of the case in the *Journal* of the American Society for Psychical Research. A lengthy unsigned "editorial note" in the April 1938 issue of the *Journal* declared that Mrs. Curran's death brought to mind "one of the most tantalizing cases in the history of psychical research." It had involved "literary genius exhibited . . . in contrast with the lack of intellectuality and the barely average education displayed by the normal mind of the medium . . . extraordinary vocabulary of Old English words used extensively in the Patience Worth scripts. This vocabulary is very puzzling to the philologist." The article went on to cite the objections registered by Professor Hyslop in 1916 and, as described earlier, went on to refute them, one by one.[27]

The same issue of the A.S.P.R. *Journal* carried the first of two articles reminiscing about Mrs. Curran and Patience Worth by a New York lady named Hettie Rhoda Mead, who apparently had known Mrs. Curran well and had attended many of the sessions in New York City. Mrs. Mead wrote: "The world has lost one of its greatest mediums. The phenomenon of Patience Worth has not been surpassed, if indeed equalled, in the annals of psychic literature."[28] The second article, appearing in the May issue of the *Journal*, summarized the religious thought of Patience Worth with many quotes from her poems.

Ten years later, in January 1948, the same Hettie Rhoda Mead wrote another article for the A.S.P.R. *Journal* on "The Songs of Patience Worth." In the article were a couple of references to Mrs. Curran that characterized her quite differently from any of the other material published about her. Mrs. Mead described Mrs. Curran as not cultured and refined, but "a trifle 'wild' and even at times vulgar." The New York friends of Patience Worth, according to Mrs. Mead, were devoted to Mrs. Curran and liked her personality, but were "often much disturbed at her incredible conduct in the presence of very conservative people."[29] The exact nature of this "incredible conduct" remains unexplained. It was the only reference of this type to Mrs. Curran that has come to my attention, and I could not otherwise verify or clarify it.

As the years went by, the story of Patience Worth and her writings largely disappeared from public attention. Yet it was too fascinating a story to remain completely buried. Billy Rose, the colorful Broadway producer, for a time wrote (or had ghost-written for him) a syndicated newspaper column called "Pitching

Horseshoes." It contained a variety of anecdotes about his own life and any other tale that made good copy. In January 1950 an entire Billy Rose column was devoted to a retelling of the Patience Worth case, which was labeled "this greatest-of-all literary riddle."[30]

In 1946 a British writer named R. F. Malone published (in Dublin) a slim volume called *Patience Worth, Temptress,* which briefly summarized the case and offered a number of samples of Patience's poetry. The material in the book seemed to me to have been mostly culled from the writings of Yost and Prince.

In 1954 *Coronet* magazine carried an article reviving the case and its never-solved mysteries, and a feature story of the same genre was run by the *St. Louis Post-Dispatch* in 1956. The latter article included a comment by Emily Grant Hutchings, who had sat at the ouija board with Pearl Curran in 1913 when Patience first appeared and who in 1956 was about eighty years old. Mrs. Hutchings told the newspaper writer that she still, after all the years, believed completely in the reality of Patience and that she never had doubted that Patience was truly the spirit of a woman who had died long before.

As mentioned early in this book, writers on psychic subjects always have referred to the Patience Worth case as a classic one. Some of the references by recent British writers already have been quoted. Arthur Ford, until his death in 1971 perhaps the best-known medium in the United States, wrote a book called *Known but Unknown* in which Patience Worth is discussed, and the case also is given considerable attention in Eleanor Touhey Smith's recent book *Psychic People* and Robert Somerlott's *Here, Mr. Splitfoot.*

Outside the realm of psychic literature, however, the story of Patience Worth has been virtually forgotten. And what is perhaps more unfortunate, her remarkable writings are seldom read any more. The books, those few that were published, are mostly gathering dust on the back shelves of libraries. And, as discussed previously, the poems have been ignored (or perhaps, by now, just forgotten) by the anthologists of poetry in the twentieth century. Typifying the disappearance of the Patience Worth poetry is the ironic fact that, of the thousands of poems written by Patience —many of which were highly praised by Reedy, Braithwaite, and other leading critics of the time—only one Patience Worth poem is even listed in the authoritative *Granger's Index to Poetry*.[31]

With the death of Pearl Curran in 1937, the voice of Patience Worth was stilled.

There have been claims on occasion that other persons have made contact with Patience since 1937. Material in the files of the Missouri Historical Society indicates that a woman in Massachusetts—presumably a spiritualist medium—has claimed communication with Patience. In St. Louis, newspapers reported in 1950 that two local couples claimed to have talked with Patience via their ouija board. (Their claims followed shortly after publication of the Billy Rose column about Patience.) Patience's main concern, according to these people, was to transmit a message from the late magician Thurston to his widow. Patience supposedly wrote that the message would require payment of $1,000 by Mrs. Thurston. (The newspaper stories noted that the claimants may have had in mind the offer of another famed magician, Harry Houdini, of a reward to anyone who could prove, after his death, that he could communicate with the living.)

Obviously none of the claimants have made public any convincing evidence. It would be simple enough to prove: They merely would have to duplicate Pearl Curran's ability, demonstrated repeatedly for twenty-four years, to produce—on request and without hesitation—comments, witty, provocative, pungent comments on thousands of different subjects while, at the same time, also producing literary materials deemed by leading critics of the day to be struck with genius. Until that slight task has been accomplished, any claims that someone has taken Mrs. Curran's place as Patience's earthly communicator must be regarded only as claims still awaiting proving.

So far as we know, the voice of Patience Worth has been silent since 1937. But while it spoke, whether from a fabled spirit land that has teased man's hopes since time immemorial, or from the depths of Pearl Curran's own being, it cast a most magical spell. No matter what her origin, Patience was indeed a unique, colorful, lovable personality—as individual and distinctive as any of your friends or mine.

And though she speaks from the shadows and we cannot, as hard as we strain, quite perceive her outline, her noble message of love and hope still comes through to us with passion and power. Even by the standards of those who say that man's only immortality lies in what he leaves behind him, Patience Worth truly still lives in the strangely beautiful words that she has left for us and for those yet to come.

10

The Analysts

DURING THE twenty-four years that Patience Worth spoke through Pearl Curran, and even after Mrs. Curran's death, a number of persons from various disciplines—fascinated and puzzled by the case—undertook to study it carefully and to offer a reasonable opinion of it.

As we have reported, the scientist of that era perhaps best qualified to investigate the matter—Dr. Morton Prince, authority on cases of personality dissociation—angrily refused to continue his study because Mrs. Curran, fearing that to be "mesmerized" might cause her to lose the ability to communicate further with Patience, would not let him utilize hypnosis. Other psychologists, psychiatrists, and neurologists showed interest in the case over the years and some of them were given cooperation by Mrs. Curran, but such interest usually terminated when the scientist demanded that his subject undergo hypnosis or psychoanalysis and was bluntly rejected.

Other scholars, however, were less dogmatic about methodology and asked only to be allowed to investigate the facts of the case as thoroughly as possible and to have Mrs. Curran honestly answer their questions. Such investigators, so far as I can tell, were given complete freedom by Mrs. Curran to inquire as they pleased and she cooperated fully with them.

The results of several of the more thorough investigations are still available for study. It seems appropriate at this point, after relating the story of Patience Worth, to summarize the major conclusions of these investigations.

The most detailed examination of the facts of the Patience Worth case was made in 1926 by Dr. Walter Franklin Prince. His findings, as mentioned earlier, were published in 1927 by the Boston Society for Psychical Research as *The Case of Patience Worth* and reissued in 1964 by University Books.

Walter Franklin Prince was one of the best known of those comparatively unsung men of psychical research—the professional investigators who devote much of their lives to checking reported cases of psychic phenomena and attempting to determine whether anything actually has occurred that can be reasonably considered to be beyond normal, naturalistic explanation. The major psychical research societies and their staff investigators are not easily awed by claims of psychic phenomena. They demand hard evidence, not simply excited hearsay. Because the vast majority of the cases they investigate do not produce the substantial evidence they require for confirmation as a legitimate psychic phenomenon, the investigators tend to be skeptical and rather hard-nosed about their cases. Such a man—cautious, studious, demanding—was Walter Franklin Prince.

Prince had been a minister in Episcopal and Methodist churches for almost three decades before he turned to psychical research. While an active clergyman he became interested in abnormal psychology and psychic phenomena and began to read widely in these fields. In 1917 he left the clergy and joined the staff of the American Society for Psychical Research as assistant to Professor Hyslop. On Hyslop's death in 1920 Prince succeeded him as Research Officer of the A.S.P.R. Five years later Prince founded the Boston Society for Psychical Research and served as its Research Officer until his death in 1934. He was the author of several books, most of them about cases he had investigated in his career.

The heartland of psychical research has been Great Britain, and its Society for Psychical Research has long been considered "first among equals" among all such organizations in the world. Prince was given the ultimate tribute for a psychic investigator in 1930 when he was elected president of the S.P.R., one of the few times that an American has been so honored. (William James had been one of Prince's predecessors in the post.)

As described previously, Prince contacted Mrs. Curran in 1926 and asked permission to undertake a full-scale investigation of the Patience Worth case, including the questioning of friends and associates going all the way back to her childhood. Permission was granted and Prince devoted much of that year to his investigation and the compilation of his findings into the book to be published the following year. Here are some of the highlights of Prince's findings:

His detailed study of Mrs. Curran's biography revealed (and Mrs. Curran made no attempt to conceal this information) that her uncle had been minister of a spiritualist church in Chicago and claimed to be a medium. She spent some time in Chicago as a teen-ager, studying music and playing piano in her uncle's church. However, she insisted that the experience with spiritualism was repugnant to her.

Prince quoted Mrs. Curran as stating: "I didn't like the crowd that came and the whole thing was repulsive to me. Since then I have had no contacts apart from Patience Worth. I never in my life attended any meetings or seances save those I have referred to. I had read, before 1913, no books on psychical research or Spiritualism whatever. Nor did the ouija-board experiments interest me until Patience Worth came." Her parents, she said, had raised her to regard spiritualism as taboo. She further stated to Prince: "I am not a Spiritualist, but am in sympathy with the furtherance of psychic facts and believe that the pioneers of today are but groping toward fact. I am not a 'medium' in the common sense."[1]

Prince questioned Mrs. Curran intensively about her early reading, and her consistent response was that she had read only the usual popular children's stories. He also tested her by quizzing her on history and found that, among other things, she was not too sure who Andrew Jackson was, although she knew he was an American, and also was under the impression that Henry VIII had been beheaded.[2]

Mrs. Curran insisted to Prince that she never had associated, before the coming of Patience Worth, with persons learned in language, philology, or history. She said, ingenuously, "I associated only with common, busy persons."[3]

Prince presented statements from several persons who had known Mrs. Curran as a young girl and their characterization of her was quite consistent: She had been a pleasant, happy-go-lucky type of youngster, not at all bookish or intellectual or religious.

John Curran's daughter by his prior marriage, Mrs. Curran's stepdaughter, also confirmed to Prince the description of Mrs. Curran provided by others. She had no interest in literature or history, the stepdaughter said, and added: "Nothing of the Patience Worth sort had ever manifested in Mrs. Curran. It was like a bolt out of the clear sky. . . . She had no hallucinations, delusions, hysteria. I never knew her to do odd or queer things—she was like other people." As to Mrs. Curran's veracity, Julia Curran told Prince: "She is the soul of truth. I used to think her too darned truthful. She is the most frank and truthful person I know, almost too much so."[4]

Prince was a scholarly man and apparently rather well versed in poetry. He devoted substantial attention in his report to a comparison of fragments of Patience Worth's poetry with the poetry of famous poets to determine possible influences on her and also the possibility that a subtle kind of plagiarism from the work of great poets had been practiced by Mrs. Curran. From this study, Prince concluded, "Patience Worth is at least as original as other poets are." There are occasional expressions in the work of Patience Worth, Prince readily agrees, that are reminiscent of other poets, but, he says, "It is incredible that poets should not by chance or the natural association of ideas hit upon the same metaphors or brief verbal combinations."[5]

Prince discussed in some detail a session in November 1917 when Patience—in a performance not particularly exceptional for her—dictated thirteen rather striking aphoristic statements in a fifteen-minute period. Of this incident Prince (foreshadowing his over-all conclusion) declared: "Since the general law is that the subconscious can occasionally surpass the feats of the conscious, but only in fields of effort where the conscious has shown aptitude or at least made effort or cherished desire to act, this mass of proverbial literature either evidences an external mind operating through Mrs. Curran's subconsciousness or makes her an exceptional case, transcending previous authentic cases and contradicting what had seemed one of the conclusions of psychology."[6]

We mentioned in an earlier chapter Prince's analysis of a brief child's prayer which Patience had painstakingly composed in 1919 and his conclusion that the prayer was the best child's prayer ever written and that it literally was a masterpiece.

Patience was famous for her "stunts," her rather showy demonstrations of verbal facility in which she often startled her listeners with her pyrotechnics. Prince describes several such incidents which he witnessed. Once he asked Patience to improvise, without pausing, in the varied styles of her several novels. She did so, with no hesitation. Another time, as already mentioned, she was asked by Prince quickly to write a poem with the lines beginning with each letter of the alphabet, except X, in order. She did so, wrote Prince, "at a speed regulated only by the ability of the scribe to take it down in shorthand." On another occasion Prince asked Patience to alternate between a dialogue and a poem, with the subjects for each to be specified by him. He gave her the subjects and, after a pause of less than ten seconds, the two works were reeled off.[7]

In the course of his study Prince came across a book of poems in the dialect of Dorset, that part of southwestern England from which Patience allegedly came. He carefully compared some of the Dorset poems with the language of Patience and pointed out some striking similarities.

So thorough was Prince that he even produced a detailed listing of the books in Mrs. Curran's personal library. He found nothing there that would seem to have a bearing on the case.

What about the crucial question of Mrs. Curran's honesty? If there was substantial question about her personal integrity, then the possibility of fraud—which skeptics always were quick to proffer—must be given additional weight. Of this, Prince concluded: "I am convinced that there has been no conscious concealment of facts. . . . Every facility for examination was given me and every question answered. . . . I have never investigated a case that seemed more free from concealment and indirection."

And, later in his report: ". . . the evidence is overwhelming that she is a person of veracity. It is vouched for by those who know her and have known her at different periods in her lifetime, whose letters and oral statements have been quoted. Mr. Reedy, skeptical at first, became willing to 'bet his head' on her truthfulness. Mr. Yost is convinced of it and so are many whose words I have not quoted. Her stepdaughter declared with emphasis that she was too frank by habit. . . . Her veracity was indicated at every step of my own drastic examination, her willingness to answer any and all inquiries."[9]

If the possibility of fraud can be ruled out, as Prince so did, what of the explanation favored by scientists and many others that Patience Worth simply was a rather unusual manifestation of Pearl Curran's subconscious?

Prince noted: "I know of no proof that a secondary personality, subliminal or alternating, can show ability so tremendously in advance of that of the primary or normal consciousness, and ability which is sustained and perpetual." And later: ". . . if a person is dissociated in a pathological and continuing extent, the fact is supposed on the basis of observed cases to be signalized by various symptoms of the type known under the group-term of hysteria. It has been usual to show the existence of such a state by pointing to the marks and symptoms. But careful interrogation of Mrs. Curran and those who have known her brings out no testimony by which this state at any period can be identified."

And still later in his report: ". . . no secondary personality ever manifested extraordinary talent in a field where the primary or conscious personality had not shown aptitude, or made earnest endeavor or felt and manifested positive ambition."[10]

Was Mrs. Curran an inherently gifted writer who, perhaps involuntarily, had chosen this unique manner of getting attention for her talents? Prince succinctly disposed of this theory: "We have now ascertained that not only is there no evidence in favor but also that all the evidence is against the theory that Mrs. Curran, prior to the announcement of Patience Worth, ever possessed and manifested any talent for poetical or other literary production, or any acquaintance with philological lore; ever showed more than the most meagre knowledge of history or the manners, customs, etc. of foreign countries; ever was endowed with and displayed unusual mnemonic or other intellectual powers of a peculiar character; or ever had or manifested a trend in the direction of deep philosophical thinking or of religiosity and mysticism."[11]

All right, so what of it all? Prince's monumental report covers more than 500 pages in the 1964 edition. But his ultimate conclusion and finding is stated in just a few words, a statement which has been widely quoted in newspaper and magazine articles about the Patience Worth case: "Either our concept of what we call the subconscious must be radically altered, so as to include potencies of which we hitherto had no knowledge, or else some cause operating through but not originating in the subconsciousness of Mrs. Curran must be acknowledged."[12]

In other words, according to Prince, psychological knowledge of the subconscious and so-called secondary personalities did not provide a satisfactory explanation for the Patience Worth phenomenon. Therefore, either such knowledge must be "radically altered" to provide for this case, or else it must be admitted that Patience Worth did not originate, consciously or subconsciously, with Pearl Curran and was, literally, a totally separate entity. The presumption of the latter alternative, although Prince carefully refrained from saying so, would be that Patience was—as she claimed to be—the spirit of a woman who had lived several centuries before.

During the years of Patience Worth's major fame, and to a lesser extent thereafter, the Curran household was frequently visited by scholars from many universities across the country, from Canada, and on occasion from other countries. Faculty members from Washington University in St. Louis were most numerous, which is understandable, given their propinquity. Two of the most distinguished academicians from Washington University were among those who wrote reports on the case of Patience Worth.

The first, Charles E. Cory, was chairman of the Department of Philosophy at Washington University during the period that Patience Worth became a celebrity. His philosophical specialty was metaphysics, but he also was extremely interested in problems of the subconscious and cases of personality dissociation. In February 1920, for example, the *Journal of Abnormal Psychology* published his report on the case of a St. Louis woman who drew many pictures supposedly without conscious control of her hands. But his report on Patience Worth preceded this by some six months.

Cory, like a number of his faculty colleagues, had become intrigued by the Patience Worth activities when he read accounts of them in local papers and *Reedy's Mirror*. He became a frequent witness to the sessions at the Curran home and was a dogged interrogator of both Mrs. Curran and Patience herself. It was Cory's persistent questioning that prompted Patience, in 1918, to dictate the defiant little statement that was to be widely quoted:

I am molten silver,
Running. Let man catch me
Within his cup. Let him proceed
Upon his labour, smithing upon me.
Let him with cunning smite
My substance. Let him at his dream,
Lending my stuff unto its creation.
It shall be no less me![13]

In 1919 Cory concluded his investigation of more than three years by writing a lengthy report on the case which appeared in the September 1919 issue of *The Psychological Review*.

Cory stated at the very outset of his article that "the case is one upon which no satisfactory report can be made without the aid of hypnosis." The two major problems posed by the case, he declared, were: 1) subconscious memory and perception, and 2) subconscious thought. "Without hypnosis," he said, "these problems lie largely in obscurity. Hypnosis had been refused because of a fear that it might injure or destroy the ability to write, and not, I believe, through a desire to avoid a thorough investigation."

The professor then went on to give the background of the case, but meanwhile revealed in so doing his judgment of the mystery by stating: "It will make for clearness if the reader will understand that Patience Worth, the writer, is a subconscious personality of Mrs. John Curran...."

After describing Mrs. Curran's method of writing and her voluminous production to date, Cory added, "A thing that gives special interest to this literature is that most of it reflects the life and manners of other times, and this it does with an intimacy that astonishes the reader. They presuppose on the part of the author, a wealth of information, a richness of contact that is normally secured only through a prolonged study."

A survey of Mrs. Curran's reading throughout her life, Cory said, leaves the problem of the source of all the knowledge unsolved. It is far more difficult, however, to determine what information might have been discussed in her presence. "But a knowledge of the interests that have dominated her life forces the conclusion that most of this material did not pass into her mind through the channel of her conscious attention. What her total environment has been, and just how that environment has been appropriated, is the question. And the problem is complicated by the fact that there have been two selves, that is, two centers of apperception drawing upon that environment. Hence no history of Mrs. Curran in terms of an ordinary biography could hope to solve the problem. Not one, but two histories must be traced."

Cory regarded as even more significant the effect of the case on the problem of what was called "subconscious reflective processes." The Patience Worth case, he wrote, "offers a new answer to the question that is of growing interest, namely: What degree of rationality may the processes of a subconscious center attain? Here there is a product showing a mentality of a very high order. It is original, creative, possessing a delicate sense of beauty, a hardy rationality, and, above all, and perhaps most surprising, a moral and spiritual elevation. . . . Mrs. Curran is an intelligent woman, but her mind is much inferior to that of Patience Worth. In short, here is a subconscious self far outstripping in power and range the primary consciousness. This is an indisputable fact, and it is a significant one for psychology."

Cory also declared that the "other self" of Mrs. Curran has somehow been given "a facile creative power amounting to genius." Thus, still another highly regarded scholar went on record as affirming that Patience Worth, even if a product of someone's subconscious, was qualitatively far removed from any other source of so-called automatic writing.

Cory went on to relate the amazing powers demonstrated by Mrs. Curran in the guise of Patience Worth: the ease of the most intricate composition, her ability to alternate facilely between several different novels, her ability to pick up—at just the right spot—a narration which had been untouched perhaps for months. Then he described Mrs. Curran's visions which appeared to her as she dictated the stories and went on to note: "Apparently the only effort required on the part of Mrs. Curran is that involved in passivity. With the proper abstraction she receives from the secondary self the letters and imagery. The meaning of what is written is, naturally enough, frequently not understood by her. Neither its form nor its substance is determined by her consciousness. They are apparently the creation of a self whose existence she is, for the most part, completely unaware of."

One may ask, Cory wrote, whether the literary works were really created while the "other personality" of Mrs. Curran was submerged. Could they not have been written as they were transmitted? No, Cory answered, "it is inconceivable that these elaborate and intricately wrought novels should not have been planned before they are so hastily written. . . . This means that, while Mrs. Curran goes about the cares of her household, the other self, unknown to her, may be deep in an English novel. The selves, to repeat, are not alternating, but coexistent or coconscious."

"I accept the judgment," Cory declared, "that Patience Worth is a genius of no mean order. And perhaps, there is in the genius of this writer a concrete illustration of what freedom a mind may achieve when released from the inhibitions that clog and check the normal consciousness." That normal consciousness, he contended, is forced by the demands of daily life to divide its attention between action and ideas. But Patience Worth is "free and unfettered." "In the realm of the idea she lives, and there she sustains herself without effort. She acknowledges no tie or bond that might take her out of her dream. She is a dreamer that never awakens. And the conditions of this spell are, in a way, the conditions of her genius. . . . In other words, she lives only in a world of thought."

What about the claims of Patience Worth that she is the spirit of a long-dead Englishwoman? Cory had affirmed the rationality of the secondary personality calling itself Patience Worth, but stated that on this one point "this mind is under an illusion." He added: "That she is honest in this belief, there is no reason to doubt. The full history of this illusion, this idea that she is a returned spirit, can be secured only by psychoanalysis."

Cory suggested that the presence of a friend, a confirmed spiritualist (Mrs. Hutchings) at the time that Patience Worth made her appearance might have caused the idea of a discarnate spirit to become a vital part of the dissociated self then developing. "This mind," Cory concluded, "that has plumbed so deeply human experience, and has touched with a sure hand its greatest tragedy, is a mind that is in error regarding its own origin and history."[14]

It should be mentioned at this point that Cory's unshakable belief that Patience Worth was purely a secondary personality of Pearl Curran was challenged at considerable length by Walter Franklin Prince in his own report, which appeared eight years later. Those readers desiring to delve more deeply into the discussion of Cory's findings are referred again to Prince's *The Case of Patience Worth*.

The second Washington University faculty member to analyze the case was Professor Otto Heller, a long-time teacher in the humanities and later the university's Dean of Graduate Studies. Professor Heller also attended many of the Patience Worth sessions before and after 1920 and was a close observer of the phenomenon. But his report has a much different perspective in time from Cory's. It was written in 1937, about two weeks after the death of Mrs. Curran.

Professor Heller noted that, "While, perhaps, it was unavoidable for the world's greatest metaphysical prodigy that her attraction as a sideshow of the literary circus outshone her performance in the main tent, it is nonetheless curious how sharply opinion was divided as to the intrinsic worth of her productions. Those who believed in their preternatural origin took their excellence for granted. Most of the others disparaged and ridiculed them unread, to demonstrate their freedom from superstition. Believing as I do that Mrs. Curran's work indeed deserves evaluation for its own sake, irrespective of its authorship, I shall briefly review the case of Patience Worth...."

Heller went on to give his personal opinions of Pearl Curran: "Mrs. Curran, when I first met her, impressed me as a decidedly comely, but also, may I say it—a rather commonplace youngish woman. On Monday and Thursday evenings when visitors were admitted to her seances with Patience Worth, she was an ingratiating hostess to a heterogeneous group of regular and casual guests. She was lively, quick at repartee, competent to entertain a roomful of company with humorous and witty small-talk. But her voluble conversation never gave the least hint of high intellectual or spiritual energy; nor did it give the slightest intimation of the store of positive information and the philosophic animation manifest in the writings of Patience Worth.

"She had, naturally, a very large circle of acquaintances. But be it from choice, be it by effect of certain characteristics—she made few friends and did not keep them long. For one thing, she was said to be capricious and of uncertain temper.

"Those who knew her well had reason to complain of the instability of her promises and decisions in important as well as trivial affairs. Another trait that was attributed to her needs to be mentioned because of its potential bearing on her own representations concerning Patience Worth. I have it on safe authority that her best friends weren't by any means sure that she was perfectly truthful. Not that she lied but—as Mr. H. G. Wells says of his newest hero—she was weak about the truth."

It is worth noting here, before continuing with the Heller report, the sharp contrast between the preceding paragraph and the evidence presented by Prince, some years earlier, concerning Mrs. Curran's veracity. For what it is worth, I can report that nowhere else did I find any question raised about Mrs. Curran's personal honesty. In interviewing several persons who had known Mrs. Curran in St. Louis, I pointedly raised the question of her truthfulness. The answers were consistent and unanimous: "She was a completely honest person . . . the soul of truth." Where Professor Heller got his information I do not know, and though I am reporting it as he wrote it, I am obligated to report also that I could not find any confirmation for his doubts about Mrs. Curran's honesty and therefore am inclined to discount them.

One of the crucial puzzles about Patience Worth, Professor Heller went on, was the "immense discrepancy" between what she knew and what Mrs. Curran had learned: ". . . the authenticity of the historic background of her narratives and the flawless accuracy of all details are beyond question. Neither can there be any doubt that the range of knowledge and power of expression displayed in all those compositions go well beyond normal capacity."

Of the many efforts to explain this mystery, Heller declared, "the most nonsensical is the explanation current in many places then and now that in early years Mrs. Curran had saturated her mind with archaic literature and that by some magic she knew how to conjure the residuum of that fugitive reading up from the low layers of her consciousness. Time does not permit me to show the silliness of that assumption."

In concluding his report Professor Heller discussed the investigation of Prince and his oft-quoted conclusion about the case. He then added: "Although Prince has been severely taken to task by the psychological fraternity for the spiritualistic implication of his verdict, none of the more realistic theories that have been advanced have a leg to stand on. . . . As for my person, I still confess myself completely baffled by the experience. I can only say that as regards the reputed cooperation between Pearl Curran and Patience Worth, the observable data of the performance excluded every chance of collusion or fraud. Mrs. Curran, seated before the board, rendered the message as it came in Ouija fashion, letter by letter, in such rapid sequence that Mr. Curran's special method of recording it was hard put to it. Already on its mechanical side the performance was scarcely short of miraculous. To realize that, spell out aloud consecutively some printed pages at a steady rate of about 36 words a minute. Unless you, too, have your connection with some invisible prompter, I predict that in less than five minutes you will be fumbling and stumbling all over your letters. But even if you should do much better than I anticipate, your reading will convey no sense to you, or anyone else. Now, Mrs. Curran, with no text whatever before her, had no difficulty in carrying on for two or three hours at a stretch . . . that stunning five-thousand word description of the Crucifixion in *The Sorry Tale* came out of a single session. And Patience Worth's dictations were finished literary compositions. As a rule, they integrated into full-length novels with an organized and coherent plot handled with real craftmanship. Then, too, it is to be remembered that they are not told in straight everyday English but consistently in the quaint idiom of a bygone century, manipulated with much dramatic effect in pathos and comedy but equally capable of great lyric tenderness; on the one hand abounding in superbly imaginative metaphors and similes; on the other hand redolent of homespun realism...."[15]

The *Journal* of the American Society for Psychical Research also got into the guessing game in 1949 with an article by Charles Waldron Clowe titled "The Case of Patience Worth: A Theory." Mr. Clowe's theory was that a person's brain cells at birth could contain "a record previously made by some progenitor, and which if subsequently agitated by the functioning of the brain will cause the child, or later the adult, to recall the information or knowledge acquired by its ancestor. Suppose we term these inherited cells of knowledge."[16]

The skeptical camp could point to a new ally in 1935 with the appearance of a book called *Wish and Wisdom* by psychologist Joseph Jastrow. The book debunked occult and psychic beliefs and devoted a chapter to Patience Worth. Jastrow, apparently using Prince's book as his primary source of information, indicated no doubt that Patience and Mrs. Curran were one and the same, and that the writing attributed to Patience was compatible with Mrs. Curran's personality and abilities. He suggested that she picked up information on English ways from her parents and that she made use of the case to lift herself out of a dull existence. It became, Jastrow argued, the most exciting thing in her life.

Jastrow also quoted a Professor Schelling, said to be an eminent Elizabethan scholar, to the effect that Patience's language was a distorted mélange of borrowed dialect words, some of which were misused and misunderstood. Schelling also judged that the wisdom credited to Patience was nothing that any naturally clever person couldn't offer and that he found nothing approaching genius in the writings. The ability to provide striking language on request was attributed by Schelling to a talent for improvisation in Mrs. Curran. He did not claim that fraud was involved, but noted that self-deception is as easy as the deception of others.

Several of the leaders in British psychical research who have written briefly about the Patience Worth case in recent years also have engaged in speculation about the mystery, although none has come up with firm conclusions akin to those of Professor Cory.

G. N. M. Tyrrell mentions, as did Heller, the suggestions by some critics that Mrs. Curran acquired the knowledge in the Patience Worth writings by either cramming her mind for years with facts from books or else listening to the talk of experts. Tyrrell commented: "It seems utterly unplausible to suppose that the knowledge shown in these automatic productions was ever acquired by the normal consciousness of Mrs. Curran." He reached the same conclusion about the strange Old English dialect she employed: "Mrs. Curran's conscious mind was innocent . . . of the verbal clothing in what that knowledge was expressed."[17]

Tyrrell is not so enthusiastic as some others about the literary value of the Patience Worth writings: ". . . there is considerable literary merit," he admits, "but . . . not here the greatness of genius but . . . a fount of inspiration which might have provided the material for a work of genius had it been expressed through the conscious mind of, say, a Coleridge, instead of finding its expression through the mind of Mrs. Curran."[18]

In discussing the common supposition that Patience was a secondary personality of Mrs. Curran, Tyrrell was careful to distinguish the Patience Worth case from most other recorded cases of secondary personality in which "the alternating phases are *complementary* to one another. . . . There is not much resemblance between secondary personalities of this kind and Patience Worth. An important fact to remember about Mrs. Curran's automatism is that she is consciously present . . . during the whole of it. . . . Patience Worth does not *supplant* the normal Mrs. Curran, nor does she seem to be an abstraction from her."[19]

Tyrrell concludes: "If Patience Worth is in some sense a secondary personality, she is, it would appear, an *additional* creation rather than a fragment of the normal Mrs. Curran. That such creations within a personality may occur is, for all we know, a possibility; but I do not think they should be confused with the cases of secondary and multiple personality occurring in hysteria, which seems to be quite a different thing. If secondary personalities of the type of Patience Worth are possible, they would afford an alternative to the view that Patience Worth is a discarnate entity; but . . . they involve astonishingly complicated assumptions about the nature of the human being. They form an alternative to the discarnate theory, but scarcely a less marvellous alternative."[20]

Tyrrell's objection to the label of "secondary personality" being too readily assigned to the Patience Worth case is echoed by Kenneth Walker, a British physician, in his 1961 book on extrasensory perception. Walker noted (p. 46) that "neither the spiritualistic nor the split personality theory of the authorship of Mrs. Curran's novels are satisfying." He quoted Mrs. Curran's comment that there never was a sharp dividing line between her consciousness and that of Patience and remarks (p. 47), "in all the well-known instances of multiple personality such as the well documented one of Sally Beauchamp, the different personalities within the person alternate with each other in their appearances and are never present at the same time. In many cases the different personalities are even ignorant of each other's existence."

Walker, it might be noted in passing, hardly endeared himself to the ghost of the St. Louis Chamber of Commerce (circa 1913) by asking: "What explanation can be offered of this astonishing intellectual feat on the part of an ill-educated American woman, a woman who had no access to libraries and who heard very little intelligent conversation in a provincial American town?" Let us hope that Walker's knowledge of extrasensory perception is more accurate than his assumptions about St. Louis in 1913.

Later in his book, and without specific reference to the Patience Worth case, Walker suggests some other alternative explanations for the mystery surrounding Mrs. Curran. He refers to Jung's theory of the Collective Unconscious and also to Tyrrell's suggestion that the mid-levels of the human mind can make direct contact with the corresponding levels of other minds. Cited also is the philosophy of the twelfth-century Moslem mystic Averroes concerning the existence of "a common mind around us of which we all partake." He discusses also the suggestion of noted American psychologist Gardner Murphy of "an interpersonal mental field possessing properties which cannot be expressed in terms of any one individual mind." Walker later stated: "In Gardner Murphy's opinion . . . man possesses, at a deeper level, the capacity to establish contact with all space and with all time."[21]

Two more opinions are worth quoting here, although they were offered in a context completely unrelated to the Patience Worth case. They are of interest as the opinions of two experts with diametrically opposed views of extrasensory perception.

C. E. M. Hansel, Professor of Psychology at the University of Wales, has established something of a reputation as a debunker of extrasensory perception and parapsychology. In his 1966 volume *ESP—A Scientific Evaluation*, writing of the seance activities of mediums, Professor Hansel made these rather strong statements: "No medium ever studied has been found to be free of deceit. . . . The trance medium, if she is not merely shamming, is a person who finds herself experiencing fits or states of changed consciousness. These occur involuntarily, but at some stage she finds it possible to elicit one at will. . . . She hears imaginary voices and may suffer from visual and kinesthetic delusions. . . . She is in fact suffering from dissociation. . . . Such a person shows features common to several psychotic as well as neurotic disorders, although hysteria would seem to be the most likely diagnosis."

One of the most renowned researchers in the admittedly controversial field of parapsychology is Dr. Louisa E. Rhine, who with her famous husband Professor J. B. Rhine has been engaged for some forty years in the study of various forms of extrasensory perception. It is noteworthy that Dr. Rhine, a firm believer in the reality of extrasensory perception, takes a very dim view of automatic writing and the ouija board. In a statement published in 1969 in the FRNM (Foundation for Research into the Nature of Man) *Bulletin*, Dr. Rhine noted a new upsurge of interest in automatic writing and the ouija board. She pointed out that, historically, before automatic processes were understood, it often was suggested that such methods might be used to get messages from the deceased.

She went on: "Today, however, the use of automatisms can be considered as a method of tapping the unconscious. It involves a sufficient degree of mental dissociation that muscular movements can be made without direct conscious intention or awareness. Consequently, in spite of the differences, the material so produced can be considered as about on a par with that of dreams. It is of interest in parapsychology only if it brings information not traceable to sense perception but which is objectively verifiable. In other words, it is of interest only if it gives evidence of ESP. The automatic method as such has no parapsychological value of its own."

Dr. Rhine continued, and these statements would seem to have strong applicability to the Patience Worth case (and I must emphasize again that Dr. Rhine's comments being quoted were in no way related to the Patience Worth matter):

"In several ways the very nature of these two automatisms makes them particularly open to misunderstanding. For one thing, because they are unconscious, the person does not get the feeling of his own involvement. Instead, it seems to him that some personality outside of himself is responsible. In addition, and possibly because of this, the material is usually cast in a form as if originating from another intelligence. In this feature it is in contrast with dream material which the person usually feels he is himself experiencing.

"Another characteristic of many automatic responses that tends to be mis-leading is the fact that it is 'unlearned.' While in some cases automatic writing must be cultivated, in others it occurs spontaneously just as does the ability to move the Ouija pointer. With that, certain individuals can and others cannot produce the movement. Thus, it can look to the naïve as if the 'gifted' person is somehow being influenced by an extraneous personality, when, as a matter of fact, the ability to dissociate is instead the magic characteristic that separates those who can perform from those who can not."

Dr. Rhine's conclusion: "The general verdict is that these automatic responses have no parapsychological significance per se; have only a slight likelihood of conveying psi information; may be intriguing to the uninformed and possibly have unhealthy effects on naïve, suggestible persons. As entertainment, they are scarcely to be recommended."[22]

There is one final group of people whose analyses—no, that's much too formal a term; make it "impressions"—of Patience Worth deserve mention before we close this account of various opinions on the case.

The first identification of Patience Worth came fifty-eight years before these lines were written, her period of greatest fame was more than fifty years ago, and the final communication from Patience was received thirty-four years ago.

Obviously the number of those persons still living who can give us a firsthand account of the sessions with Patience is very limited. Yet I was fortunate enough to find a few of them and talk with them. They are ladies in their seventies and eighties who, as young married women, attended the Patience Worth sessions with their husbands or, perhaps, served as hostesses in their own homes for some of the meetings.

It was fascinating to discuss with them the strange case, to hear their memories of Pearl Curran and her conversations with Patience, and to ask for their opinions as to the explanation, if any.

I found a complete unanimity of opinion among them: They regard the Patience Worth case as the most remarkable activity in which they ever participated; they considered Mrs. Curran to be completely honest; they remember her as an exuberant, witty, "cut-up" type of person but one who took Patience Worth with deadly seriousness; they remember Pearl's attitude of great thankfulness that she had been blessed with the companionship of Patience; their husbands, to a man, never were convinced of the genuineness of the phenomenon, but also could never explain it away.

One of the ladies told me of a session she had attended at which a college professor was present. Patience began speaking on a topic which she brought up with no previous explanation. The professor was completely amazed. He had been discussing this very topic with his class the previous day and there was no apparent way in which Mrs. Curran could have known about this.

I was told about another professor, described as an expert in archaic English dialects, who heard Patience utter a word with which he was completely unfamiliar. Quite sure that the word, in fact, had never been spoken in England, he went home to his reference books. He telephoned the Currans later to report, also in amazement, that the word used by Patience, which he could not remember ever hearing before, had indeed been spoken in England at the time Patience claimed to have lived but had dropped from usage thereafter and had been almost forgotten.

Another of the ladies told me of a trip to England taken by a close friend of hers, who went to Dorset. As had Casper Yost (as we described earlier), she looked for landscapes and landmarks to fit those mentioned by Patience. She reportedly found a remarkable congruity between the actual Dorset scenes and the descriptions given by Patience. In one case, I was told, she asked local residents about a building described by Patience on a spot she found to be occupied by a gas station. She was told that the villagers remembered as children hearing of a building at that location, exactly as described by Patience.

And on and on and on. There is no way to document or verify these comments; they are the reminiscences of elderly ladies who, in some cases, were at my request thinking again about Patience Worth for the first time in decades. Yet I don't think they can be facilely discounted, either. In every case these were ladies of culture and refinement, as well educated as almost any women of their day. They were and are not the type to fall victim credulously to some sort of mass suggestion or hysteria.

They felt, without exception, that they were fortunate to have had the chance to witness something mystifying and wonderful as they watched and listened to Pearl Curran and Patience Worth.

They can offer no answer to the riddle of Patience Worth and do not attempt to. But they are thankful that they were part of it and remember it with awe and with love.

It is a good way to be remembered.

11

Who Was Patience Worth?

AND FINALLY, when all is said and the story of Patience Worth is ended, we come round again to the question that has perplexed everyone since 1913: Who was Patience Worth?

I have been immersed in this strange case for some two years now, and I readily confess: I do not have an answer.

The possibility of hoax or fraud never can be completely ruled out, although all the evidence of the case, the testimony of countless witnesses, and simple logic seem to argue overwhelmingly against it. Yet—it would be stupid to say that fraud was impossible.

Although fraud cannot be unequivocally ruled out of the Patience Worth case, it must be considered a very remote possibility. How could it have been carried out? Was there, as some rumors had it, a secret genius who provided Mrs. Curran with the writings? If so, who was it? It couldn't have been John Curran, for the Patience Worth communications continued, with no apparent change in quality or style, for fifteen years after his death. Casper Yost and Billy Reedy were not even involved in the case until many months after the writing had commenced. Emily Grant Hutchings was not part of the activity after 1915 and, indeed, was engaged in "spook writing" on her own and hardly would have been content to be a silent partner to Pearl Curran. Most significant, no single individual except Pearl Curran was present at *all* the sessions wherein Patience made impromptu statements on a variety of requested topics. There is no doubt that the material was emanating from Pearl Curran and not from any other individual.

Could Pearl have been busily cramming herself with information from books, meanwhile spending her days frantically composing the writings and then memorizing them to orate during the evening ouija-board sessions? It would be an incredible feat to carry out and, too, this theory just can't account for Patience's ability to ad-lib with a facility and literacy that amazed a skilled investigator such as Walter Franklin Prince. Also, it doesn't seem possible that a relatively uneducated woman, no matter how ambitious (or tireless) or innately talented, could force-feed herself enough information to so skillfully write a life of Christ that a professional historian of high standing would call it the greatest since the Gospels.

What could have been the motivation for fraud? The most obvious is money—and the plain truth is that the Currans never made any out of Patience Worth. That her books would not find a mass market became obvious by 1918, yet Pearl Curran continued to produce the Patience Worth literature for nineteen more years. It seems hardly logical that money was the goal. Well, what about fame, publicity, notoriety? Yes, there were these benefits and it seems obvious that Mrs. Curran enjoyed them and, to an extent, basked in them. Yet she continued patiently to carry out her role long after most of the publicity had faded.

If Pearl Curran herself knowingly had the ability to write books that would rate high praise from critics, wouldn't it have made much more sense, as Henry Holt and others pointed out, for her to write such books under her own name and reap all the rewards for herself, rather than share them, or really surrender them to another shadowy figure in the background?

If there was fraud, the motivation, the objective, is scarcely apparent. And to point to fraud as an explanation we would have to label as utterly credulous a long list of intelligent observers and analysts who emphatically had ruled it out.

Was Patience Worth, as she claimed and as Mrs. Curran apparently believed with whole heart, the spirit of a woman who had lived in the seventeenth century? Many persons simply will not countenance such a possibility, including virtually all scientists. To them it smells so badly of superstition and ignorance that they won't even consider it.

I, for one, am willing to give it the same consideration as any other theory in the case. Dogmatically to rule out *any* alternative because it offends one's sensibilities or because it is considered beneath contempt seems to me both unscientific and illogical.

We face here the same problem in considering this possibility, as arises in virtually every instance of spiritualistic mediumship. Information is provided by a medium or a "sensitive" that purportedly comes from the spirit world. Sometimes the information is amazingly accurate—so much so that it has a startling effect on the witnesses, some of whom may have been related to or intimately known the dead person with whom communication supposedly has been effected.

Yet the fact remains that rarely, if ever, has the evidence been so convincing that skepticism has been completely vanquished. Seldom or perhaps never is information provided at the seance which could be coming *only* from the spirit of a dead person. For one thing, there is the very live possibility that the information is being obtained by the medium telepathically from living persons. All concerned may be quite unaware of the true nature of this communication. It is because this possibility exists that most reputable researchers in extrasensory perception have largely abandoned efforts to study purported communication with the dead. These researchers believe that all their effort must go into the study of telepathy and other forms of extrasensory perception in order to determine the extent to which they exist. (This assumes, of course, that extrasensory perception is a fact; a majority of scientists today still refuse to concede that this has been demonstrated.) When more information about the range of extrasensory perception is obtained, say the researchers in the field, then they might be in a better position to judge whether mediums perhaps obtain their often startling bits of information from living persons by telepathic means

For the sake of argument, however, let us assume for a moment that Patience Worth was actually a spirit. This leads to a host of other questions for which we have no answer: Why did she select Pearl Curran? When Pearl died, why didn't Patience continue transmitting through someone else? Patience was a woman from rural England; where did she obtain the ability to write like that? If it was miraculous for Pearl Curran to have such writing skill, it was equally so for Patience Worth. If Patience lived in the seventeenth century, as she claimed, how did she know enough of Victorian England to write *Hope Trueblood*? And, conversely, where did she get her intensive knowledge of Palestine at the time of Christ?

And we come, finally, to the same question that arises about all other cases involved with spiritualism. The spirit seems to want so badly that everyone believe in man's immortality. Why, then, with all the powers and knowledge at his command, doesn't he (or she) provide really conclusive, totally compelling evidence that spirits of the dead do exist and can communicate with us? Why is the information provided always of a nature that can be explained in other ways, so that the skeptics remain as unconvinced as ever? In other words, if someone can speak to us from the world of the dead, would he not also have the power convincingly to demonstrate his existence?

There are, of course, other possibilities besides that of spirit communication that fall elsewhere into the psychic arena. We have mentioned the suggestion that Mrs. Curran might have been receiving her information and her literary materials telepathically from some other living person. Is it conceivable that some sort of involuntary line of communication had been set up between Pearl Curran and the subconscious mind of a noted, living writer, who was producing these materials—perhaps in his sleep—without even being aware of it? This idea doesn't seem very persuasive (and it doesn't account for Patience's ability at impromptu repartee) but it deserves consideration along with theories offered by many persons over hundreds of years of a universal unconscious—a sort of grand, collective mind on which Pearl Curran may have been drawing, which she somehow had discovered how to tap without even being aware of her power.

WHO WAS PATIENCE WORTH? / 269

The great majority of persons who have heard of the Patience Worth case, and probably close to 100 percent of scientists and scholars, would subscribe to the solution that—from the very beginning of the case—shared equal billing with the spiritualist one; namely, that Patience Worth was entirely a figment of Pearl Curran's subconscious, that Mrs. Curran had dissociated to the point that she was living her life with two entirely separate personalities coexisting in her body.

It is the easiest, least disturbing of the alternatives. Intellectuals can blithely accept it without any risk of compromising their integrity. One can safely, comfortably point to it without leaving the security of scientific propriety.

Yet, for me, this explanation also has certain weaknesses which make it impossible to proclaim that it *has* to be the answer.

The biggest hole, or at least unexplained aspect, is what Casper Yost referred to as the "problem of knowledge." Even if Patience was only a secondary personality, she did display a vast erudition. If there was an output of such information, there had to be a prior input. Where was it?

It is convenient to respond, "Oh, well, she undoubtedly picked up bits and dabs of information here and there throughout her life, then put them all together when she needed to use them." It is easy to make such a statement, but not so easy to prove it. It was shown time and again that Pearl Curran had no apparent access to the information contained in the works of Patience Worth. She was not a reader, she did not consort with learned men, she did not memorize the encyclopedia. Where, then, was the input?

Admittedly, there are numerous cases on record where an individual spouts some bit of arcane information and no one can figure its source. Further study reveals some unexceptional origin. For example, Professor G. H. Estabrooks in his book *Hypnotism*[1] described a case in which a woman, under hypnosis, began talking in classical Greek of a type spoken some 2,000 years ago. She could give no explanation as to her knowledge of the language. Further analysis eventually disclosed that, as a child of three or four, she often had been taken by her mother to visit a family friend, an elderly classical scholar. He was wont to walk around the house reciting passages of classical Greek poetry. Apparently she retained these scraps of Greek in her subconscious and eventually brought them to the surface again. This kind of situation, however, would hardly seem adequate to explain the vast amount of knowledge displayed in the Patience Worth literature and its amazing diversity, both in time and in subject matter. Incidentally, Professor Estabrooks—a psychologist—briefly discusses the Patience Worth case in his book. Admitting that the case is an unusually complex one from a psychological point of view, he nevertheless regards Patience as patently a creation of Mrs. Curran's subconscious.

Another obstacle to the theory of subconscious personality is the technical question raised by some of the analysts of the case concerning the manner in which Pearl and Patience coexisted (e.g., Pearl dictating a poem by Patience while waving a greeting to a friend entering the room). The usual case of split personality, according to these analysts, involves the alternation of two or more personalities, rather than their coexistence. (A rather graphic example of this was provided in the movie *The Three Faces of Eve*.) This, however, is an issue which is best left to the psychologists and psychiatrists to fight out.

Right up to the present day, other cases with some aspects of similarity to that of Patience Worth have continued to pop up around the world.

On April 14, 1970, for example, CBS Television's "60 Minutes" program carried a segment about a London medium who had composed music which she claims was dictated to her by the spirits of Liszt, Chopin, Brahms, Rachmaninoff, *et al.* The woman was untrained in music except for three years of piano instruction as a child, yet the music she displayed was complex and sophisticated. Composers Virgil Thomson and Andre Previn were interviewed about her music. Previn noted that for a person even to forge this kind of music would require a good deal of technique and ample knowledge of the "hieroglyphics" that is musical notation. He felt, however, that the quality of the music was third- or fourth-rate, the sort of stuff that famous composers would have discarded if they had written it. Thomson considered the music somewhat reminiscent of the composers to whom the medium attributed it, but insisted that there was an underlying similarity between the various works, indicating that they all had been written by the same person. (Apparently not all the experts have been quite so unimpressed. *Time* magazine also recently [July 6, 1970, p. 68] did a story on the medium, Rosemary Brown, and quoted British composer Richard Rodney Bennett as commenting, "If she is a fake, she is a brilliant one and must have had years of training. Some of the music is awful, but some is marvelous. I couldn't have faked the Beethoven." The article notes that several other well-known British musicians have become interested in the case. The *Time* writer said of the music: "The pieces all are characteristic of their alleged composers. Some of them are good enough to have been written by a Liszt or a Beethoven in a nodding moment, though they also suggest the possibility of highly skilled parody.")

The CBS program also featured a psychiatrist from the University of London who had examined the medium. She definitely was not schizophrenic or neurotic, he said, but probably had long repressed a desire to write music and to associate with musicians and, unconsciously, she had meanwhile picked up a good deal of technique and musical information that she now was expressing.

The parallels of this case to the Patience Worth affair are quite obvious. Yet there still is the one essential difference that has separated Patience Worth from all the other cases of automatic writing that have cropped up through the years: She produced work that many of the most eminent critics of her day, by the literary standards of that day, pronounced absolutely top-grade and in some cases labeled as sheer genius. This must be contrasted to the opinions of Thomson and Previn that the music of the London medium, while interesting, was really nothing very extraordinary. Patience Worth continues to stand apart from all other cases that do bear some similarity insofar as she created literary material that was judged by highly qualified persons to be utterly unique in style and superb in quality. It is on this point that simple comparisons with other cases must inevitably break down.

During the fifty-eight years that have passed since the emergence of Patience Worth in a muggy St. Louis parlor, science has been unable to provide a clear, unequivocal answer to the question: Who was Patience Worth? There have been, however, some recent developments in science which—if someone will apply them to the Patience Worth case—might conceivably produce the answer, or at least a part of it.

One such advance is the use of the computer as an aid in settling difficult philological and etymological questions. Scholars in these fields have been experimenting with the computer in seeking to determine the authorship of disputed literary works. The experiments are based on the hypothesis that every individual has certain prevalent patterns that constantly recur in his language, whether spoken or written. The pattern is an unconscious one and the speaker or writer usually is unaware of it. The pattern becomes almost a verbal fingerprint in stamping language with the authorship of a given individual.

In Israel, for example, a scientist recently has been conducting such computer experiments on portions of the Bible. He has come up with a theory, based on his research, that one particular book of the Bible—long regarded by most biblical scholars as having been written by a single individual—actually had two authors, each of whom wrote a portion of the book, as manifested in the two distinct lingual patterns of the book brought to light by the computer used in the research.

Someday, perhaps, such a scientist will take the language of Patience Worth and subject it to a detailed analytical comparison on the computer with the language of Pearl Curran. Samples of the latter are available in the form of an article or two written under her own name, the short story that was published, and a few of her letters that have been preserved.

If such a computer analysis were to show the hidden patterns of construction and diction in the language of Patience Worth and Pearl Curran to be identical, then such a finding would go a long way toward proving once and for all that Patience actually was a product of Mrs. Curran's subconscious.

It is likely that, even given such a result, diehard proponents of the spiritualist position would still contend that the computer proved nothing because Patience transmitted her works in the form of thought waves and they were verbally constructed by

Mrs. Curran, thereby reflecting her own personal language patterns. But such an argument, I suspect, would not be very persuasive to most objective judges in the face of suitable evidence to the contrary.

It is true that a simple finding that Patience was a secondary dissociative personality of Pearl Curran still would not answer the other questions posed by the case. Where did Mrs. Curran get the ability to produce in great volume and with astounding facility a language so drastically different, at least on the surface, from her own? And how was she able to transmit vast amounts of information on subjects about which she consciously knew almost nothing —information which seemingly had no way of entwining itself into her subconscious.

Progress constantly is being made toward a greater understanding of the human personality and its myriad of abnormalities. As our understanding deepens, answers presumably will be found to all the questions concerning the mysterious appearance of Patience Worth.

What do I think? As mentioned, I have no answer to put forth. I leave the case sharing with Walter Franklin Prince, Otto Heller, and most of the others who have examined it closely through the years a sense of continuing bafflement. As I did at the outset of my investigation, I still lean slightly in the direction of the theory that Patience was a product of Mrs. Curran's subconscious, yet I readily admit that this leaning stems more from my own temperament and value system rather than from any strong weight of evidence supporting this position.

I'm content at this point, frankly, to enjoy the mysterious music that is the case of Patience Worth without concerning myself too much over who composed it or the techniques of the counterpoint. It is somewhat like a unique, engrossing mystery story which has not yet come to the climactic moment when the detective announces that the butler did it. Having to wait a while longer for the solution of the mystery shouldn't prevent us from relishing all the earlier scenes of the melodrama that have passed before us.

And, ironically, to leave the mystery still unsolved seems very much in accord with the wishes of Patience Worth.

Again and again during the years that she spoke, Patience reiterated that the details of her life and her present existence were of no importance whatever. It was her message, she insisted, her song of love for man and love for God that was the reason for her presence. Give all your attention to my words, she pleaded, and not to me as an individual.

Because we are unable to answer our questions concerning Patience Worth and her strange visitation, we find ourselves forced to return to her written words again and to ponder once more their beauty, their nobility, and their stirring song of hope.

And this, after all, is just what she asked of us, isn't it?

It seems to me that the most fitting way to conclude this chronicle of Patience Worth is with her own words of farewell. Here, then, are two of Patience's short poems of parting:

> *How sweet*
> *That parting is naught*
> *But the opeing of a door*
> *And closing it!*
> *Thy soul and mine*
> *Know not the mask*
> *Called parting.*
> *Farewell is a jest,*
> *A wasted word.*
> *Yesterday is now,*
> *Today is now,*
> *And tomorrow too*
> *Is now.*
> *Think, my Beloved*
> *Need we then fear*
> *What we already know?*

> *Parting*
> *Is but the opeing*
> *And the closing*
> *Of a door.*
> *It meaneth naught.*
> *Farewell is a jest,*
> *A wasted word.*

That I have sung, be not enough;
That thou hast lent thy heart, be not enough;
That the cup hath been proffered
And filled, be not enough;
Leave within the empty thing, remembrance,
Will ye?

Anight.

NOTES

CHAPTER 1
1. Patience Worth Record, pp. 3-4. This will henceforth be referred to as the PW Record and is the complete bound compilation of all the Patience Worth materials, except for the full-length works otherwise published. The PW Record is in the archives of the Missouri Historical Society, St. Louis.
2. Arthur Walter Osborn, *The Meaning of Personal Existence*, London: Sidgwick and Jackson, 1966, pp. 32-33.
3. Rosalind Heywood, *Beyond the Reach of Sense*, New York: E. P. Dutton & Co., 1961, pp. 107-11.
4. G. N. M. Tyrrell, *The Personality of Man; New Facts and Their Significance*, West Drayton, Middlesex: Penguin Books, 1948, pp. 134-43.
5. Tyrrell, *op. cit.*, states that she was born of British parents and this is also mentioned by Kenneth Walker, presumably based on Tyrrell. I could find no evidence that her parents were born in Britain (and there are some contrary indications), but if they were, this could have been the source of Patience Worth's intimate knowledge of the flora and fauna of rural England. My impression is that Mrs. Curran's parents were native-born Americans, though their ancestry may have been British, and that Tyrrell's statement is in error.
6. Walter Franklin Prince, *The Case of Patience Worth*, Boston: Boston Society for Psychical Research, 1927; New Hyde Park, N.Y.: University Books, 1964, p. 11.

278 / NOTES

7. Mrs Chas. P. Johnson, *Notable Women of St. Louis*, St. Louis: Mrs. Chas. P. Johnson, 1914, pp. 110-14.
8. *The Book of St Louisans*, St. Louis: St. Louis Republic, 1912.
9. Heywood, *op. cit.*, p. 24.
10. *Ibid*, p. 81.
11. *Ibid*, p. 93.
12. Frank Gaynor, ed., *Dictionary of Mysticism*, New York: Philosophical Library, 1953, p. 132.
13. Casper S. Yost, *Patience Worth: A Psychic Mystery*, New York: Henry Holt & Co., 1916, p. 5.
14. *Wall Street Journal*, October 23, 1969, p. 20.
15. PW Record, *op. cit.*, p. 1. Also quoted in Prince, *op. cit.*, p. 33.
16. *Ibid*, p. 1.
17. *Ibid*, p. 2.
18. *Ibid*, pp. 2-3 Also partially quoted in Prince, *op. cit* , p. 33.
19. Prince, *op cit.*, p. 31.
20. PW Record, *op. cit.*, pp. 3-5. Also quoted in Prince, *op. cit.*, pp. 33-36.
21. Yost, *op. cit* , pp. 188-89.
22. PW Record, *op. cit.*, pp. 5-6.
23. *Ibid*, p. 7 Also quoted in Prince, *op. cit* , p. 36.
24. *Ibid*, p. 9. Also quoted in Prince, *op. cit.*, p. 37.
25. *Ibid*, pp. 11-12. Also quoted in Prince, *op. cit.*, pp. 37-38.
26. *Ibid*, p. 14. Also quoted in Prince, *op. cit.*, p. 39.
27. *Ibid*, p. 22.
28. *Ibid*, pp. 28-29.
29. *Ibid*, pp. 38-39. Also partially quoted in Prince, *op. cit.*, p. 181 and Yost, *op. cit.*, p. 30.
30. *Ibid*, pp. 39-40. Also partially quoted in Prince, *op. cit.*, p. 44.
31. *Ibid*, p. 1.
32. *Ibid*, pp. 39-40. Also quoted in Prince, *op cit.*, p. 89.
33. *Ibid*, p. 45. Also partially quoted in Yost, *op. cit.*, p. 47 and Prince, *op. cit* , p. 45.
34. *Ibid*, p. 62 Also quoted in Yost, *op cit* , p. 29.
35. *Ibid*, pp. 68-69. Also quoted in Yost, *op cit.*, p. 31.
36. *Ibid*, p. 78. The play is quoted in full in Yost, *op. cit.*, pp. 111-121.
37. Prince, *op. cit.*, p. 26.

CHAPTER 2

1. Obituary, *St. Louis Globe-Democrat*, May 31, 1941, p. 1.
2. *Ibid*, p. 2A.
3. *Ibid*, p. 2B.
4. *Missouri Historical Review*, Vol. 41, p. 110.
5. Memorial by James Malcolm Breckenridge, given at a meeting of the Missouri Society, Sons of the American Revolution, April 17, 1943.

CHAPTER 3

1. Max Putzel, *The Man in the Mirror, William Marion Reedy and His Magazine*, Cambridge: Harvard University Press, 1963, p. vii.

2. *Ibid*, p. 4.
3. Fannie Hurst, *Anatomy of Me*, Garden City, N.Y.: Doubleday and Co., 1958, p. 100.
4. John T. Flanagan, article "Reedy of the Mirror," *Missouri Historical Review*, January 1949.
5. Jean Winkler, article "William Marion Reedy," *St. Louis Review*, January 28, 1933.
6. Putzel, *op. cit.*, p. 287.
7. *Reedy's Mirror*, February 26, 1915, p. 3.
8. Reedy's memory apparently was mistaken here or else, for some reason, he chose to omit mention of his earlier visit. The PW Record shows that he attended a session with Patience on August 31 before returning on September 13.
9. *Reedy's Mirror*, October 1, 1915, pp. 219–20.
10. *Ibid*, p. 221.
11. *Mirror*, October 8, 1915, p. 241.
12. This is presumed to mean John Livingston Lowes. More of his visits to Patience Worth are related in Chapter 4.
13. *Mirror*, October 1, 1915, pp. 217–21.
14. *Ibid*, October 8, 1915, pp. 239–43.
15. Meeting program, Papyrus Club of St. Louis, November 2, 1915, in Archives, Missouri Historical Society.
16. *St. Louis Globe-Democrat*, November 3, 1915.

CHAPTER 4

1. PW Record, March 4, 1915, pp. 90–92.
2. *Ibid*, March 16, 1915, pp. 98–99.
3. *Ibid*, March 26, 1915, pp. 107–8.
4. *Ibid*, April 2, 1915, p. 111.
5. *Ibid*, April 7, 1915, p. 113. Also quoted in Yost, *op. cit.*, p. 38.
6. *Ibid*, May 26, 1915, p. 133. Also quoted in Prince, *op. cit.*, p. 298.
7. The essay also may be found in Prince, *op. cit.*
8. Patience Worth, *Telka*, New York: Patience Worth Publishing Co., 1928, pp. 247–52.
9. Quoted in Prince, *op. cit.*, p. 343.
10. *Telka, op. cit.*, pp 252–58.
11. *Ibid*, p. 260.
12. *Ibid*, p. 270.
13. PW Record, July 7, 1915, p. 168. Also quoted in Yost, *op. cit.*, pp. 171–2.
14. *Ibid*, July 9, 1915, p. 171.
15. Patience Worth, *The Sorry Tale*, New York: Henry Holt & Company, 1917, preface by Casper S. Yost, p. v.
16. *Ibid*, pp. v, vi.
17. *Ibid*, p. iv.
18. *St. Louis Post-Dispatch*, November 10, 1915.
19. *Ibid*.

280 / NOTES

20. *St. Louis Republic*, November 11, 1915.
21. *Ibid*, November 18, 1915.
22. *St. Louis Post-Dispatch*, November 18, 1915, and PW Record, pp. 310-11.
23. *St. Louis Post-Dispatch*, *St. Louis Star*, *St. Louis Republic*, November 18, 1915.
24. *Ibid*, *St. Louis Star*.
25. *Ibid*, *St. Louis Republic*.
26. PW Record, p. 314.
27. Article in *The Unpopular Review*, January 1916, pp. 187-88.
28. *Ibid*, pp. 188-90.

CHAPTER 5

1. There is considerable exaggeration in this account; the sessions with the ouija board generally were limited to two a week, which would have allowed ample time for Mrs. Curran to recuperate between sessions.
2. *St. Louis Republic*, November 21, 1915.
3. *Reedy's Mirror*, October 15, 1915.
4. *Ibid*, October 22, 1915.
5. *Ibid*, October 29, 1915.
6. *Ibid*, November 12, 1915.
7. *Ibid*.
8. *Ibid*, November 26, 1915.
9. *Ibid*, December 3, 1915.
10. *Ibid*, November 19, 1915.
11. *The Unpopular Review*, January 1916, pp. 192-93.
12. *Ibid*, p. 194.
13. *Ibid*, p. 196.
14. Yost, *op. cit.*, p. iii.
15. *Ibid*, p. 3.
16. *Ibid*, p. 9.
17. *Ibid*, p. 14.
18. *Ibid*, p. 15.
19. *Ibid*, pp. 33-34.
20. *Ibid*, p. 18.
21. *Ibid*, p. 35.
22. *Ibid*, p. 57.
23. *Ibid*, p. 174.
24. *Ibid*, p. 224.
25. *Ibid*, pp. 226-27.
26. *New York Times Book Review*, February 27, 1916, p. 69.
27. *Reedy's Mirror*, February 25, 1916, pp. 117-18.
28. *Literary Digest*, May 6, 1916, pp. 1316-25.
29. *Journal* of the American Society for Psychical Research, April 1916, pp. 189 ff.
30. *Ibid*, April 1938, p. 111 ff.
31. *Reedy's Mirror*, June 2, 1916, pp. 370-71.

32. *Ibid*, June 16, 1916, p. 406.
33. *Ibid*, p. 407.
34. *Ibid*, June 23, 1916, pp. 418–19.
35. *Ibid*, June 30, 1916, p. 439.
36. PW Record, p. 561.
37. *Ibid*, p. 488.
38. *Ibid*, p. 515. Also quoted in Prince, *op. cit.*, p. 201.
39. *Ibid*, p. 636.
40. Not really so remarkable, since Patience had several days in which to compose it. It would have been a much more striking feat if the phrase of 120 letters had been given immediately, when it was first proposed to Patience.
41. PW Record, pp. 337–39. The inscription also was quoted in *The Unpartizan Review*, March-April, 1920.

CHAPTER 6

1. Quoted in Prince, *op. cit.*, p. 178.
2. The account of the baby's birth was pieced together from the PW Record, newspaper stories, *Reedy's Mirror* for October 20, 1916, pp. 659–60, and Henry Holt's article "That Patience Worth Baby" in *The Unpopular Review*, January 1917.
3. Quoted in Prince, *op. cit.*, pp. 144–45.
4. PW Record, June 16, 1917, p. 947.
5. *Reedy's Mirror*, October 27, 1916, p. 682.
6. PW Record, August 26, 1916, p. 661.
7. *Ibid*, November 15, 1916, p. 742.
8. *Ibid*, December 9, 1916, p. 765.
9. *The Unpopular Review*, January 1917, pp. 193–98.
10. PW Record, February 17, 1917, p. 821.
11. Patience Worth, *Hope Trueblood*, New York: Henry Holt & Company, 1918, p. 3.
12. PW Record, December 9, 1916, p. 766. Also quoted in Prince, *op. cit.*, pp. 298–99.
13. *The Sorry Tale*, *op. cit.*, p. vi.
14. *Book Review Digest* for 1917, New York: H. W. Wilson Co., p. 617.
15. A.S.P.R. *Journal*, March 1919, p. 194.
16. *Ibid*, January 1918, p. 311.
17. *St. Louis Globe-Democrat*, July 8, 1917.
18. *Reedy's Mirror*, March 30, 1917, pp. 225–26.
19. *Ibid*, July 6, 1917, pp. 442–43.
20. *The Forum*, January 1917.
21. *The Bookman*, November 1917, pp. 350–53.
22. *Reedy's Mirror*, August 4, 1916, p. 504.
23. *Ibid*, August 18, 1916, p. 534.
24. Fred Wilhelm Wolf, *William Marion Reedy: A Critical Biography* (doctoral dissertation), Vanderbilt University: 1951, p. 212.

282 / NOTES

25. *Reedy's Mirror*, August 4, 1916, pp. 503-4.
26. *Ibid*, July 20, 1917, p. 469.
27. *Ibid*, June 21, 1918, p. 374.
28. A S.P.R. *Journal*, July 1917, p. 361.
29. *Reedy's Mirror*, August 10, 1917, pp. 511-12.

CHAPTER 7

1. PW Record, August 11, 1917, p. 997.
2. *St. Louis Republic*, September 24, 1917.
3. *St. Louis Post-Dispatch*, December 5, 1937, p. 3.
4. *Patience Worth's Magazine*, September 1917, p. 5.
5. *Ibid*, p. 8.
6. PW Record, September 30, 1917, p. 1049. Also quoted in Prince, *op. cit.*, p. 130.
7. Quoted in Prince, *op. cit.*, p. 79.
8. PW Record, December 25, 1916, pp 782-83.
9. *Ibid*, December 22, 1917, p. 1144. Also quoted in Prince, *op. cit.*, p. 49.
10. *Reedy's Mirror*, November 9, 1917, p. 704.
11. Program for "A Patience Worth Evening," Archives, Missouri Historical Society.
12. William Stanley Braithwaite, ed , *Anthology of Magazine Verse for 1916 and Year Book of American Poetry*, New York: Laurence J. Gomme, 1916, pp. 40, 117, 232.
13. *Ibid* for 1918, Boston: Small, Maynard & Company, pp. 24, 81, 139, 149, 154, 218-20.
14. *Ibid*, p. 276.
15. PW Record, March 20, 1918, pp. 1239-40.
16. *Ibid*, January 19, 1917, p. 804.
17. *Ibid*, March 19, 1917, p. 851.
18. *Hope Trueblood, op. cit.*, jacket cover.
19. *Book Review Digest* for 1918, New York: H. W. Wilson Co., p. 486.
20. Prince, *op. cit.*, pp. 76-77.
21. Yost, essay on "The Problem of Knowledge" quoted in Prince, *op. cit.*, p. 373.
22. *Ibid*, p. 375.
23. Prince, *op. cit.*, pp. 76-77.
24. PW Record, August 18, 1919, p. 1948.
25. Article by Professor W. T. Allison in the Winnipeg *Evening Bulletin*, as reprinted in the *St. Louis Globe-Democrat*, September 29, 1918.
26. Agnes Repplier, article "Dead Authors," *Atlantic Monthly*, August 1918, pp. 156-64.
27. PW Record, August 5, 1918, p. 1409.
28. *Ibid*, April 18, 1919, p. 1688.
29. *Ibid*, December 30, 1918, p. 1591. Also quoted in article by Professor Cory in *The Psychological Review* for September 1919.
30. *Ibid*, July 31, 1919, pp. 1912-13. The incident involving the creation of the child's prayer also was described in Prince, *op. cit.*, pp. 272-73.

31. Prince, *op. cit.*, pp. 271–72.
32. PW Record, April 22, 1918, p. 1291.
33. *Ibid*, September 1, 1919, p. 1962.
34. *Ibid*, September 8, 1919, p. 1968.

CHAPTER 8

1. PW Record, November 12, 1919, p. 2069. Also quoted in Prince, *op. cit.*, p. 62.
2. *St. Louis Republic*, November 13, 1919.
3. *Ibid*.
4. PW Record, November 7, 1919, p. 2046.
5. *Ibid*, November 14, 1919, p. 2078. Also quoted in *Light from Beyond*, Poems of Patience Worth selected and compiled by Herman Behr (New York: Patience Worth Publishing Company, 1923) p. 47.
6. *Ibid*, November 21, 1919, p. 2097. Also partially quoted in Prince, *op. cit*, p. 33n.
7. *Ibid*, November 24, 1919, p. 2104.
8. *Ibid*, May 6, 1920, pp. 2421–22. Also quoted in Prince, *op. cit.*, pp. 285–6.
9. Clipping, St. Louis *Post-Dispatch*, date obscured, apparently from April 1920.
10. This referred to statements previously made by Mrs. Curran that her only physical reaction while receiving the words from Patience was a feeling of slight pressure at the top of her head.
11. *The Unpartizan Review*, March–April 1920, pp. 357–72.
12. PW Record, July 29, 1920, p. 2554.
13. *Ibid*, August 16, 1920, pp. 2580–81. This incident also was described in Prince, *op. cit*, pp. 305–6.
14. *Ibid*, August 23, 1920, p. 2590.
15. *The Unpartizan Review*, October 1920, pp. 336–47.
16. PW Record, June 3, 1921, p. 2909.
17. *Ibid*, July 4, 1921, pp. 2934–54. This session is described more fully in *Light from Beyond*, op. cit., pp. 259–66.
18. Letter from Casper Yost in PW Record, August 12, 1921, p. 2986.
19. PW Record, November 14, 1921, p 3035. The poem "My Staff of Faith" also is quoted in Prince, *op. cit.*, pp. 163–4.
20. *Ibid*, December 12, 1921, p. 3052.
21. *Ibid*, March 13, 1922, p. 3112.
22. *Ibid*, July 10, 1922, p. 3157.
23. *Ibid*, September 4, 1923, p. 3269.
24. Prince, *op. cit.*, p. 64.

CHAPTER 9

1. *The Censor*, November 19, 1925, p. 11.
2. PW Record, February 24, 1924, p. 3374.
3. Notes of Williamina Parrish, dated January 1928, in Archives, Missouri Historical Society.

284 / NOTES

4. *Ibid.*
5. PW Record, February 17, 1925, pp. 3495–97. Also quoted in Prince, *op. cit.*, pp. 333–34. Prince analyzes the incident in some detail and concludes that Patience took the whole thing as a joke and did not provide Ticknor's words.
6. *Ibid*, March 9, 1925, p. 3515. Also quoted in Prince, *op cit.*, p. 202.
7. *Ibid*, January 22, 1925, p. 3478.
8. *Ibid*, March 12, 1923, p. 3196.
9. *Ibid*, January 12, 1926, p. 3675. Also quoted in Prince, *op. cit.*, p. 210.
10. *Ibid*, January 14, 1926, p. 3686.
11. *Ibid*, February 15, 1926, p. 3696 ff.
12. *Ibid*, March 8, 1926, p. 3718.
13. *Proceedings of the Society for Psychical Research* (London), Vol. 37, Part 103, November 1927, pp. 573–76.
14. PW Record, April 14, 1927, p. 3812.
15. *St. Louis Post-Dispatch*, October 27, 1929.
16. PW Record, January 18, 1929, p. 3985.
17. *Ibid*, October 28, 1930.
18. *Ibid*, February 27, 1929, p. 3992.
19. *Ibid*, July 29, 1930, p. 4094 ff.
20. *Ibid*, September 2, 1931, p. 4223.
21. Found in separate bound volume titled *Odds and Ends of Patience Worth* in Archives, Missouri Historical Society.
22. PW Record, June 27, 1933, p. 4300.
23. *Ibid*, March 13, 1937, p. 4364.
24. *Ibid*, inserted communication from Max Behr, November 25, 1937.
25. Letter from Mrs. Smith to Charles van Ravenswaay of the Missouri Historical Society, dated May 28, 1957, in Archives, Missouri Historical Society.
26. This poem also is quoted in *Light from Beyond, op. cit.*, p. 161.
27. A.S.P.R. *Journal*, April 1938, p. 111 ff.
28. *Ibid*, p. 114.
29. *Ibid*, January 1948, p. 15.
30. *St. Louis Globe-Democrat*, January 27, 1950.
31. *Granger's Index to Poetry*, Fifth Edition, New York: Columbia University Press, 1962.

CHAPTER 10

1. Prince, *op. cit.*, pp. 11, 15.
2. *Ibid*, p. 15.
3. *Ibid.*
4. *Ibid*, p. 26.
5. *Ibid*, p. 80 ff.
6. *Ibid*, p. 271.
7. *Ibid*, pp. 282–91.
8. *Ibid*, pp. 341–42.

9. *Ibid*, pp. 420, 489.
10. *Ibid*, pp. 439, 449, 502.
11. *Ibid*, p. 494.
12. *Ibid*, p. 509.
13. PW Record, December 30, 1918, p. 1591. The poem also is quoted in Professor Cory's article.
14. *The Psychological Review*, Vol. 26, No. 5, September 1919, pp. 397–407.
15. Report by Professor Otto Heller in Archives, Missouri Historical Society; quoted by permission of Mrs. Otto Heller.
16. A.S.P.R. *Journal*, April 1949, p. 70.
17. Tyrrell, *op. cit.*, pp. 140–41.
18. *Ibid*, p. 141.
19. *Ibid*, p. 142.
20. *Ibid*, p. 143.
21. Kenneth Walker, *The Extra-Sensory Mind*, New York: Emerson Books, Inc., 1961, pp. 194, 212, 240.
22. As reprinted in the Newsletter of the American Society for Psychical Research, Number 5, Winter 1970.

CHAPTER 11

1. New York: E. P. Dutton, 1943; revised 1957.

INDEX

Abnormal Psychology, Journal of, 77, 251
Adams, Franklin P., 100
Alden, Henry Mills, 101
Allison, W. T., 169-170
American Society for Psychical Research, 3, 102, 146, 189, 228, 235, 246
    Journal of, 103, 104, 132, 146-147, 240-241, 258
Arnold, Mr. & Mrs. Fred, 23-24
Athenaeum (London), book review, 168
Atlantic Monthly, 5, 171
Austin, Mary, article by, 201-203
Automatic writing, 8-10, 261-262
Averroes, 260

Baldwin, Roger, 207
Barrymore, Ethel, 186
Beauchamp, Sally, 260

Behr, Herman, 178, 186, 209, 210, 211, 228, 232, 236
Behr, Max, 235, 237, 238, 239
Belmont, Dr., 235-236
Bemis, Mrs. William N., 214
Benet, William Rose, 159
Bennett, Richard Rodney, 271
Beyond the Reach of Sense (Rosalind Heywood), 3
Blewett, Miss Avis, 158
Book Review Digest
    for 1916, 98
    for 1917, 131-132
    for 1918, 165-166
Bookman, The, 139
Bookseller, The (London), book review, 168
Boston Society for Psychical Research, xi, 219, 227, 246
Boston Transcript, book reviews, 131, 166
Boynton, H. W., 139-141

288 / INDEX

Braithwaite, William Stanley, 159–161, 212, 242
Brentano's, 228
Brown, Rosemary, 271
Butcher, Prof. Henry, 9

Cambridge University, 135
Catholic World, book review, 132
Censor, The, 214
Chaucer, Geoffrey, 3, 55, 57, 63, 70, 91, 104, 105, 107, 108, 109, 110
Chicago, 5, 11, 209, 247
Chicago Evening News, 153
Chicago Evening Post, poetry review, 99
Chicago Mail, book review, 167
Chicago Tribune, poetry review, 99
"Child's Prayer," writing of, 178–180, 249
Chriskios—Divine Healer (Emily Hutchings), 5
Christ, Jesus, 3, 10, 54, 57, 93, 111, 112, 128–132, 134, 136, 137, 138, 139, 170, 188, 196, 210, 266
Christianity, 20, 188
Clowe, Charles Waldron, 258
Columbia University, 102
Communicating With the Dead (Martin Ebon), ix
Computer, use of, 272
Congress, U.S., 218
Corliss, Judge, 215
Coronet magazine, 242
Cory, Prof. Charles, 178, 251–255
Cosmopolitan, 5
Culver City, California, 235
Curran, Eileen, 208
Curran, John H., 5–6, 12, 13, 27, 28, 35, 44, 48, 57–58, 62, 75, 76, 77, 82–83, 101, 103, 104, 106, 109, 110, 112, 113, 114, 118, 122, 149, 150, 152, 161, 179, 181, 192, 203, 205–208, 210, 213, 220, 248, 265

Curran, Patience Worth (Patience Wee), 115–121, 123, 209, 210, 213, 236, 239, 240
Curran, Pearl Lenore (Mrs. John H.)
  article by, 194–199
  attitude toward spiritualism, 11, 247
  capabilities of, 32, 57, 86–88, 95–96, 104, 123, 124–125, 138–139, 180–185, 193, 200–202, 243, 247–248, 250–251, 259, 269
  death of, 239
  deflated by Patience, 28–29, 85, 162–163
  demeanor during sessions, 30, 161–162, 224–225
  early life, 4–5
  first contacts with Patience Worth, 1–2, 10–17
  honesty of, 37, 55, 86, 96, 101, 103–111, 137, 249–250, 256, 257–258, 263, 265–266
  letter from, 123–125
  memories of, 262–264
  moves to California, 232
  remarries, 229, 235, 39, 44–45, 48, 60–61, 62, 74, 75–77, 80, 82–85, 149, 208–210, 241, 272–273

Damrosch, Mrs. Walter, 217
Delroy, Arthur, 76–77
Dial, book reviews, 131–132, 166
Dissociation of a Personality, The (Morton Prince), 77
Dorset Press, The, 203
Dorsetshire, 203–205, 249, 263–264

Ebon, Martin, x
Einstein, Albert, 231
England, reaction to *Hope Trueblood*, 167–169
ESP—A Scientific Evaluation (C. E. M. Hansel), 261

INDEX / 289

Estabrooks, G. H., 269-270
Extra-Sensory Mind, The (Kenneth Walker), 4, 71

Fairbanks, Mr. & Mrs. Douglas, 233
Flanagan, John T., 41
Fool and the Lady, The, 30-31, 39, 84
Ford, Arthur, 242
Forest Park (St. Louis), 6
Fox Sisters, 7
Francis, Mrs. David R., 111, 158
Fraud, possibility of, 265-266
"Friends of Patience Worth," 157-158
FRNM (Foundation for Research into the Nature of Man) *Bulletin*, 261

Gandhi, Mahatma, 233
Garland, Hamlin, 159, 186
Garland, Mrs. Hamlin, 217
Gerald, Earl of Balfour, 9
Gilman, Lawrence, 99
Granger's Index to Poetry, 243

Haberman, Dr. Victor, 187
Hadley, Gov. Herbert (of Missouri), 6
Hannibal, Missouri, 5
Hansel, C. E. M., 261
Harcourt, Alfred, 83, 84, 85
Harper & Brothers, 145
Harper's Magazine, 101
Harris Teachers College, 193
Harvard University, 65, 135
Hays, Mrs. Lola, 144, 146
Hedges, Mrs. Isaac, 158
Heller, Otto, 255-258, 259, 273
Here, Mr. Splitfoot (Robert Somerlott), 242
Heywood, Rosalind, 3, 8, 9
Hill, Dr. John Wesley, 152
Holt, Henry, 75, 83-85, 93-94, 102, 103, 104, 105, 112, 118, 123, 124, 125, 180, 194, 201, 266

Holt, Henry & Company, 75, 128, 157, 163, 176, 192
Holt, Mrs. Jack, 233
Hoover, Herbert, 233
Hope Trueblood, 127, 156, 157, 158, 163-165, 170, 188, 205, 268
  reviews of, 165-169, 170
Hoskier, Mr., 215
Houdini, Harry, 243
Huckle, Dr., 188
Hurst, Fannie, 41, 128, 154
Hutchings, C. Edwin, 5, 62
Hutchings, Emily Grant (Mrs. C. Edwin), 1, 2, 5, 11-16, 20-24, 27-29, 34, 39, 57, 62, 108, 143-146, 173, 242, 255, 265
Hypnotism (G. H. Estabrooks), 269
Hyslop, James H., 102-111, 132, 133, 146-147, 170, 175, 189-190, 195, 219, 235, 241, 246

Immortality, 207, 235-236, 237-238
Independent, book review, 98
Independent (Sheffield, England), book review, 168
Israel, research in, 272

James, William, 247
Jap Herron (Emily Hutchings from a ouija board), 144-147, 173
Jastrow, Joseph, 258
Johnson, Mrs. Charles P., article by, 86-88
Johnston, Mary, 91
Joint Committee of Literary Arts of New York, 158-159
Jung, Carl, 260

Kansas City Star, poetry review, 100
Kennerly, Mitchell, 144
Kerlin, Robert T., 90, 107-108, 110
Kingston, Countess, 128
Known But Unknown (Arthur Ford), 242
Kroeger, Ernest R., 62, 158

Ladies Field (London), book review, 168
Lady's Pictorial (London), book review, 168
Lay, Dr. Wilfred, 139, 141–142
League of Nations, 214
Leete, Mrs. Hazel, 215
Light from Beyond, 211, 228
Literary Digest, 102
Liverpool Post, book review, 168
Lodge, Sir Oliver, 171, 188
London, Jack, 7
London, University of, 271
London Times, book review, 168
Los Angeles Times, book review, 167
Louisiana Purchase Exposition (St. Louis World's Fair of 1904), 6, 112
Lowell, Amy, 128, 159, 160
Lowes, John Livingston, 65–68, 75, 79, 80, 93
Luntz, Charles, 4

Malone, R. F., 242
Manitoba, University of, 169
Masters, Edgar Lee, 40, 42, 159, 186–187
Maupin, Julia Curran, 31–32, 248
Mead, Hettie Rhoda, 241
Meaning of Personal Existence, The (Arthur Osborn), 3
Merry Tale, The, 111, 127, 156, 189
Millay, Edna St. Vincent, 160
Missouri, University of, 5
Missouri Historical Review, 212
Missouri Historical Society, xii–xiii, 243
Missouri State Capitol, 113–114, 198
Mound City, Illinois, 4, 207
Murphy, Gardner, 260
Myers, Frederic, 9

Nation, The, book review, 132
Nevin, Mrs. Ethelbert, 217
New Republic, The, book review, 98
New York Call, book review, 132

New York Evening Sun, book reviews, 99, 167
New York Herald-Tribune, 240
New York Times, book reviews, 3, 98, 131, 166–167, 212
New York Tribune, 42
   poetry review, 100
   book review, 166
North American Review, book review, 99

Olin, John M., Library, xii
On the Cosmic Relations (Henry Holt), 75
Osborn, Arthur, 3
Ouija board, 7, 10, 60–61, 83, 103–104, 150, 154, 190–191, 199, 240, 261–262
Outlook, book review, 132
Oxford University, 3, 135, 227
Ozarks, dialect of, 104, 106, 108, 109, 181

Pan-Germanism (Roland G. Usher), 135
Papyrus Club of St. Louis, The, 62–63
Parrish, Mr. & Mrs. Dinks, 216–217, 239
Parrish, Grace, 214
Parrish, Williamina, 214–217, 221, 224
Patience Worth
   coming of, 1–2, 11–15
   final communication from, 238–239
   first identification of, 2
   language of, 17–19, 43, 55, 57–58, 66, 69–71, 76, 96–97, 104, 105, 109, 127, 140, 165, 173–174, 258
   life of, 16, 20, 37, 58–59, 68, 80–81, 121, 161, 203–205
   literary production, 2–3
   personality of, 16, 37, 59, 73–74
   personification of, xi–xii

philosophy of, 49–51, 92–93, 97, 151–152, 188, 235–236
previous books about, xi
"stunts" of, 176–177, 198, 226–227, 249
Patience Worth, The Case of (Walter Franklin Prince), xi, 227, 246, 255
Patience Worth "Clan," 117, 121
Patience Worth Publishing Company
of New York, 213, 228
of St. Louis, 149
Patience Worth Record, xii, 12–13, 73, 78, 207–208, 210, 220, 237, 240
Patience Worth: A Psychic Mystery (Casper S. Yost), x, xi, 75, 85, 93, 95–101
Patience Worth, Temptress (R. F. Malone), 242
Patience Worth's Magazine, 69, 128, 147, 149–154
Payne, Dr. E. George, 62
Payne, Mrs. E. George, 62
Peattie, Elia W., 99
Personality of Man, New Facts and Their Significance, The (G. N. M. Tyrrell), 4
Pilsbury, Miss, 83
Piper, Mrs. Leonora, 8–9
Plotinus, 200
Pollard, George, 4
Pollard, Mrs. Mary, 1–2, 4, 12, 14, 16, 21–23, 24–25, 27, 28, 39, 44, 48, 208, 210, 213
Pot Upon the Wheel, The, 192, 203
Previn, Andre, 270, 271
Prince, Dr. Morton, 75, 77–83, 92, 94, 103, 105, 107, 141, 245
Prince, Walter Franklin, xi, 166, 168, 180, 211, 219–228, 229, 246–251, 255, 257, 266, 273
Psychic People (Eleanor Jouhey Smith), 242
Psychological Review, The, 252
Putzel, Max, 149

Ray, Mrs. E. Lansing, 157
Red Cross, benefit for, 157–158
Red Wing, 44, 59, 67, 69, 152
Reedy, William Marion, 40–63, 88–92, 100–101, 105–108, 120, 121, 126, 134–135, 142–147, 148, 149, 158, 187, 199–200, 212, 242, 250, 265
Reedy, Mrs. William Marion, 44, 45, 46, 47, 48, 51–54
Reedy's Mirror, 40–42, 44, 54, 60, 61, 65, 88, 90–93, 100, 105–111, 120, 126, 134, 136, 142–145, 149, 158, 159, 199, 252
Reincarnation, 119, 139, 235
Relativity, Theory of, 231
Repplier, Agnes, 175, 176, 202
article by, 171–175
Review of Reviews, book reviews, 132, 166
Rhine, Prof. J. B., 261
Rhine, Dr. Louisa E., 261–262
Road to Xanadu (John L. Lowes), 65
Rogers, Dr. Henry H., 229
Ronchi, Nino, 224
Rosa Alvaro, Entrante (short story by Pearl Curran), 181–185
Rose, Billy, 241–242, 243

St. Louis, x, xii, xiii, 1, 5–6, 9, 145, 260
St. Louis Globe-Democrat, 5, 6, 33, 36, 37, 38, 42, 43, 44, 56, 62, 75, 126, 149
book reviews, 99, 133
St. Louis Post-Dispatch, 75, 242
St. Louis Public Library, xiii
St. Louis Republic, 5, 86, 119
St. Mark's-in-the-Bouwerie Church, 229
Samuel Wheaton, 161, 189, 213–214
Santa Monica, California, 232
Saturday Evening Post, 182
Schelling, Prof., 258

292 / INDEX

Schiller, F. C. S., 227–228
Scientific American, 226
Selborne, 200
Shakespeare, William, 3, 46–47, 54, 55, 56, 57, 70, 90, 91, 97, 107, 137, 139, 143, 235, 237, 238
Sinclair, Upton, 233
"60 Minutes" (CBS Television), 270
Smith, Mrs. Alexander ("Dotsie"), 178, 191–192, 210, 213, 229, 232, 233, 234, 237, 239
Smith, Eleanor Touhey, 242
Society for Psychical Research (London), 3, 7, 8, 9, 56, 227, 246–247
   proceedings of, 227–228
Sockman, 215
Somerlott, Robert, 242
Sorry Tale, The, 45, 57, 59, 72–75, 83, 89, 111, 112–113, 115, 118, 123, 124, 125–127, 128–142, 152, 154, 156, 158, 159, 165, 170, 173, 174, 178, 188, 196, 257
   reviews of, 130–139, 170
Spamer, Richard, 62
Speer, A. A., 113, 114
Spenser, Edmund, 3, 55, 63, 91, 107
Spiritualism, 7–11, 247, 267–268, 272–273
Stadler, Mrs. Ernst A., xiii
Stephens, Edward, 113, 114
Stranger, The, 39, 88, 90
Sunday Associated Magazine of Chicago, 5

Task, The (Casper S. Yost), 127–128, 176, 178, 192
Telka, 44, 59, 65, 68–71, 112, 198, 227, 228
Theosophical Society of St. Louis, 4, 230
Thomson, Virgil, 270, 271
Three Faces of Eve, The, 270

Thurston, 243
Ticknor, John W., 217–218
Time magazine, 271
Tindall, Miss Elizabeth, xiii
To Have and To Hold (Mary Johnston), 91
Tower Grove Park (St. Louis), 5
Town Hall Series (Detroit), 229
Twain, Mark (Samuel L. Clemens), 5, 144–147, 173
Tyrrell, G. N. M., 4, 259–260

University Books, xi, 246
University Club (Evanston, Ill.), 209
Unpartizan Review, The, 194, 201
Unpopular Review, The, 93, 123, 194
Usher, Roland Greene, 135–138, 169
Usher, Mrs. Roland G., 158

Verrall, Prof. A. W., 9
Verrall, Mrs. A. W., 9
Virginia Military Institute, 90

Wales, University of, 261
Walker, Kenneth, 4, 71, 260
Wall Street Journal, 10
Wallen, Professor, 66, 67
War, poems on, 154–156
Washington University, x, xii, 6, 65, 128, 135–136, 176, 251, 255
Weisse, Dr. John H., 70
White, Gilbert, 200
Wickliffe's Bible (John), 70
Willett, Mrs. (Coombe-Tennant), 9
Williams, Mrs. Tyrrell, 158
Williams, William Carlos, 159
Wish and Wisdom (Joseph Jastrow), 258
Wood, Clement, 132
Worth, Patience. See Patience Worth
Wyman, Robert, 235

Yost, Casper S., x, xi, 10, 32, 33–39, 42, 44–45, 55, 57, 62, 63, 68,

69–71, 73, 74, 75, 86, 92, 93, 94, 95–99, 100, 101, 102, 103, 104, 105, 106, 107, 108, 109–110, 111, 112, 126, 127–128, 130, 131, 133–134, 139, 140, 148, 149, 150, 151, 152, 153, 156–157, 163, 166, 167, 168, 169, 172, 173, 174, 175, 176, 188, 189, 190, 191, 192, 194, 198, 199, 200, 203, 204, 205, 208, 215, 227, 250, 265, 269

Yost, Mrs. Casper S., Jr., x, xiii
Yurka, Blanche, 186

ABOUT THE AUTHOR

Irving Litvag is the author of two books, articles for national magazines, newspaper feature stories, radio scripts, and prize-winning one-act plays. In addition to free-lance writing, he has been a journalist and public relations executive. His other book is THE MASTER OF SUNNYBANK: A BIOGRAPHY OF ALBERT PAYSON TERHUNE.

AUTHORS GUILD BACKINPRINT.COM EDITIONS are fiction and nonfiction works that were originally brought to the reading public by established United States publishers but have fallen out of print. The economics of traditional publishing methods force tens of thousands of works out of print each year, eventually claiming many, if not most, award-winning and one-time bestselling titles. With improvements in print-on-demand technology, authors and their estates, in cooperation with the Authors Guild, are making some of these works available again to readers in quality paperback editions. Authors Guild Backinprint.com Editions may be found at nearly all online bookstores and are also available from traditional booksellers. For further information or to purchase any Backinprint.com title please visit www.backinprint.com.

Except as noted on their copyright pages, Authors Guild Backinprint.com Editions are presented in their original form. Some authors have chosen to revise or update their works with new information. The Authors Guild is not the editor or publisher of these works and is not responsible for any of the content of these editions.

THE AUTHORS GUILD is the nation's largest society of published book authors. Since 1912 it has been the leading writers' advocate for fair compensation, effective copyright protection, and free expression. Further information is available at www.authorsguild.org.

Please direct inquiries about the Authors Guild and Backinprint.com Editions to the Authors Guild offices in New York City, or e-mail staff@backinprint.com.